STERLING REVIEWS FOR

# The
# GOOD
# marriage

🐾

"Written in a masterful style that often reads like the best popular fiction. . . . Wallerstein and Blakeslee again combine their substantial talents . . . deftly and entertainingly exploring the foundations of good marriages."

—*San Francisco Examiner & Chronicle*

"The lessons in [Wallerstein's] book . . . are drawn from vivid snapshots of the couples in her study."

—*Seattle Post-Intelligencer*

"A lagniappe to enduring couplehood. . . . Judith S. Wallerstein, a gifted interviewer, persuades the couples to reveal their interior lives in rich, explicit detail."

—*New York Times Book Review*

"I have read THE GOOD MARRIAGE with real pleasure. . . . This book should inspire people with the conviction that a good marriage can succeed. Bravo!"

—*T. Berry Brazelton*

"Solid . . . impressive. . . . Those interested in social policy should be pleased that so well-respected a liberal academic as Ms. Wallerstein has written a book that celebrates marriage and points the way toward restructuring it."

—*Wall Street Journal*

"Should prove a lifesaver for many couples."

—*Publishers Weekly*

*more . . .*

"If there's one runaway hit this year, it's THE GOOD MARRIAGE."
—*American Bookseller*

"At last. A book that takes a serious look at how happily married couples can build their relationship."
—*Arizona Republic*

"Will stir controversy and conversation."
—*Milwaukee Journal Sentinel*

"Fascinating . . . beautifully written."
—*Book Page*

"A great resource for both married and unmarried couples in search of guidelines."
—*Nashville Tennessean*

"Should be required reading for all who are interested in marriage."
—**W. Walter Menninger**

"Miss Manners is scandalized to read about people who dare to defy modern convention by brazenly carrying on happy marriages. It is high time that they were made to explain themselves."
—**Judith Martin**

"Historically informative as well as profoundly wise psychologically."
—**Joan M. Erikson**

"A very appealing book . . . clearly written and clearly thought out."
—*Library Journal*

"Wallerstein's major contribution is not about how and why love lasts, but about how and why love develops. It is in such a context, less idyllic, but more realistic, that the book will prove to be a lasting contribution."
—*Readings: A Journal of Reviews and Commentary in Mental Health*

Books by Judith S. Wallerstein

SURVIVING THE BREAKUP
*How Children and Parents Cope with Divorce*
(*with Joan Berlin Kelly*)

SECOND CHANCES
*Men, Women, and Children a Decade after Divorce*
(*with Sandra Blakeslee*)

THE GOOD MARRIAGE
*How and Why Love Lasts*
(*with Sandra Blakeslee*)

*The*

# GOOD
# marriage

*How & Why Love Lasts*

## Judith S. Wallerstein
## & Sandra Blakeslee

**WARNER BOOKS**

A Time Warner Company

Warner Books Edition
Copyright © 1995 by Judith S. Wallerstein and Sandra Blakeslee
All rights reserved.

This Warner Books edition is published by arrangement with Houghton Mifflin Company, 215 Park Avenue South, New York, NY 10003

Warner Books, Inc., 1271 Avenue of the Americas, New York, NY 10020

Visit our Web site at http://warnerbooks.com

W A Time Warner Company

Printed in the United States of America

First Warner Books Printing: October 1996
10 9 8 7 6 5 4

Library of Congress Cataloging-in-Publication Data
Wallerstein, Judith S.
         The good marriage : how and why love lasts / Judith S. Wallerstein
& Sandra Blakeslee
             p.   cm.
         Originally published: Boston: Houghton Mifflin, 1995.
         Includes bibliographical references.
         ISBN 0-446-67248-3
         1. Marriage.   I. Blakeslee, Sandra.   II. Title.
HQ734.W194   1996                                        96-7793
306.81—dc20                                                  CIP

Cover design by Michaela Sullivan
Cover photograph: Photonica/Joe Squillante

FOR MY BELOVED GRANDCHILDREN

*In the order of their appearance:*
*Jonah, Hannah, Benjamin,*
*Alexei, Nicole*

# Contents

*The*
# GOOD
## marriage

# PART ONE
# Thinking about Marriage

# 1

# Happy Marriages

## Do They Exist?

O N A RAW SPRING MORNING in 1991, I shared my earliest thoughts about this book with a group of some one hundred professional women — all friends and colleagues — who meet each month to discuss our works in progress.

"I'm interested in learning about good marriages — about what makes a marriage succeed," I said cheerfully. "As far as our knowledge is concerned, a happy marriage might as well be the dark side of the moon. And so I've decided to study a group of long-lasting marriages that are genuinely satisfying for both husband and wife." I looked around the room at these attractive, highly educated women — women who had achieved success in our high-tech, competitive society and who appeared to have it all. "Would any of you, along with your husbands, like to volunteer as participants in the study?" I asked.

The room exploded with laughter.

I felt disturbed and puzzled by the group's reaction. Their laughter bore undertones of cynicism, nervousness, and disbelief, as if to say, "Surely you can't mean that happy marriage exists in the 1990s. How could you possibly believe that?"

Many of the women in the group had been divorced. Some had remarried, but a good number remained single. Some had come to feel that marriage should not be taken all that seriously. "Happy marriage doesn't exist," protested one woman, "so I'm going to get on with my life and not worry about it." Yet when their sons and daughters decided to marry, these same women announced the marriages with great pride and accepted heartfelt rounds of congratulations from the others in the group. No one acknowledged the apparent contradictions involved.

When I pondered the meaning of their laughter later that night, I realized I had hit a raw nerve. For many, my innocent mention of a study of successful marriages seemed to strike below the well-defended surface, bringing to life buried images of love and intimacy. For a brief moment, I believe, the women had reconnected with passionate longings, only to confront again their disappointment that their wishes had not been fulfilled. And so they had laughed, dismissing their longings as illusory — vain hopes that could only lead to sorrow.

This duality of cynicism and hope is familiar to me, as it is to millions of men and women in America today. We share a profound sense of discomfort with the present state of marriage and family, even wondering sometimes if marriage as an institution can survive. At the same time, we share a deeply felt hope for our children that marriage will endure. I do not think this hope is misplaced.

We have been so preoccupied with divorce and crisis in the American family that we have failed to notice the good marriages that are all around us and from which we can learn. In today's world it's easy to become overwhelmed by problems that seem to have no solution. But we *can* shape our lives at home, including our relationships with our children and marriage itself. The home is the one place where we have the potential to create a world that is to our own liking; it is the last place where we should feel despair. As never before in history, men and women today are free to design the kind of marriage they want, with their own rules and expectations.

Fortunately, many young people have not yet become cynical and are still able to speak directly from the heart. After spending some wonderful hours talking to college students about their views of marriage, I received the next day a letter from Randolph Johnson, a twenty-one-year-old senior at the University of California in Santa Cruz. He wrote: "What I want in a wife is someone whom I know so well that she is a part of who I am and I of her. Someone to fill all that I am not but aspire to be. My wife is someone not just to share a life with but to build a life with. This is what marriage is to me, the sharing of two lives to complete each other. It is true that people change, but if people can change together then they need not grow apart."

Randolph speaks for a new generation that is still capable of optimism about love and marriage and "the sharing of two lives to complete each other." He also speaks for a society that is tired to death of the war on marriage, escalating divorce rates, and the search for new partners in middle age. All of us want a different world for our children. When we're honest, we want it for ourselves.

It is absurd, in fact, to suggest that the need for enduring love and intimacy in marriage is passé. The men and women I've seen in twenty-five years of studying divorce begin actively searching for a new relationship even before the divorce is final. In every study in which Americans are asked what they value most in assessing the quality of their lives, marriage comes first — ahead of friends, jobs, and money. In our fast-paced world men and women need each other more, not less. We want and need erotic love, sympathetic love, passionate love, tender, nurturing love all of our adult lives. We desire friendship, compassion, encouragement, a sense of being understood and appreciated, not only for what we do but for what we try to do and fail at. We want a relationship in which we can test our half-baked ideas without shame or pretense and give voice to our deepest fears. We want a partner who sees us as unique and irreplaceable.

A good marriage can offset the loneliness of life in crowded cities and provide a refuge from the hammering pressures of the competitive workplace. It can counter the anomie of an increasingly impersonal world, where so many people interact with machines rather than fellow workers. In a good marriage each person can find sustenance to ease the resentment we all feel about having to yield to other people's wishes and rights. Marriage provides an oasis where sex, humor, and play can flourish.

Finally, a man and woman in a good, lasting marriage with children feel connected with the past and have an interest in the future. A family makes an important link in the chain of human history. By sharing responsibility for the next generation, parents can find purpose and a strengthened sense of identity.

These rewards take root in the soil of a strong, stable marriage. But, surprisingly, we know very little about what makes such a marriage.

As a psychologist who has been studying the American family for most of my professional life, I have observed many changes in relationships between men and women and in society's attitudes about marriage and children. In 1980 I founded a large research and clinical center in the San Francisco Bay Area, where my colleagues and I have seen thousands of men, women, and children from families going through first or second divorces. Presently I am conducting a twenty-five-year follow-up of sixty couples who underwent divorce in 1971, with an emphasis on the lives of their 131 children, who are now grown and involved in their own marriages and divorces.

These young men and women, whom I have been interviewing at regular intervals as part of the longest study ever done on divorce, provide unique insights into its long-term effects on the American family. I have seen a great many children who, ten and fifteen years after their parents' divorce, are still struggling with unhappiness. On the threshold of adulthood, they are still in the shadow of that event. I am poignantly aware of how unfamiliar these children are with the kinds of relationships that exist in a happy family. Many tell me that they have never seen a good marriage.

I'm also concerned about the many men and women who remain lonely and sad years after a divorce. I'm doubly worried about the high divorce rate in second marriages with children, which compounds the suffering for everyone. I am sometimes criticized for being overly pessimistic about the long-term effects of divorce, but my observations are drawn from the real world. Only if you see the children and parents of divorce day in and day out can you understand what the statistics mean in human terms.

I want to make it clear that I am not against divorce. I am deeply aware of how wretched a bad marriage can be and of the need for the remedy of divorce. But divorce by itself does not improve the institution of marriage. Some people learn from sad experience to choose more carefully the second time around. Others do not. Many never get a true second chance.

In the past twenty years, marriage in America has undergone a profound, irrevocable transformation, driven by changes in women's roles and the heightened expectations of both men and women. Without realizing it, we have crossed a marital Rubicon. For the first time in our history, the decision to stay married is purely voluntary. Anyone can choose to leave at any time — and everyone knows it, including the children. There used to be only two legal routes out of marriage — adultery and abandonment. Today one partner simply has to say, for whatever reason, "I want out." Divorce is as simple as a trip to the nearest courthouse.

Each year two million adults and a million children in this country are newly affected by divorce. One in two American marriages ends in divorce, and one in three children can expect to experience their parents' divorce. This situation has powerful ripple effects that touch us all. The sense that relationships are unstable affects the family next door, the people down the block, the other children in the classroom. Feelings of intense anxiety about marriage permeate the consciousness of all young men and women on the threshold of adulthood. At every wedding the guests wonder, privately, will this marriage last? The bride and groom themselves may question why they should marry, since it's likely to break up.

To understand how our social fabric has been transformed, think of marriage as an institution acted upon by centripetal forces pulling inward and centrifugal forces pulling outward. In times past the centripetal forces — law, tradition, religion, parental influence — exceeded those that could pull a marriage apart, such as infidelity, abuse, financial disaster, failed expectations, or the lure of the frontier. Nowadays the balance has changed. The weakened centripetal forces no longer exceed those that tug marriages apart.

In today's marriages, in which people work long hours, travel extensively, and juggle careers with family, more forces tug at the relationship than ever before. Modern marriages are battered by the demands of her workplace as well as his, by changing community values, by anxiety about making ends meet each month, by geographical moves, by unemployment and recession, by the vicissitudes of child care, and by a host of other issues.

Marriage counselors like to tell their clients that there are at least six people in every marital bed — the couple and both sets of parents. I'm here to say that a crazy quilt of conflicting personal values and shifting social attitudes is also in that bed. The confusion over roles and the indifference of the community to long-term conjugal relationships are there, as are the legacies of a self-absorbed, me-first, feminist-do-or-die, male-backlash society. The ease of divorce and changing attitudes about the permanence of marriage have themselves become centrifugal forces.

Our great unacknowledged fear is that these potent outside forces will overwhelm the human commitment that marriage demands and that marriage as a lasting institution will cease for most people. We are left with a crushing anxiety about the future of marriage and about the men and women within it.

My study of divorce has inevitably led me to think deeply about marriage. Just as people who work with the dying worry about death, those of us who work with troubled marriages are constantly forced to look at our own relationships. So I have carefully taken note of my marriage and those of my three grown children. As our fiftieth wedding anniversary approaches, I have thought long and hard about what my husband and I have done to protect our marriage. Why have we been able to love each other for so many years? Did we begin differently from those who divorced? Did we handle crises differently? Or were we just lucky? What have I learned that I can pass on to my children and my grandchildren?

I certainly have not been happy all through each year of my marriage. There have been good times and bad, angry and joyful moments, times of ecstasy and times of quiet contentment. But I would never trade my husband, Robert, for another man. I would not swap my marriage for any other. This does not mean that I find other men unattractive, but there is all the difference in the world between a passing fancy and a life plan. For me, there has always been only one life plan, the one I have lived with my husband. But why is this so? What makes some marriages work while others fail?

An acquaintance of mine — a highly regarded psychologist who has done extensive marriage counseling — called me when she became engaged. She said, "I want to spend several hours with you, drawing on your experience. My fiancé is several years older than I am and has been through one divorce. He's afraid of another failure. I'm thirty-eight years old and have for many years been frightened of marriage. What wisdom do you have for me based on your own marriage, which has always looked so ideal to me, and also based on your many years of work with divorce? Help me anticipate what lies ahead for Jim and me, so I can be prepared." Her request intrigued me. What wisdom did she seek? She did not want shortcuts or hints but a realistic vision that could guide their efforts in building a successful marriage.

Not long after her call I decided to design a qualitative study of fifty couples who had built lasting, happy marriages, couples who had confronted the same obstacles, crises, and temptations as everyone else and had overcome them. As I began setting up the study, I drew up a list of questions that would guide my inquiry. Are the people in good marriages different from the men and women whose marriages fall apart? Are there common ideas, ways of dealing with the inevitable crises? What can we learn about selecting a partner, about sex, the stresses of the workplace, infidelity, the arrival of a baby or of adolescence, coping with midlife, aging, and retirement? What is happy in a marriage when people are in their twenties, thirties, forties, or fifties, or when they reach retirement? What are the central themes at each life stage? What makes men happy? What makes women happy? What does each spouse value in one another? What do they regard as the glue of the marriage?

From the beginning I was aware of the limitations of this kind of research, including the risk that it would attract vulnerable couples seeking a stamp of approval on their marriage, as well as the risks of selection bias, reliance on volunteers, and the small size of the sample. But I felt that these limitations were far outweighed by the potential understanding to be gained from exploring subjectively defined happiness in marriage. I planned to interview all of the individuals separately and each couple together over a two-year period.

Although fifty couples may seem too small a number from which to make sweeping conclusions about marriage, my conclusions are not meant to explain all there is to know about this subject. My intentions are much more modest. I have looked for commonalities as well as individual differences, hoping to find patterns on which to build general hypotheses. To me this is a fertile method of inquiry, but I should emphasize that I regard this as a pilot study. Further investigation would include more subjects and greater ethnic, geographic, and economic diversity, as well as homosexual couples.

The couples I studied, all of whom lived in northern California, were predominantly white, middle-class, and well educated. They do not represent the entire country and were not selected as typical. In a country as heterogeneous as ours, finding "typical" couples has limited value; the payoff comes from understanding different subgroups within the whole. The fifty couples represent a "first cut" within a particular socioeconomic group — but a group that is influential in setting social and cultural trends for the nation. Californians, who make up a sixth of the country's population, are more likely than other Americans to be distant from their families of origin and regions of birth — circumstances that are increasingly the norm in our highly mobile society.

The sample divided almost evenly among people who had married in the 1950s, 1960s, 1970s, and early 1980s. This provided a panoramic look at the changes that have overtaken marriage in the last four decades: the sexual revolution, the women's movement, the rise of dual-career couples.

I recruited the fifty couples by casting a wide net into the community, starting with the group of women who had heard my earliest thoughts on the study. For a while, whenever I spoke to professional groups, schools, social clubs, or other organizations, I requested as my fee the names of couples willing to participate in the marriage project. I found others with the help of my graduate students in the Department of Social Welfare at the University of California at Berkeley. These couples were younger and less affluent than the others in the study, and they had young children.

My criteria were straightforward. Both husband and wife had to consider their marriage a happy one. They had to have been married at least nine years, because the number of divorces peaks in the early years, and I wanted my subjects to be past that danger point. The shortest marriage studied was ten years, the longest forty years. The participants had to agree to lengthy interviews. I asked to see each spouse separately and then together in interviews that often lasted up to three hours each. Most people were interviewed at home, and a few at their place of work. I wanted to observe them in the surroundings they had created.

Although I had hoped to study only first marriages, it soon became clear that that was too limiting, so I included second marriages with children. The couple had to have produced children by the marriage, except in remarriages in which each partner brought at least one child from a previous marriage. I included children because all of my professional work has focused on families and because married couples without children either by choice or incapacity are psychologically and socially very different from those with children over the course of their lives. In some cases I met the children, and in a few instances I interviewed or played with them.

All of the participants understood that the questions and answers were on the record, that I could use all dialogue and family histories in this book, but that I would fully disguise their identities — not

simply their names but their occupations and aspects of their surroundings. No one was paid; their only reward was in helping other
people learn about good marriages. I was pleased at how open these
people were — at how completely they trusted me. Because I promised
full confidentiality, I was often privy to information that even the
person's spouse did not have.

One very important goal of the study was to find out what people in
these marriages meant by "happy." To what did they attribute their
happiness? Were they happy from the start, and if not, what made the
difference? I've always believed firmly that in a great many areas of life,
especially in the realm of human relationships, ordinary people know
a lot more than the experts. One of the major mistakes of my field is
that we don't learn from people's expertise: we ask questions, but we
don't listen to their wisdom.

Many years of working with divorcing couples have taught me how
little one can tell about a marriage from the outside. Consider how
surprised everyone is when the picture-book couple next door files for
divorce. The interior does not match the facade. "Our family represents to some people a Camelot, when they view it from the outside,"
one woman told me. "Even those who know us don't see the nitty-
gritty that every marriage goes through. But he and I know it. And our
children do, now that they're grown." The problem, then, is how to
gain entry into the inner sanctum of a marriage and not be misled by
the front door.

I began each interview by asking "Tell me what's good about this
marriage." My second question was "What's disappointing about your
marriage?" This opening allowed each person to start wherever she or
he was comfortable. More important, it gave my subjects no clues
about what I might want to hear, and it anchored the discussion to
the reality that all relationships are a mixture of good and less good
elements.

I asked many questions about each person's parents, siblings, and
other significant figures and about the major events of early life. I was
interested in their view of the parents' marriage and their own relationship with each parent. I asked about experiences in adolescence
and young adult life, including early sexual relationships, the steps that
led to the marriage, and any misgivings they had had. I tried to elicit
a full history of all domains of the marriage, including conflict, sex,

extramarital relationships, household routines, work experience, friends, extended family, crises, including deaths, and, of course, the children. My intent was to understand their life experience prior to the marriage, the factors that had brought them together, and the changes that had occurred during the marriage. I was also interested in fantasies, roads not taken, and wishes that remained unfulfilled. Finally, I wanted to know their perspective on their past and any advice they had for others.

These couples spoke of their love for and friendship with each other and of the pleasures and frustrations of parenting. They talked about sex and passion, commitment and shared values. They described stormy conflicts and long-standing differences. They recounted their childhood histories and the relationships in their original families. They talked about their first reactions to each other and to each other's family and about their decision to marry. They made it clear that they were not happy all the time. Many admitted that at times they wanted out. Some confessed that on occasion they felt they had made a mistake. But each person felt strongly that on balance their marriage had a goodness of fit in needs, wishes, and expectations. Although everyone was reluctant to define love, they spoke movingly, often lyrically, about how much they valued, respected, and enjoyed the other person and how appreciative they were of the other's responsiveness to their needs.

They stressed different aspects of the relationship. Some said that their marriage had given them a sense of continuity and of hope for the future. One thirty-eight-year-old man said, "We share a vision about how our lives will unfold — like when we're seventy, our kids will be good and responsible people who care about the world and other people."

Others emphasized the security that marriage afforded. One woman said, "I feel safer in this marriage than I have ever felt in any other place in my life." Another said, "I knew we would go through forty years of ups and downs, but it would be absolutely inconceivable to me that we wouldn't make it to the end of our lives. And I think that he feels that way too. It gives you this incredible feeling of safety and comfort, so that you don't have to ask those wrenching questions over and over again. And I know that is at the core of our sense of security in an insecure world."

Happy marriages are not carefree. There are good times and bad times, and certainly partners may face serious crises together or separately. Happily married husbands and wives get depressed, fight, lose jobs, struggle with the demands of the workplace and the crises of infants and teenagers, and confront sexual problems. They cry and yell and get frustrated. They come from sad, abusive, neglectful backgrounds as well as from more stable families; all marriages are haunted by ghosts from the past.

Every good marriage must adapt to developmental changes in each partner, bending and yielding to the redefinitions that all men and women go through. It must expand to accommodate children, close ranks when the children leave home, and metamorphose at retirement. But somehow, for reasons that are critically important and that I explore here, these people have stayed married despite the *Sturm und Drang* of modern life. They feel, and say with conviction, that the marriage will last. After ten, twenty, thirty, or more years of being together, they regard the marriage with contentment and feel confident about its survival.

By observing these couples, I learned how much marriage has changed over the past decades. The changes are reflected in the different expectations and experiences of the men and women who married in each of the decades from the fifties to the early eighties. A particularly striking change is in the sexual experiences of women prior to marriage and in the woman's role within the marriage. All of the women who married in the fifties were either virgins or pregnant at the wedding, whereas none of those who married during the early eighties were virgins. Some had had sexual experiences with many lovers, beginning when they were fifteen. The rise of dual-career families and the increased anxiety about divorce are also seen in the experiences of these couples.

Marriage is an ever-changing relationship, and it must be examined at several points along the way. A snapshot cannot substitute for a portrait of a marriage over time. Two years after the first interview with each couple, I contacted them again, and everyone agreed to a second interview. In that short time, a period of economic recession, all kinds of changes had occurred. People were really worried about making ends meet. Some middle-aged husbands had lost jobs that they could never hope to match. One man got the job he'd wanted his whole life and had moved his family to London.

The shock waves of adolescence had rocked many families. Some children won prizes; one boy was expelled from school for smoking marijuana. In one family the child of a former marriage turned up without warning. There had been unexpected promotions, accidents (including one head-on collision on the Golden Gate Bridge in which three family members were seriously hurt), and life-threatening illnesses. Several grandparents had died. In short, a lot of life had happened. But no couple had divorced.

Many therapists seem to think that the people in a faltering marriage are made of real flesh and blood, struggling with tangible problems, while those in a good marriage are something like Balinese shadow puppets. But the people who describe the inner workings of their marriages in this book are fully dimensional human beings.

It's important to stress that I am not writing about lasting marriages per se. People can be held together for decades by lethargy, fear, mutual helplessness, or economic dependency, in marriages that are, to my mind, empty shells. This is a book about marriages in which both husband and wife agree that the relationship is satisfying. With justification, these men and women consider their marriages to be personal triumphs.

I should also say that this is not a how-to book. It will not tell you how to fight with your husband so that you can strengthen your marriage, how to have a better sex life with new techniques, or what to do if a guy at the office keeps telling you that his wife doesn't understand him. It will not give you ten easy steps to happiness or a vaccine against family strife. I believe in my heart not only that these approaches do not help but that they trivialize and demean the central relationship of adult life. Instead, what I have tried to write is a book about the intimate interiors of some successful marriages. To my mind this book offers an opportunity to look behind closed doors, to see in detail how people struggle with the central journey of adulthood. By getting to know these couples, by sharing their disappointments and triumphs, the reader will be able to use the insights they provide. I hope every part of this book will be helpful to young people contemplating marriage, to convey the enormous pleasures that await them and to tell them where the mines are hidden. I especially want them to learn that romance does not have to end when the honeymoon is over.

Early in this century Carl Jung told us that marriage is the most complex of human relationships. Today marriage is more fragile than ever. But I am committed to the view that if a man and woman begin their marriage with a healthy respect for its complexity, they stand a much greater chance of success. If they can grasp the richly nuanced, subtle needs that people bring from their childhood experiences and can understand how the past connects with the present, they can build mutual understanding and love based on true intimacy. If they can see how each domain of marriage connects with every other — especially how their sex life affects every aspect of their relationship — and if they can acknowledge the central conflicts in all marriages and the importance of friendship and nurturance in muting those conflicts, they will be well on their way toward building an enduring relationship. Finally, if they can appreciate the myriad ways that people grow and change through the years and realize that a happy, lasting marriage is challenged and rebuilt every day, then they will have acquired the only map there is for a successful lifetime journey together.

Many conservatives say we should go back to the days of that ideal couple, Ozzie and Harriet; but in fact, the children raised in the days of that television show grew up to become pioneers in the new landscape of marriage. Only five of the hundred spouses I interviewed wanted a marriage like their parents', even though many genuinely loved (or at least felt compassion for) their parents. The men consciously rejected the role models provided by their fathers. The women said that they could never be happy living as their mothers did. Clearly, few people really do want to turn back the clock.

Some therapists advocate teaching people to reduce their expectations of marriage, so that disappointment will not ensue — as if divorce occurs because of a gap between people's high expectations and the realities they confront after marriage. But what kind of response would you get if you told your son or daughter not to expect very much from marriage? Would cynicism and lower expectations make for better marriages and happier families? For better or worse, Americans have high expectations of marriage and show no signs of backing down from the pursuit of individual happiness.

I am convinced that the kind of society we have in the future will depend on how we address relationships within the family. As the external forces keeping modern marriages together weaken, the forces holding them together from within grow ever more important. To understand these forces, we need a whole new body of knowledge. We need guidelines that will enable men and women to fulfill their deep longings for love and friendship. We know a great deal about marriages that fail, for many couples seek counseling when their relationships are unable to weather the inevitable crises of life. But while studies of marital problems and divorce now overflow many library shelves, the entire body of research on happy marriage would fill less than half a shelf.

It has always been easier to identify the dark forces that spell misery than to understand what contributes to happiness. Illness and anger are more easily explored than health and love. Research on happy marriage is in its infancy. Considering the importance of the subject, it's astonishing how little work has been done. I found only a handful of studies — and only one that relied on individual interviews with happily married couples. Beyond this one study, which involved only twelve families from a religious community, I could find no other qualitative studies, which are fundamental to understanding complex social issues and human behavior. The case-study method, which is central to clinical work in medicine, psychology, psychoanalysis, and ethnology, is a major tool in qualitative research. It is the method of choice in building psychological theory.

Reviewing the recent quantitative research — studies in which large data sets are analyzed statistically — on the general subject of marriage, the distinguished sociologist Norval Glenn expressed disappointment. He noted that for several decades researchers have tended to test simple propositions that don't advance our understanding of marriage. He concluded that we need more qualitative research to generate new ideas.

To glean insights about human feelings, motivations, and emotions, the researcher must meet people face to face. Telephone surveys or mailed questionnaires do not penetrate to the subtleties and nuances of life. A survey asking "How often do you see your father?" will not reveal how a woman feels about her father. The question "How often have you been unfaithful?" doesn't touch the emotional impact of infidelity. A researcher can ask for a yes-or-no response to "Have you ever considered divorce?" but a questionnaire cannot provide an adequate answer to the potent question "What would break your marriage?" During a face-to-face interview expressions often tell more than any words could — as when a mature man breaks into tears when asked "What would happen if you lost your wife?" or when a woman crosses her legs and smiles like the Cheshire cat when asked "How faithful have you been?" Experimental psychologists say that in predicting divorce a husband's body language is more useful than his words. And what people *don't* say can be more important than what they do say.

To study the visceral questions of life, one needs to do case studies, working with individuals or small groups in intimate settings, asking open-ended questions and listening carefully to the answers that flow spontaneously, giving each person time to describe his or her feelings in words and gestures. In my studies I have tried to get to know each individual as intimately as possible. I listen to and absorb not just people's life stories but the sequence in which they tell them, as well as their casual remarks, smiles and tears, dreams and fantasies. They open their hearts to me and, in a figurative sense, the very doors to their bedrooms.

While designing my own study of good marriages, I did come across a few interesting recent studies by others. John Gottman and his colleagues have researched different styles of marital conflict and their physiological concomitants in men and women. They distinguish the kind of conflict that can destroy a marriage from conflict that occurs within its bounds. They also propose that a good marriage is best maintained by striking a balance between positive and negative interactions. They suggest that the "magic number" of five positive interactions will undo the impact of one negative interaction. Gottman has also worked on the prediction of divorce according to patterns of detachment observed in men experiencing conflict with their wives.

In 1981 Arlene Skolnick examined marriages selected from a large longitudinal study of adult lives. Comparing data from two interviews ten years apart, without any observations about the couple's interactions, she concluded that marital relationships have a high potential for change and do not necessarily decline over the years. She proposed that situational factors such as money, health, and career success were of major importance in marital contentment or unhappiness.

Two recent studies of long-lasting marriages, by Robert and Jeanette Lauer in 1987 and Florence Kaslow and Helga Hammerschmidt in 1992, were based largely on data from mailed questionnaires. Both studies reported the importance of friendship, commitment, and shared values, and both found many long-lasting marriages that were unhappy. Plans are under way for replicating the Kaslow and Hammerschmidt study in other countries and different cultures.

I could find only one study of healthy families. Jerry M. Lewis and his colleagues, in 1976, assessed twelve families who belonged to a Protestant church in Texas and who were selected by church staff, from a group of volunteers, as functioning well. The researchers concluded that there was "no single thread" to healthy family functioning. These families were characterized by mutual affection and trust in one another and in the community, respect for individual differences in perception and feelings, the ability to communicate, the ability to accept loss, and clear-cut boundaries between parents and children. Although the study was small, it has been influential in family therapy. It provides one of the few examples of good family functioning that therapists can use to compare with the troubled families in their care.

I could find no research in which happy marriage, as subjectively defined by both partners, was the specific focus of an in-depth inquiry.

After completing the first round of interviews with the men and women in my study, I spent some time thinking about why these couples had stepped forward. Some clearly felt that what they had achieved together was a triumph. Others were intrigued by the notion of examining their marriage. Still others were flattered to be included in a "happy" sample. But I think the main reason for their participation was that I gave them an opportunity to tell their story. Marriage in America is a private affair. When people divorce, they may broadcast their difficulties to the world, but those who are quietly and happily married don't discuss it openly — not even with their children or close friends. It isn't dinner table conversation, nor is it grist for the television talk shows or movie scripts.

And this is precisely why we have so much to learn from these quiet successes. The erotic excitement and voyeurism of the television shows do not prepare us for life because they don't teach us how to solve real problems.

This book, then, is an attempt to map new territory: the internal life of good marriages in a culture of divorce. Like other early cartographers, I have probably missed major oceans or inadvertently combined continents. Undoubtedly there are more kinds of happy marriages than are reported in these pages. But this is an exploration, a pilot effort, with all the caveats and strengths of such a study. I hope that many other studies will follow.

# 2

# Patterns in Marriage

THE FIRST INTERVIEW I conducted for this study was full of surprises. I met the husband of one of my couples, a fifty-two-year-old engineer, outside a conference room at his main office in San Jose. As he left the meeting for our interview, he told me, his colleagues had ribbed him about participating in a project on happy marriage. He turned and said, "Look, you bastards, you wouldn't qualify."

After leading me to his office, he sat down behind a desk cluttered with charts, reports, and computer paraphernalia. He began with a warning. "I hope it won't offend you if I use strong words." I assured him that it would be hard to offend me. "When I married my wife, at age thirty," he announced, "I liked her. I had been a bachelor in the fast lane and had had plenty of sex with beautiful women. But what I wanted from her was different. I didn't love her when I married her. But somehow, two to three years into the marriage, I realized she was the first woman I had ever really loved."

"What did you love about her?"

"She's beautiful through and through. She's a no-bullshit lady with a set of moral values that are visible, and she doesn't wear them like a badge. She stands for certain things and makes no bones about it." These were not the words that readers of *Cosmopolitan* ever hear about how to catch and keep your man.

Later I asked, "How faithful have you been?"

"I've strayed."

"How much?"

"Two times," he said. "Briefly, when I was on the road." He guffawed. "Judy, if this is what infidelity is about, they can keep it."

Several days later I conducted my second interview. The wife I was visiting set out a sterling silver coffee service and the most beautiful strawberries I had ever seen. It was nine o'clock in the morning; shafts of sunlight fell through a casement window, accentuating the high polish of this woman's immaculate furniture. I began, "What's happy about your marriage?"

"What's wonderful about my marriage," she said, pouring coffee in an elegant manner, "is that I have chosen a very supportive man who's allowed me to grow up within the marriage. I live a very full life. I've changed careers a number of times, and he's supported that. I've raised three men I'm very proud of. And he's had a big input as a father."

Later I asked her, "What do you think he would say about the marriage?"

She laughed. "He would say that I bewitched him thirty years ago so that he hasn't noticed a lot of my faults. He would say that I make him very happy and that we both have kept our sense of humor."

"And humor is important?"

"Yes," she said, "because life is so serious."

The next day I drove up and down hills looking for the house of my third family. At last I found it, set back from the street behind a wild tangle of honeysuckle, ivy, sword ferns, and bamboo. On the path to the front door, I stepped over a bicycle, a washtub, and a truck tire. The wife opened the door, smiled broadly, pushed a large dog out of the way, and greeted me graciously in a finishing-school accent. "Dr. Wallerstein, please come in, we're so happy to meet you." I noticed the portraits of four young children on the piano, a cage full of fluttery finches, and two cats. The house looked as if it had been hit by a hurricane, with stuffing coming out of the sofa, papers strewn on every table, and toys lying about, yet the wife greeted me as if I were being ushered into a chateau. I had entered a hideaway.

I realized then that each of these marriages was a different world, a sovereign country unto itself. Rather than a single archetype of happy marriage, I found many different kinds. Like a richly detailed tapestry, each relationship was woven from the strands of love, friendship, sexual fulfillment, nurture, protection, emotional security, economic responsibility, and coparenting. But the patterns in the marital weave varied, and gradually I began to see several distinct types.

I learned that at the heart of any good marriage is a core relation-ship created out of the conscious and unconscious fit of the partners' needs and wishes. This core reflects what each partner wants and expects from the other — expectations influenced by relationships that begin in infancy, childhood, and adolescence but that are ultimately shaped within the marriage. It also reflects what each person considers undesirable or unacceptable. The core relationship includes each person's perceptions of the other: "She is so gentle," "He is so exciting"; and what each values in the other: "She is entirely honest," "He will be a wonderful father." The marital core represents a shared vision of what brought these two people together and what they see for their future as a couple and as a family — Me and You and Us through time.

As my study proceeded, I began to see that these good marriages naturally sorted themselves into distinguishable types. Once the study was completed, I decided to propose a typology that consists of four marriage forms, which I have labeled romantic, rescue, companionate, and traditional. Although a relationship rarely falls neatly into a single category, the couples in this study were largely captured by this typology. Some of the marriages clearly belonged to one type or another, while others were hybrids. Undoubtedly other types of marriage exist. In many cultures throughout the world, marriages are more embedded in the extended family than they are in America. Some long-lasting homosexual relationships would fall into these categories, while others would require an extension of my typology.

Although the types overlap, they are unquestionably distinct forms. Each gives priority to some needs and relegates others to second place. It is inevitable that in weaving one pattern, we exclude others. Every marriage has roads not taken. Each offers a different menu of possibilities and limitations.

Thus each type of marriage provides a different degree and kind of closeness between husband and wife. The views of the roles of the man and the woman vary among the different types; so do the views of the appropriate division of labor and responsibility for child care. For some couples a single pattern of connectedness remains constant throughout the marriage. In others the core relationship may shift gradually or change radically at a critical developmental transition, such as the birth of the first child, the time when the children leave home, the arrival of midlife, or retirement.

Sometimes the man and woman are in accord from courtship on. More often they come to agree about fundamental issues during the early years of the marriage. The core relationship emerges gradually as the partners weave the tapestry of their relationship. If the fit is right, the marriage itself helps shape the closeness in values and shared expectations. A marriage in which two people have incompatible expectations or unmodifiable demands is likely to fail.

The first of my proposed types is the romantic marriage, which has at its core a lasting, passionately sexual relationship. A couple in a romantic marriage often shares the sense that they were destined to be together. Exciting, sensual memories of their first meeting and courtship retain a glow over the years and are a continuing part of the bond between them.

The second type I identified is the rescue marriage. Although every good marriage provides comfort and healing for past unhappiness, in a successful rescue marriage the partners' early experiences have been traumatic. They are "walking wounded" as they begin their lives together. The healing that takes place during the course of the marriage is the central theme.

I call the third type companionate, and this may be the most common form of marriage among younger couples, as it reflects the social changes of the last two decades. At its core is friendship, equality, and the value system of the women's movement, with its corollary that the male role, too, needs to change. A major factor in the companionate marriage is the attempt to balance the partners' serious emotional investment in the workplace with their emotional investment in the relationship and the children.

The fourth type is the traditional marriage, which has at its core a clear division of roles and responsibilities. The woman takes charge of home and family while the man is the primary wage earner. Today women in this form of marriage define their lives in terms of chapters: the time before marriage and children, the chapter when children are young, and a later chapter that may include a return to work or a new undertaking.

All marriages need to be renegotiated as they mature, but renegotiation is especially important in second marriages. Although they come in every form — they can be romantic, traditional, companionate, or rescue — second marriages carry a particular set of challenges. They are accompanied by a host of characters from the past: the ex-wife, the ex-husband, children from the first marriage. As I learned from my study, people who enter a second marriage have a specific agenda: to undo the trauma they experienced and prevent its recurrence.

Also worthy of special mention is the retirement marriage. While there were only a few retired couples in this study, they shared many characteristics, providing insight on happy marriage in older age. The most notable feature is that the couple spends more time together than they have at any earlier time. This togetherness enriches, challenges, and surely changes their relationship.

Each of the four marriage types has a dangerous hidden potential within its design that I call the "antimarriage." The antimarriage emerges when the negative aspects that exist in every marriage begin to dominate. At that point the relationship can become a lifeless shell or a collusive arrangement in which the neurotic symptoms of the partners mesh so well that the marriage endures indefinitely. Thus the romantic marriage has the tragic potential for freezing husband and wife into a self-absorbed, childlike preoccupation with each other, turning its back on the rest of the world, including the children. The rescue marriage can provide, instead of healing, a new forum for replaying earlier traumas. Spouses have the capacity to wound and abuse each other, and one may suffer the abuse without leaving or protesting — mistakenly concluding that this is what life is about. The hopes for rescue and comfort that led to the marriage are buried and forgotten.

The danger in a companionate marriage is that it may degenerate into a brother-and-sister relationship. Invested primarily in their respective careers, husband and wife see each other only fleetingly, sharing a bed with little or no sex or emotional intimacy. And a traditional marriage may focus so narrowly on bringing up the children that the partners view each other only as parents; they dread the time when the children will leave home, knowing they will be left with little in common.

A second marriage also contains the potential for antimarriage. The marriage may be so preoccupied with the earlier failures that it is unable to take off on its own. Sometimes, in their zeal to avoid repeating the earlier suffering, the man and the woman unite as allies in battle, projecting all their current difficulties onto the prior partners. The fighting fueled by shared hostility can absorb energy and large sums of money when it involves children. This form of antimarriage cements the relationship but falls far short of a good marriage.

Marriage today provides a wider range of choices than ever before. Each kind of marriage has its strengths, its limitations, and its hazards. Understanding what each choice entails would enable a couple in the early years of marriage to get their bearings quickly and plan ahead. For example, a companionate marriage requires the couple to make careful decisions about when to have children and how they will be cared for. It also requires them to take special precautions against becoming too separate. Similarly, a traditional marriage depends on having a single sufficient income so that one parent can stay home with the children. It, too, requires particular nourishments in order to flourish.

The choice of a type of marriage is of course not entirely conscious. At its best the choice reflects the partners' unique conscious and unconscious fit. But it is within the couple's power to nurture the marriage and prevent its deterioration.

A good marriage is a process of continual change as it reflects new issues, deals with problems that arise, and uses the resources available at each stage of life. All long-lasting marriages change, if simply because we all change as we grow older. People's needs, expectations, and wishes change during the life cycle; biological aging is intertwined with psychological change in every domain, including work, health, sex, parenting, and friends. The social milieu and external circumstances change as well. Thus the individuals change, the marriage changes, and the world outside changes — and not necessarily in sync with one another. As one woman said, "John and I have had at least six different marriages."

Many men and women are still becoming adults as they work on the first chapter of their lives together — getting to know each other sexually, emotionally, and psychologically. This time of absorbing exploration is critically important for defining the couple's core relationship. Sadly, many couples find they cannot navigate this difficult first leg of the course. But if they do succeed, they will have a sturdy foundation for the structure of their marriage.

The birth of a child entirely revamps the internal landscape of marriage. Becoming a father or mother is a major step in the life course, a step that requires inner psychological growth as well as changes in every part of the marital relationship and in the extended family. It is also usually a time when one or both partners have made career commitments; the tough road of the workplace stretches ahead, and its stresses are high.

For many people the years when the children are growing up is the busiest time of their lives. A central issue is balancing the demands of work and of home. Children's needs for parental time and attention multiply along with the continuing demands of the workplace and often of school. Many couples cannot find enough time to be together even to exchange greetings, let alone make love.

The course of marriage changes again when children become adolescents, when parents dealing with midlife issues and presentiments of aging are suddenly faced with sexually active youngsters. The growing dependency, illness, or death of the spouses' own aging parents adds further turbulence to this period. When the children leave home, the couple must find each other again and rebuild their relationship. This new stage provides an opportunity to re-create the marriage in a different mold, perhaps with time to travel and play together. If a husband and wife have not succeeded in building a good marriage by now, they may find themselves merely sharing a household.

A later part of the journey is retirement, when issues of dependency and illness, as well as the opportunity to pursue new hobbies and interests and the continuing need for sexuality, take center stage. Once again the marriage is redefined, as the couple face life's final chapters and inevitably consider the loss of the partner and their own deaths.

All through adulthood our internal lives change as we create new images of ourselves and call up old images from the past. At each stage we draw on different memories and wishes, pulling them out like cards from a deck held close to the heart. The birth of a child draws on the memories and unconscious images of each parent's own infancy and childhood. That child's adolescence evokes the memories and conflicts of one's own teen years. Parents, watching their teenagers assert their independence, remember their own risk-taking behavior and realize that they were often saved from disaster by the skin of their teeth. And as old age approaches, every person draws on the experiences of prior losses in the family.

We have for many years told our children that marriage requires hard and continuing work, but since we could not tell them where or how to begin this work, we soon lost their attention. How could we tell them what we did not know?

I believe that the happy marriages I explore in this book can tell us a great deal about the kind of hard work that is required. I propose that a good marriage is built on a series of sequential psychological tasks that the man and the woman address together. I am convinced that the achievement of these goals is central to the success of the marriage.

The concept of psychological tasks is drawn from psychoanalyst Erik Erikson's blueprint of the life cycle. Erikson explains that at each stage, from infancy to advanced old age, the individual confronts specific challenges. If these are not dealt with, psychological development stops dead in its tracks. For example, the task of the child during the elementary school years is to acquire the capacity to learn in the classroom and to get along with peers in play and friendship. If the child fails to master these tasks, she is handicapped in her future development. The psychological task of the adolescent, the best known of Erikson's formulations, is to establish a secure base of identity — who she is and what she expects to be in the future, separate from her family.

As a result of this study, I have extended Erikson's classical concept of tasks that the individual must master. I suggest that the young married couple faces nine life challenges or psychological tasks, which I discuss and illustrate throughout this book. These tasks are not a set of instructions for achieving success, not a checklist to be tacked up on the kitchen wall and marked off as each is completed. I have lifted these tasks out of the living experience of all marriages, including my own, and given them names and shapes. They are not imposed on the couple from the outside, to be accepted or rejected as they wish; they are inherent in the nature of marriage. They represent the essence of living together as man and wife and making it work.

Whether the couple is aware of it or not, they are necessarily engaged in these tasks if the marriage is on track. And indeed, in many of the divorced families I have studied, these tasks were hardly begun, or their resolution was so brittle that it broke apart at a time of crisis. My goal is to describe the tasks so that people building a marriage can proceed with greater sophistication and confidence.

Folk wisdom captures some of these issues in the story of the three little pigs. Although this is a parable about leaving home, it is also a story about building one's house — an excellent metaphor for marriage. When the first little pig builds a house of straw, the wolf comes along and blows the house down instantly. The second little pig, a bit older and wiser, builds a stronger house of twigs, but it cannot withstand the wolf's onslaught either. The third little pig (who may really be the same pig at a later stage of development) builds a solid house of bricks, which the wolf cannot destroy. The wily wolf then slides down the chimney, but the third little pig has put. a pot of boiling water into the fireplace and thus defeats the enemy inside the house. A house built of bricks by a wise pig will withstand not only the wolves outside the door but also those on the inside.

The metaphor of building a strong house applies to every marriage; when children arrive, the "walls" are extended to accommodate the needs, wishes, and emotional growth of the whole family and to withstand the wolves outside the door and those that lurk within. Because crises are inevitable, a marriage is never out of danger. Threats from without include such unpredictable events as the loss of a job, a forced move to a new area, a natural disaster. The stresses on a marriage inside its walls include the maturational changes associated with parenthood, midlife, retirement, and aging, and tragedies such as illness and death. The threat of divorce lurks both outside and inside the house. All major changes — accidental or developmental — have the potential for either weakening the walls of the marriage or leading to their reinforcement, depending on whether the couple blame each other or work together to deal with the threat and move on.

Many of the divorcing families that I have observed failed to construct a marriage strong enough to withstand the inevitable, acute, and ongoing stresses of life. By comparison, the good marriages examined here have maintained their integrity and staying power because they were built of sturdier materials and were reinforced over the years as the menacing wolves appeared. It is the lifetime process of building that distinguishes good marriages and the people in them.

The nine tasks I have identified are as follows:

- To separate emotionally from the family of one's childhood so as to invest fully in the marriage and, at the same time, to redefine the lines of connection with both families of origin.
- To build togetherness by creating the intimacy that supports it while carving out each partner's autonomy. These issues are central throughout the marriage but loom especially large at the outset, at midlife, and at retirement.

- To embrace the daunting roles of parents and to absorb the impact of Her Majesty the Baby's dramatic entrance. At the same time the couple must work to protect their own privacy.
- To confront and master the inevitable crises of life, maintaining the strength of the bond in the face of adversity.
- To create a safe haven for the expression of differences, anger, and conflict.
- To establish a rich and pleasurable sexual relationship and protect it from the incursions of the workplace and family obligations.
- To use laughter and humor to keep things in perspective and to avoid boredom by sharing fun, interests, and friends.
- To provide nurturance and comfort to each other, satisfying each partner's needs for dependency and offering continuing encouragement and support.
- To keep alive the early romantic, idealized images of falling in love while facing the sober realities of the changes wrought by time.

The first two tasks require psychological growth and subtle accommodation to the other person. Moreover, each requires giving up the independence and freedom of the single life for the satisfactions of being husband and wife. When the task of becoming a parent is added, the baby has the power to throw the relationship out of balance. This strain can break a marriage that is too fragile to contain a child.

The early years of marriage can be difficult because the first several tasks do not come single file. Usually they have to be addressed simultaneously and at least partially resolved to create a firm foundation for the marriage. On the other hand, many of the tasks coincide with the individual psychological tasks of adulthood. Building a marriage profoundly changes and strengthens both people. And as they build the marriage and protect it, they continue to change and grow as individuals.

One of the many pleasures of writing this book has been that it enabled me to reflect on my own marriage. As I retraced the steps my husband and I took together, it was clear to me that no one executes the nine tasks with ease. No amount of communication can eliminate the inherent conflict as two people try to live together and make decisions that will simultaneously further their individual interests while protecting the partner and the marriage itself. Nevertheless, although the tasks are serious, accomplishing them is a richly reward-ing process.

The couples you will meet in the following chapters have taught me a great deal, not only about creating a good marriage but also about maintaining it. Here is what I learned.

# PART TWO

# Romantic Marriage

# 3 ⁊

# Matt and Sara Turner

I T IS FASHIONABLE to think that passionate or romantic love is short-lived, that disenchantment sets in after a year or two, and that realism descends with a nine-to-five job and diaper pails. We've all been told that the cold light of day is different from the enchantment of starlight. Songwriters, after all, do not pen verses that begin "Daylight becomes you . . ."

But even before I undertook this study of happy marriage, I knew long-married couples who had maintained a loving, romantic, and often passionate vision of each other during their thousands of days and nights together. I wondered how common such romantic marriages were. Did they happen only to the lucky few? Were they as rare as the blue moon?

I was surprised to find that some 15 percent of the happily married couples in the study fell into the romantic marriage category. After twenty, thirty, even forty years of marriage, they talked of mutual love and passion, excitement and ecstasy.

"I've never not felt in love with my wife," said a man who had been married for sixteen years. "She is very feminine, and that's important to me. She's beautiful, soft, and warm. What's masculine about her is her fire. It's scary. She doesn't back down, she doesn't play a passive role. She's nurturing and accepting and exciting." His wife told me, "We have great sex. That's a very important part of our relationship, because of the intimacy and how much we understand each other's needs and fantasies. Our connection is very deep, our spirits are connected. There is something about the level of our intimacy and our love that was meant to be."

In speaking about their relationships, the men and women in romantic marriages said that their mate had brought joy to their lives, and when they spoke of hopes for their children they looked at their own marriage as the richest legacy they could bestow. After twenty-five years of marriage, a man told me, "My wish for my children is that they feel the joy of loving someone that I've felt in our marriage."

I soon realized that I had been granted a special opportunity. We've all heard stories of star-crossed lovers, like Romeo and Juliet, and of betrayal, as in *Anna Karenina*. But I was privileged to enter the interior landscape of truly happy, long-lasting romantic marriages — the kind every bride and groom dream about when they utter the words "I do."

The existence of these marriages constitutes an important discovery, for they widen our view of what is possible in a lasting marriage. They offer indisputable evidence that men and women can love each other passionately throughout their lifetimes.

I met Matt and Sara Turner through two of my colleagues, who knew them through their work for environmental organizations. Matt is a senior policy analyst at a major think tank, and Sara helped found a land trust organization. They married in the late 1950s, on the day she graduated from college. "They're still in love, Judy," said the woman who recommended them for the study. "They're an inspiration!"

In the spring of 1991 I set out to meet Matt and Sara. I found their house, a small but attractive shingled bungalow, behind a neat hedge on a narrow street in the Oakland hills. Inside, the knotty pine walls and bright Mexican carpets created a sense of warmth and coziness, while a tiny bay window scooped up sunlight like a bouquet of buttercups.

Sara invited me into a living room cluttered with inexpensive-looking furniture. A fine Chinese lacquer chest near the bay window, Sara later told me, was an heirloom from Matt's grandmother. She poured two cups of coffee, and we settled down to talk. At fifty-one, Sara was a slim, casual woman whose down-to-earth demeanor put me instantly at ease. Her strawberry-blond hair was cut short in a style that set off her eyes and her high cheekbones. She sat cross-legged, elbows propped on knees, and leaned forward to hear my first question.

When I asked Sara what she felt was happy about her marriage, she didn't hesitate. "What's happy about my marriage? Matt," she said, smiling. "Magic. It's always felt magical, and it continues to feel that way, thirty-two years later."

Reading my expression, she went on, "I know you're going to ask what I mean by magic. And I guess it's like most deeply religious questions. When you get down to the bottom line, I don't know what it is. Just that it still feels like magic. When things were toughest, that quality was still present, always present. There's something when we're together. I don't know what I'm describing, Judy. Is that love?"

Clearly Sara had a lot to say on this subject, and she was wonderfully expressive.

"We both felt the magic within the first hour we met. We talked about it then, and we still talk about it." She shrugged. "I guess I should tell you how we met. The story has its own kind of magic. I was dating someone, and he took me to this big off-campus party one night. I must have been all of nineteen, but I was certain that we were in love and that it would last forever." As she smiled at the memory, crow's feet crinkled around her lovely gray-green eyes. "I remember standing next to a partition in the room when I heard someone laugh. I turned to my boyfriend and said, 'Who has that wonderful laugh?' And he said, 'It's my ex-roommate, Matt.' I said I wanted to meet him, and when we got past the partition and I got close to him, it was the first time in my life that I had feelings about smelling a human being."

Sara paused just long enough to note my interest, then continued. "This ought to be embarrassing — but it isn't. I got near him, and I smelled a male human smell for the first time in my consciousness. It was wonderful, the most wonderful smell. Like I remember my babies smelling. I realized that I wanted to be near that smell. And I remember the smell as being safe." (It is interesting to note that the word "safe" came up in the stories of a surprising number of these marriages — not just in romantic marriages but in all of the types.)

This incident had occurred three decades earlier, yet it was fresh and vivid in Sara's memory. She moved back to that first meeting with ease, evoking all the sensuous emotion of Matt's laugh and male smell.

Many couples in romantic marriages, I would learn, have a sense that they are connected by a magic that transcends time and space. Like Sara, many feel that their relationship is out of the ordinary, that it possesses a fantasy quality. They sometimes speak in mystical terms, as if their meeting were preordained or the answer to a prayer. These are not New Age people, nor are they particularly religious, yet they speak of a love that crosses the reality of the present and extends to a hidden past and to a future beyond death.

One woman said, "He's an old soul. Sometimes I think we have met in another reincarnation." And a man told me, "When I went to Boston to meet her family, I felt as if I had been there before, although I never had. I had the word 'forever' engraved on our wedding ring, and I mean just that."

A woman confided, "My greatest fear is, if there is an afterlife, how long will it take me to find him?" This fear was echoed by another man, who said, "What frightens me about my next life is that I don't know where she'll be. I'll have to go looking for her again and again."

A man in his fifties told me, "I have a friend who tells the story that sometime, long ago, Earth was invaded by aliens, and a couple of women from this alien group were left behind. They are a special group of women. They are very exciting and have a special presence. They're not aliens in a bad sense but in a good sense — they have a special exuberance. I think of my wife as being one of them, as exciting and different."

Sara continued the story of meeting Matt at a party with her boy-friend. "The three of us went out to dinner afterward, and we talked about the laughter that comes from the right place. It's what you say about a musician — the music comes from the right place. And that's the way it was. I really hadn't dated that much, but I tended toward very sophisticated, complicated guys. And here was his refreshingly open, uncomplicated laugh — a belly laugh, like the kind of laugh you associate with Santa Claus. It was from the right place."

The laugh and the smell, she said, had always remained the same for her, as fresh and erotic today as they were thirty-two years ago. "It's been beautiful and tender and loving. I made the only right choice for myself. I feel addicted to him."

What kind of background, I wondered, led to Sara's ability to throw herself into a passionate relationship with such intensity? Do young women today fall in love with abandon, or are they too anxious about failing? Was marriage safer thirty years ago?

"I was surrounded by loving men from an early age," Sara began in answer to my question. "There was me, my brother, my uncle, my father, my mother, and my grandfather. We lived in Alturas, a little town in northeast California. It's surrounded by ranchland — real rural, pure *American Graffiti*."

Sara turned and took a framed photograph from the windowsill. "Here we all are," she said, handing me the faded black-and-white print. She pointed to each male and named him. She skipped her mother and pointed to a little girl in a polka-dot sunsuit sitting on her father's lap. He was a lean, bearded fellow with large hands and smiling eyes. "That's me. Age five. I never smiled in photographs. Life was too serious."

I asked what she meant by too serious.

"My father," she continued, sidestepping my question, "was the most wonderful man in the world. He was always there for me. He was loving — of me, and really of all women. He loved girls, women, and I don't mean in a sexual way. His mother died when he was young, and he raised six siblings by himself and with his father. My friends always said that to be my friend was to be loved by my father."

As she portrayed it, Sara's central relationship was with a father who loved and admired her. She moved her hands from the coffee cup to her cheeks. "On a Sunday morning, in this tiny town, we'd get up and walk down the main street, and it was his way of including me. And then we'd get pancakes, and he'd introduce me to whomever he met, and I would feel his pride. I knew it was an act of love, taking our Sunday walk together. He was bestowing me on the town." What a memorable phrase: "bestowing me on the town." And in this wonderful story, which probably telescoped many such incidents, he showed her off with pride and joy.

The only part of her background Sara had not volunteered was about her mother. When I asked directly, her expression changed. "My mother didn't want children," she said quietly. "Having us was a duty. Her family wanted her to produce a male child, and there was a lot of rejoicing when she gave birth to my brother. When I was a child, my aunts told me that the only reason she had me was so that my brother wouldn't be spoiled. My mother hated females, and she had no use for me. My father knew that, and that's probably why he protected me."

Then she said, in a rush of memories, "She would sometimes run away for a week at a time." Sara slumped in her chair. "She'd walk down the stairs, go to the bus stop, and visit her sister in San Francisco, but she'd never say good-bye or tell me when she was coming back. I was certainly deprived of maternal affection and love. She says she never touched me until I was six months old. But I figure she had to have, if she nursed me. She once told me that her milk dried up and that she sent for a wet nurse. I'm not sure what's true anymore. But I know that she never took care of us when we were sick. The truth is, I never had a mother. I never had a mother who touched me."

Sara's story about her background and her courtship with Matt illustrates a central theme in any marriage. Long before she met Matt, Sara's expectations of love and marriage had been shaped by the relationships within her family.

All courtship begins with a fantasy — a fervent desire, bordering on delusion, that another person can step in and magically undo all of life's hurts and disappointments. The new loved one will adore you forever, protect you, drive away wicked people, make you feel whole, valued, beautiful, worthy, and honorable — forever. But courtship also begins with the fear that none of these fantasies will materialize, that earlier disappointments will be repeated, that you will be hurt, betrayed, and rejected for a more beautiful princess or a more dashing prince. Even the Beatles, hardly out of their teens, sang, "Will you still need me, will you still feed me, when I'm sixty-four?"

Our fantasies and fears about love grow out of our earliest experiences in life. Each person's concept of a human relationship — its potential for providing steady nurturance and love or hostility and abandonment — is forged in infancy and continually honed by subsequent relationships and experiences. Infants are not born with knowledge of love and hate, but they begin learning from the moment they are placed in their mother's arms. An infant's earliest attachment — usually to the mother in the first year of life — strongly influences how the child views all future relationships. The nurturing, love, and comfort given or withheld by the mother affect how the adult views his or her partner. Will he be there when I need him? Will she come willingly when I call out to her?

Expectations are formed early. If a child is left to cry in the crib for hours on end, he learns that crying brings no help. If, in the years that follow, he continues to find that no one is responsive to his hungers, pleas for help, or feelings of discomfort, he is likely to grow up with the sense that life is sad, that people are neglectful, that his efforts to reach out to others will be disappointed. He may conclude that he is unworthy because he is funny-looking, or a boy, or too small, or whatever explanation he chooses from the infinite possibilities the human mind can conjure. And tragically, his low expectations, anxious manner, and diffidence are likely to evoke rejecting and hurtful responses in his subsequent relationships.

Another child is the delight of her parents, and they are responsive to all her needs. They talk to her long before she can understand them; they smile at her and take obvious pleasure in her first achievements. The inner template created for this child is different. She has the sense that life holds rich promise, that people are trustworthy, available, responsive, and sensitive, and that she is a worthwhile human being who will give and receive love. These expectations will color her future relationships.

For most of us, early experiences are a mixed bag of gratification and deprivation, of love and rejection. Also, in ways we don't yet understand, each person's world-view is shaped by inborn temperament and personality traits. Some children have inherent difficulty with change; others are flexible. Some are born optimists; others are shadowed by storm clouds.

The mother-child attachment is soon enlarged by relationships with the father, siblings, grandparents, and other caregivers. In the family circle and the surrounding neighborhood, the child learns not only how people treat him or her but how they treat one another. The child sees that people can be loving or rejecting, available or unavailable, nurturing or depriving; adults are reliable or unpredictable or dangerous, fair or unfair, moral or corrupt. The child may come to see the world as a place that values and cares for him or as a place that values him while neglecting a sibling or as a place in which something is always missing for everyone. Each of us carries an image formed in childhood into our adult relationships. One person might say, "I was the child who was brought out to sing"; another, "I was the child who was hidden away"; and another, "I was the child who sat in the dark on the staircase while others danced in the light."

Every child experiences some hurts and losses while growing up, no matter how loving the parents. Of the people in romantic marriages, a high proportion had sustained severe losses during childhood, including the death or physical or mental illness of a parent. Sara and, to a lesser extent, Matt did not feel loved by their mothers. Both spoke of having a "hole" in their childhoods. The sense of magic and of a relationship that extends beyond time and space may rest on the unconscious connection between the adult lover and the lost beloved person from childhood.

Our internal images are formed not by experience alone but also by our interpretation of the experience. One child will say, "My mother hits me because she can't help it." Another says, "My mother hits me because I deserve it." The objective truth may have little to do with what the child feels. A little girl may feel abandoned by her ill mother, even though the mother loves and cherishes her. A little boy may feel angry at his parents even though they are acting in his best interests. In both instances it is the child's inner experience that becomes the lasting reality.

A child's ultimate conclusion about herself and the world depends on a complex balance sheet that contains the sum of all her relationships and observations. A little boy with an abusive mother but a nurturing grandmother may be protected by the good relationship and conclude that he does not deserve his mother's abuse. A little girl whose father tells her she is worthless may be protected by a teacher who tells her she is outstanding.

Each new relationship serves to reinforce or modify our images, positive or negative, which we can think of as an internal cast of characters, forever warning us what to expect. How will I respond to the person before me? How will he or she treat me in return? How will this all play out between us? Our internal voices are answering these questions long before we even think to ask them.

When I teach this notion of an inner world of characters who guide our expectations, I like to use the example of a college student arriving on the first day of class in a course I'm teaching. Standing on the threshold, the student may think, "Well, I have a fifty-fifty chance of being bored to death. Maybe she'll be the exception and I'll really learn something useful. Maybe I'll be disappointed again." The images of all the teachers that student has ever had are standing on that threshold too, influencing the pending relationship. Is school a place where you expect to be rewarded or punished? Will it be boring or interesting? Can you get by with a little work, or are you expected to put out real effort? No one enters a classroom without some preconceptions of what will occur.

Similarly, a graduate student goes to a party in a new town. As he enters the room, he may think, "No one is going to notice me or talk to me, as always. How can I arrange to leave early?" Or he may think, "I'm going to meet a lot of new and wonderful people. Maybe I'll fall in love. I'll start out by talking with the dark-haired girl over there." The party is well under way in his unconscious long before he enters the house.

The classroom, the party, the house (every house) — all are packed with what psychoanalysts call transferences, the shadows of past experiences that fall on present relationships. These transferences reflect our unconscious expectations of other people, of ourselves, and of the relationship that is likely to ensue. But even though they can be strongly influential, transferences do not dictate what happens in the classroom or at the party. The teacher may in fact be a crashing bore. The beautiful woman may turn out to be a cold fish, a bitch, or the love of your life. And these discoveries, in turn, exert an influence on subsequent encounters.

It's important to realize that transferences are unconscious. Although we are aware of our behavior, we may not be aware of the fears, expectations, and wishes governing it. And psychologists don't really know why people with similar experiences take different paths. A young child whose father or mother dies may spend a lifetime looking for someone to fill that void or may decide that people disappear and it's not safe to love anyone. A child of divorce may enter into many relationships to avoid the pain of losing an important one or may stay forever on the sidelines. Each person responds to past experiences in his or her own way.

During courtship and early marriage, especially, the entire cast of transferences springs dramatically to life. No other stage in the relationship draws more on our self-image — on how we expect to be treated and on what we believe ourselves capable of in return.

When two people fall in love and the courtship flowers, they begin a pas de deux of conscious and unconscious bargaining. The conscious part, which is very much governed by each person's values and family background, defines who is acceptable and who is not acceptable in socioeconomic and cultural terms. You choose someone who is in accord with, or perhaps in open defiance of, your upbringing.

The unconscious part flows from the transference images formed earlier in life. You may be looking for someone who will meet your fantasies or someone who will take care of you or even, perhaps, someone who will betray you. The courtship also brings your worst fears to the surface. You are afraid that Prince Charming will turn out to be a frog, or the princess will fall asleep or fail to spin gold. In one way or another, you fear that the lover will fail at the tasks ahead. Hopes and fears are infused with tremendous power at this time. When someone comes along and ignites your deepest fantasies, the blaze can be overpowering.

When Sara stood beside the partition and heard a "Santa Claus laugh" that came from "the right place," she was captivated by a symbol. After all, who is Santa Claus? He is the transference image of the always-loving parent, the man who fulfills wishes and brings the gifts you've always wanted. In Sara's childhood, Santa Claus arrived on time with a full sack of goodies. Matt's laugh was a symbol of what Sara most wanted, her wish come true. "I want to meet that man," she said with confidence, and began to explore whether the man with the Santa Claus laugh would fit her other conscious and unconscious agendas.

What is striking in many stories about first meetings and instant attraction is the presence of an evocative symbol or image that is long remembered. Sara would always remember how Matt smelled the night they met, and she would always hear that laugh.

A woman in her late forties told me, "He was and is my first and only love. I love that he loves me as much as I love him. I noticed him immediately when we met. I was eighteen. You'll laugh at this, but after our third date, my roommate asked me why I was so excited. I told her I didn't know his last name, but he was the man I was going to marry. I don't know what it was, but I knew that he was the right choice for me."

Another woman said, "When I met John I was afraid of him. When I looked at him, I said to myself, with this kind of man there is no bullshit. You are not messing around here. You are going to have to be really real and put your cards on the table. It scared the hell out of me. In the beginning I tried to avoid him."

The roots of Sara's capacity for passionate love are revealed in her story of a genuinely warm and loving relationship with her father. Unlike many girls growing up in the 1940s, Sara didn't feel that she was a second-class citizen. She felt adored not only as a child but as a girl and, later, as a young woman. Having grown up with an affectionate and moral father, Sara as an adult saw herself as attractive, lovable, and virtuous. She was able to make choices among suitors, secure in her belief that she would be sought after.

In the romantic marriages I studied, all the women except one said their father was the more nurturing parent. The relationship with their mother was more conflicted and somewhat less nurturing. The women spoke of their fathers as moral; one said her father was "a saint." Several mentioned that they had been their father's favorite child. Sara's father filled both the maternal and the paternal role.

The husband in these romantic marriages inherits some of the young girl's idealization of her father along with her confident expectations that her mate will be a reliable person who will love and admire her. Contrary to the popular view that the daughter models herself after her mother, in these cases the father-daughter relationship sustained the woman's capacity to love a man wholeheartedly. We have underestimated the father's role in laying the foundation for his daughter's future relationships. We have also underestimated the capacity of one parent's great love for a child to make up for deficiencies in the other parent. In Sara's case the father filled in for both parents.

On the dark side of Sara's childhood was a mother who neglected and rejected her. But on the other hand the mother made no attempt to interfere with the father's love for his daughter. As a result, although Sara always felt the pain of being rejected by her mother, she was able to commit herself to a man with all her heart. She did not expect to be betrayed or abandoned. Symbolically, Matt stood on the shoulders of her loving father.

Several of the men in romantic marriages had lonely, isolated childhoods in which fantasy probably played an important role. Others had sustained losses as children; the mothers of two had been hospitalized for many years. These men came to adulthood with intense, long-postponed needs for love and closeness.

The men's sense of making up for early losses may help explain why they felt almost physically connected to their wives. The couples in romantic marriages often seemed to have an unusual unity, not only on an emotional level but on a physical level as well. "I've never not felt in love with her. I've never even had dreams in which I was with someone else. She is very much a part of me, a soul mate," said one man. His wife said, "I feel whole when he's in the house."

In fact, each partner's central identity was defined by the marital bond, as if they were halves of a whole, halves that could not exist independently. As Sara said, "Who am I? I am the woman who is loved by him." This sense of unity, combined with the intense continuing idealization of early courtship fantasies and real gratitude for the fulfillment of the relationship's promise, reinforces the romantic marriage.

One man was particularly poignant in describing the connection between his early losses and his love for his wife. He was an only child, and his father was killed in an airplane crash when he was ten. His mother became a falling-down drunk who developed delirium tremens. Family life was nonexistent. He ate when he was hungry and slept "wherever and whenever I wanted to." He said, "It hurt me a great deal personally. I guess what I carried with me always was the rejection. She chose the bottle over me, that's the way it came out."

Growing up in a Detroit slum, the boy discovered the television program *Father Knows Best*. "I remember thinking to myself, I wish I had a family like that. I knew I was missing something. It was a stable family. It was a father, the mother, the three children. They respected each other, and they dealt with the little foibles of life. Nothing could destroy that stability. That's what I wanted then, and that's what I want now."

That television show kept his hope alive; it was the church of his childhood. And in his marriage his passionate love for his wife reflected his joy, his sense of having been granted a miracle, and his sheer incredulity at finding her. He said, "A light went off when we met. At that moment, there was just no way I was going to spend the rest my life without her. I knew that then and I know it now, twenty-five years later. There is no way to explain logically how I feel. I never thought you could love somebody that way. I love the sum total of her, the goods and the bads. It's just the way it is."

When I met Matt, I was curious to see whether he would match Sara's description of him. I was not disappointed. We met on a late Thursday afternoon in his office in downtown San Francisco. At fifty-three, balding and a little overweight, he seemed relaxed and very much a gentleman who had dedicated his life to high purposes. He wore wire-rimmed eyeglasses, a blue oxford shirt, and casual slacks. There was nothing stuffy about him.

During our interview I was impressed by the ease with which Matt

expressed his passionate feelings for Sara. I sensed that this was not
how he related to the rest of the world. When I asked, "What is good
about your marriage?" he replied, "We like each other and love each
other. I feel nurtured and cared for by Sara, in a loving and supporting
way. I feel better when she's here and" — his words came in a crescendo of feeling — "I don't feel complete when she is not by my
side."

"Did this ever happen to you in other relationships?"

"Never. I never met anybody like her before. I had other relationships with women that I felt were emotionally strong, but those relationships were never filled with the compassion she has and the
sensibility she brings to it. I've never shared as much with anybody as
I do with her. It has a kind of magic for me. She's so beautiful, so
sensitive, so sweet in many ways." I noted his use of the word "magic,"
which Sara had emphasized.

"You see," Matt went on, "we care about each other and for each
other."

"How are those two different?"

"By caring *for* me, I mean that she loves me. By caring *about* me, I
mean that she shares and defends my interests. She understands what
I do. None of what I do now would have happened without her active
support. She encourages me all the time."

"Can you give an example of what you mean?"

"Yes," he said, leaning forward in his chair, "I sure can. The major
turning point of my life was when I changed careers. I was in international trade, working twelve hours a day, and I came home exhausted every night. It was exactly the kind of work my mom and dad
admired — entirely in accord with their values — and you might say
I had been groomed for that job and I was doing exactly what they
expected." He shook his head sadly at the memory. "One day, out of
the blue, Sara said, 'Matt, you're in the wrong job in the wrong place
at the wrong time. Why don't you give up international business? I
don't need a lot of money to be happy. Do what you love.' It took my
breath away, she said it so straight. She really meant it."

"How did you react?"

"I didn't believe it. There was no way I could believe her. I'd never
thought about it in my whole life. I guess I must have, but I sure
buried it. But she kept saying it until I finally did believe her, and then
I did a hundred-and-eighty-degree turn. I applied for a job in an

environmental organization and got hired. It was a low-level job at first, but I soon started to use some of my professional skills. I loved the people there, the ambience. Mostly I loved the cause. It was like music, my passion. I'm eternally grateful to Sara for helping me break away from being my Dad's junior partner and living my life in accord with his values and not mine." Matt leaned back in his chair, smiling.

As Matt went on to speak about his family, I learned that his background was different from Sara's. His family was socially prominent and wealthy. His father, a well-known attorney, hobnobbed with politicians and at one point was an assistant secretary in the Commerce Department in the Eisenhower Administration. His mother, too, came from a well-to-do family. The atmosphere of the home was formal, with frequent elegant dinner parties.

"I adored my father," Matt said. "I grew up hoping to be exactly like him someday. But my mother was another story. My father treated her like she was made of glass, on the verge of shattering. I grew up tiptoeing around her at a respectful distance. She was volatile and unpredictable, so I had to be careful. I used to be embarrassed at the way she abused people who were weaker, like waitresses. I suppose I loved her, but I never thought much about it. I wasn't an only child, but I felt like one." He described a lonely childhood. He did well at school but suffered from a lack of self-confidence. "I was always on the periphery of the in-group among my friends."

I wondered whether his mother had wanted him to marry a woman from a wealthy, prominent family, so I asked him point-blank.

"You're probably right," he said grimly, "but that's not all. I never got angry at my mother until I became an adult. That happened when she was so bitchy and hateful to Sara. My marriage changed my relationship with both parents. I never thought about it before, but you might say my marriage set me free."

I asked him to tell me about the first time he met Sara.

"I was attracted to her instantly — to her spirit as well as to her as a female. I liked the way she looked physically, her expressive face, her laughter, her ease with people. Her personality was so spontaneous, so unlike the way I was raised. We had a very romantic courtship, which we both loved. I wanted to be with her all the time, see her all the time, talk to her all the time. I was captivated. I didn't have a really important relationship with a woman before I met her, although I certainly had had several sexual relationships, some with older women. Actually, our first important date was on Valentine's Day, and we fell in love immediately. She broke it off once, because she thought I was rushing her, and I was devastated. But we got back together.

"It's a natural fit, the two of us," he said, smiling. "I love the way she is with the world." Matt leaned forward. "Let me tell you a story about Sara, something that also won me over. Not long after we started dating, we were walking along a trail on the coast near Inverness and there was this little girl — maybe seven or eight years old — who was sitting on a rock, crying. She had fallen but wasn't hurt badly. She was more scared than anything else. I remember that Sara took water from her canteen and tenderly washed the tears away and insisted on staying with the child until her parents returned. As I watched her, I remember thinking what a loving, caring woman she was and what a sweet wife and tender mother she would be someday." He sighed happily. "It was a harbinger of good things to come."

During the courtship Matt considered the many roles he hoped his future wife would play. Would she laugh with him and break into his reserve? Would her easy access to her feelings help him unlock his? Would her engaging manner with people enrich their lives together? Would her attractiveness be a source of sexual excitement and pride? Would she take care of him and take care of their children and of the child in him? Using small observations and symbols, Matt was asking and answering the big questions that would determine his choice.

All lovers feel a sense of urgency — a feeling that it is time to requite the past. Charged with both hopes and fears, they are in a profound dilemma, and to escape its push and pull they suppress their darkest doubts, at least for a while. They engage in a full-blown idealization of the other — an idealization rooted in the wishes and hopes of childhood. The new love is larger than life, endowed with the magical ability to deliver whatever one's heart desires. Generations of parents have learned that it is impossible to introduce a different perspective at the height of a new romance because the lovers have blocked out reality. No one can argue with them.

But my observations showed clearly that idealization and fantasy are not necessarily doomed to end when the honeymoon is over. In fact, many early idealizations translate well into reality and are even strengthened by life experiences. Matt made every effort to gratify Sara's wishes in their life together, even though he wasn't Santa Claus and didn't always understand exactly what she wanted and needed.

In happy marriages the high expectations of courtship are modified to fit life's inevitable disappointments, but they are never entirely given up. "I'd rather spend an evening with him than with anyone I've ever met," said a wife after thirty years of marriage. In the romantic marriages I studied, these idealizations were more powerful, more erotic, and more closely linked to vivid memories of the wonder of the first meeting than in the other marriage types. The mutual sense of physical and emotional connection was evident in those memories, which were filled with tingling sensory impressions and suffused with light.

One woman described meeting her husband-to-be at an art gallery. "He talked over my shoulder. I just turned around, and as I was turning around I was just mesmerized. I was completely electrified by his voice. I thought, who is this person? And it just continued from there." A very sober banker in his mid-fifties described meeting his wife-to-be. "We met at a party. I looked at her across the room and said, 'That's my girl.' Just like that. The minute I saw her. I liked her exuberance, I liked her personality. I remember the light shining on her hair. I was eighteen."

Marriage without fantasy or idealization is dull and dispirited. Many of the divorced couples I've seen appear to have never idealized each other. I've learned to ask myself about a divorcing couple (obviously I can't ask it directly), was there ever a marriage here? Was there ever love, joy, hope, or idealization in this relationship? Often I'm hard put to find it. Divorce does not always represent an erosion of love or high expectations; in many cases the expectations weren't high enough.

Idealization of the other is part of every happy marriage. In a romantic marriage the early idealizations remain very powerful.

I said to Matt, "Tell me about the early years of the marriage. What were they like?"

His eyes twinkled. "Sexual," he said, "although it took Sara six months to figure it out. To be fair, I was working my head off and finishing my degree, and she was going back and forth to her parents. But things fell into place pretty quickly after that. Once I got drafted and we were out from under those pressures and had time to spend with each other, our sex life took off. I think we spent that first year in Europe in bed. But first we had to get something settled."

I looked at him quizzically.

"You remember, Judy, that in those days women were virgins or pregnant when they got married. Sara was a virgin. And our sex life didn't begin until we had this crazy conversation. She turned to me and asked if we couldn't just live like brother and sister." Matt exploded with laughter, a deep belly laugh that sounded just as Sara had described it. "And suddenly I realized she hadn't had an orgasm. And what's more, she was probably too naive to be sure or to even know the difference. And so," he chuckled, "I looked her in the eye and said, 'No way! Forget it.' And soon after that, Judy, she had her first orgasm. She was thrilled and excited and from then on she wanted sex as much as I did."

Matt continued, smiling at the memory. "Back then, we were even more tactile with each other — we'd hold hands, kiss each other a lot, tell each other we loved each other a lot, more than our friends. In those early years, sometimes people didn't want to be around us because we never paid attention to anyone else. For a while we were antisocial."

He laughed again. "We went on vacation one summer. I remember one Saturday morning that we didn't get out of the hotel because I'd bought Sara a new white bikini. Once she put it on, we never made it out the door. We'd make love, rest, then she'd put on the bikini and we'd make love again. I believe we made love nine times in twenty-four hours. We counted it up. It was the most intense, tactile, physical, emotional experience of my life. So, yes, it was very sexual from the start."

Clearly, for this man sexuality was a source of great pride. And he felt triumphant about the sexual relationship and the performance he described.

I was fascinated by Matt's story that Sara wanted to live as brother and sister and his forceful reaction, demanding that she be an adult sexual woman and encouraging her to achieve this. Obviously this validated his manhood and pride as well.

I was interested that Sara's sexual passion developed within the marriage. At the beginning of the relationship with Matt she was almost childlike in her view of adult sexuality. What developed was a spontaneous combustion born of his insistence that she meet him halfway sexually. It grew from her full trust in him and eventually in herself and in her capacity to give and receive sexual pleasure.

"Sex has been great for both of us, except for the early months of the marriage," Sara had said during my interview with her. "It was frequent, it was easy, it was wonderful. Actually, it's been hard for me to keep my hands off him."

I said to Matt, "I take it sex is pretty central to your marriage."

"It sure is," he said emphatically. "I think the sexual bond is essential." He added more reflectively, "But more than that, it's a clear indication of how close and open we are with each other. Look, sometimes you do it just because someone wants to make love, but we could just as easily have gone to sleep. But I'm talking about the times when we are *really* making love. It's a voyage. It's what we love and what we look for during intimacy. It doesn't happen all the time, and we don't expect it to happen all the time. But sometimes when I've made love to Sara, I disappear. It's really incredible."

In these romantic marriages the holy ground, if you will, is the couple's sex life. Sexual passion remains central throughout the marriage. Husband and wife are proud of having achieved a satisfying sex life and speak about it frankly and easily. "We're both pretty accomplished lovers with each other and are in tune most of the time with what we need," said one man.

"I don't think we've ever had a period when sex wasn't good for us. It's a very tight bond," another man said. "I'm a very sexual person," said his wife. "I like a lot of foreplay. Not just the actual hands-on type of thing but setting the mood. I love candles and music and making love on the beach, hiking in the woods and finding a hollow redwood tree and making love there."

Although for many of these couples the intensity and frequency of sex diminish over time, sex remains central to the marriage. A romantic marriage is a genuinely creative act forged of hope and an inner vision. Most of these men and women were raised in conservative, even repressive, homes, but unlike their parents, they take special pleasure in frankly expressing their sexual feelings. They are not rebels who set out to do things differently; rather they have drawn on the new images of men and women that came out of the sexual revolution, when women began to fully recognize their own sexual needs and when many men realized what they had always wanted — a woman who is an equal sexual partner.

# 4

# The First Task

*Separating from the Family of Origin*

LIKE A SLY PUSS who has bested the ogre, Sara was telling me, with relish, about an important skirmish that almost blocked her marriage.

"Three weeks before the wedding," she said, "Matt's mother invited me to tea. After polite conversation with tea and petits fours, she said to me — and I'll never forget this till the day I die — 'Sara, you're a lovely young woman. You have many wonderful qualities. But I want you to know that I'm never wrong about people, and you and Matt are not good for each other. It's not going to be a good marriage.'"

Sara's eyes widened. "Judy, the ground fell out from under me. I was too upset to say anything except 'Thank you,' and I almost bowed my way out, choking. After I closed the door behind me, I burst into tears and sobbed all the way to the street corner, where there was a telephone. I called Matt — thank God I got him right away — and sobbing, crying, said, 'Your mother said she's never wrong about people and that you and I will never make it together.' I'll never forget his voice at the other end. I really think it launched our marriage. Instantly he said, 'Don't worry about it. I'm going to call my mother right now and tell her she's not invited to our wedding.'"

Sara grinned. "Of course that was only the beginning."

"Of what?" I asked.

"Of other problems. The first battle of my marriage wasn't with Matt. It was with his mother. She wanted a key to our house. I said no, and believe me, it took all my courage. Remember, I was a small-town girl, and my mother-in-law was a woman of the world. When I said no, she flushed with rage and then, in a very nice way, she said, 'How is it that your mother should be the only person who has a key?'" Sara smiled with triumph. "I said, 'But my mother does not have a key.' She couldn't believe it and backed down."

"Was that the skirmish or was that the war?"

"You get the picture." She laughed. "It was one of many skirmishes. Some I lost, some I won. But most I won because I had a trump card. I had Matt, and he backed me every time. It took a while, because he had no idea his mother wasn't a saint. And he had no idea she wanted a foothold in our living room and probably in our bedroom."

"You were a very young woman. How did you get so wise?"

Sara smiled conspiratorially and said, "There are some things women are born with. But I tell you, if I hadn't stood up to her, we wouldn't have had a marriage. I knew in my bones that unless we fought for it, we wouldn't have a marriage."

Marriage is a *laissez-passer,* a passport to travel in tandem on life's journey. Even if the bride and groom have been partners for some time, they are never fully prepared for this journey. Thinking about the road is not the same as moving down it.

They need to take along appropriate luggage and leave behind any emotional baggage that will encumber them on their trip. They need to decide the direction in which they will travel and the conveyance they will use. Will it be the fast lane or the slow lane? How much money and what kind of provisions are available? What pace is most comfortable, and where are the stopping places? How will they deal with bends in the road and with sudden landslides that temporarily block their path? Today the road maps of their predecessors are unreliable because the landscape and the destinations have changed.

You do not have to be an adult to begin this journey, but unless you are working toward adulthood the journey is likely to end in failure. For people who marry young, the tasks of early marriage coincide with the tasks of consolidating adulthood. A good marriage can help each partner become an adult, while a poor marriage can block or delay adulthood.

The first task in any first marriage — romantic, rescue, traditional, or any other type — is to separate psychologically from the family of origin and simultaneously create a new kind of connectedness with the parents' generation. These intertwined tasks, seemingly in opposition, are mutually necessary.

Psychological separation means gradually detaching from your family's emotional ties. It does not mean driving across the country in a Volkswagen bus or taking a three-year assignment in the oil fields of Saudi Arabia. It doesn't mean just sharing an apartment with someone you love. It doesn't even mean getting married and having children — for you can do all that without separating psychologically from your original family. To have a good marriage, you must establish an independent stance and be able to rely on your own moral judgment and your own ability to make choices. Most of all, you must shift your primary love and loyalty to the marital partner and your primary focus to establishing a new family. This emotional shift from being a son or daughter to being a wife or husband is accomplished by internally reworking your attachments to and conflicts with your parents.

Sara's "skirmishes" with her mother-in-law were major steps in the process of giving the marriage priority. Such struggles are familiar in many young marriages. Matt's mother, trying to hold on to her son, probably did not comprehend the devastating impact of telling Sara that she and Matt were not right for each other. Had Matt said to Sara, "Let's postpone the wedding" or "Why don't you talk to her again and see if she'll come around?" the marriage would have started off on a different foot — and gone down a different road. By declaring his loyalty to Sara and the marriage, Matt instantly rearranged the priorities of his life and provided a turning point for the young relationship. By refusing to give her mother-in-law a key, Sara too was making a stand for their marriage.

Matt was forced by his mother's apparent intrusiveness to choose early between the role of husband and that of son. In choosing the adult role, he came face to face with his long-standing resentment of his mother. Emboldened by his adult love for Sara, he was able to break away from the dominant pattern of his boyhood, that of deferring to her wishes. By forcing the issue, his mother's words of warning had the unintended effect of pushing him toward Sara. She had overestimated her power and underestimated Matt's sense of himself as an adult. Had she won, there would not have been a real marriage.

Sara later told me another story about her gradual move into the role of married woman. "The first six months of our marriage were hell," she said flatly. "I was having trouble learning what an orgasm was all about. And Matt was finishing up his Ph.D. in economics at Berkeley and was utterly immersed in his dissertation, plus he was working at night to make money to help support us. I had a part-time job during the week, and because he was studying all the time I volunteered on weekends in an animal shelter. It seemed to me that Matt was hardly ever home. We didn't fight, Judy. But I was so lonely. I think it was the loneliest time of my life. I washed my hair every night. I groomed the cat. I ate. I was so lonely that I gained twenty pounds, and I had always been slender. I moped around."

Sara's body tensed as she recalled this unhappy time. "Then one day I woke up and said to myself, 'My God, I'm married. I'm not ready to be married!' I hadn't realized the import. I woke up to what I had done. I missed my dad, my home. I missed having people around. I missed them physically. So I packed and went home."

"How long did you stay?"

"Three weeks," she said, somewhat sheepishly.

"What did you do there?"

She laughed. "Not much. I went to the grocery store, and then I started to cry because I realized that was something Matt and I liked to do together. So I didn't belong here and I didn't belong there. After the first twenty-four hours, the longer I stayed away, the sadder I got."

"What did your dad make of this?"

"I think he knew I was confused. We'd go on long walks together, not saying a word. But one time he turned to me, took both my hands in his, and said, 'I think you've made a very wise decision in marrying Matt.' I just stood there and burst into more tears."

"What did you say to Matt during this time?"

"Oh," she said airily, "thank God, he didn't have any idea of why I left. He thought I was just visiting my folks. He'd call every night, and that just made me feel worse. The problem was that I was comfortable nowhere. I didn't feel like a daughter at home, and I didn't feel like a wife with Matt."

In separating emotionally from their families of origin, young people move into new identities. In the first year of marriage, these new identities should begin to take priority, but this doesn't usually happen without pain. When Sara went home she felt like an alien. When she returned to Matt she felt homesick. Psychologically she was wearing two hats — the old hat as daughter and the new hat as wife. Although a newly married woman may vacillate between roles, she has to settle for the wife's hat in a reasonable amount of time. If she keeps going back and forth in her mind, she's not a wife, and the marriage is compromised. In praising Matt and her wisdom in selecting him, Sara's father helped her make the move toward being a wife. He subtly reaffirmed her new status and made it easier for her to return to her new home.

Separation is particularly tricky for women because the ties between mother and daughter, made up of strands of compassion, love, and sometimes guilt, are so powerful. Three major milestones in this relationship are the daughter's marriage, motherhood, and the mother's death. Each change activates powerful feelings and conflicts. Marriage may be particularly hard for the daughter whose mother is lonely and unhappy or is caring for an ill sibling or spouse.

As was true in Sara's case, it is tremendously hard to leave a relationship in which strong, enduring hungers for the mothering were unfulfilled. When Sara returned home she tried to engage her mother in discussing her new life, including her unhappiness and frustrations. But once again she faced an unbridgeable gulf. Her mother insisted on shopping for expensive antiques, which Sara could not afford and did not admire. Sara had to give up the hope that her relationship with her mother would change for the better. It is as difficult to give up unmet needs and hope for fulfillment as it is to give up real love.

The customs of the marriage ceremony reflect the anxiety that accompanies this major step. The bride is expected to fret, cry, and have a last-minute temper tantrum. Folklore instructs us not to leave the bride alone before the wedding ceremony, because she is in danger of being snatched away by evil spirits. Even in the 1990s the bride wears something borrowed, something blue, something old, something new — talismans to ward off the evil eye.

The psychological move away from the parents to the marriage is part of the script of the wedding ceremony in all Western religions. In the Jewish ceremony, for example, the change is symbolized by the *chupa*, a canopy held aloft on four poles by family members. Under it the bride and groom stand symbolically beneath their own roof. The first task of marriage is to provide walls for that *chupa* with gateways over which the young couple exercise reasonable control.

The bride's ties to her father also need to be loosened, so that desire can be transferred to the bridegroom. It is no small task. Sara and her father adored each other. He had been the primary parent, playing both mother and father in her young life. But when it came time for her to marry, they had to separate. Each had to mourn the loss of the other's daily presence. During the first year of her marriage, Sara struggled with this bittersweet separation by going home and then going back to Matt. Gradually her need to be with her father diminished, and she attached with love and passion to her husband.

Another aspect of separation is ending the self-absorption of adolescence and young adulthood. As one woman remarked to me, "Suddenly I realized I wasn't playing anymore. There's a real person at the other end of this who might get hurt." Even in young adulthood we are protected by our adolescent sense of timelessness, by the ease with which we can assume and discard a role (as when Sara went home to Daddy), and by a sense of unreality. At marriage the young woman moves into the unknown. With or without her family's support, she experiences internal shifts along with the external changes. It's easy to underestimate the courage this process takes.

For a young man separation also takes time. Matt was aided by his mother's attempts to dominate his young wife. When he rose to Sara's defense, he sharply defined the boundaries of their new relationship with his mother. As Matt said very clearly, his powerful identification with his father and his wish to please both parents governed his choice of a career — which he did not enjoy. He later succeeded in separating from his father — but only with his wife's direct intervention and encouragement. His marriage allowed him to make this important separation.

For most young men, separation from the family, especially from the mother, begins in childhood and is usually well along by young adulthood. But entry into marriage begins another life chapter. Now the young man must relinquish the freedoms and pleasures of bachelorhood and extended adolescence and assume responsibility. His primary struggle involves his conscious and unconscious reluctance to move into adulthood and his fears of marriage, of women, of emotional intimacy, and of being trapped by the chains of obligations and commitment. These are all part of the fear of becoming an adult and the wish to remain like Peter Pan, perpetually young and able to fly away.

The notion that the groom cannot be trusted to remember to bring the wedding ring captures this inner ambivalence, as does the Lerner and Loewe song "Get Me to the Church on Time": along with regret that playtime is over, there is anticipation of a new life. Like his bride, the young man is afraid and needs courage to take this momentous developmental step.

The process of separating from parents and redefining the ties to family continues throughout the marriage. Each partner helps the other achieve greater independence. In Sara and Matt's case, it was not until several years into the marriage that she helped him separate his own values and wishes from those of his parents by changing his career.

Matt told me that after their first child was born, his parents kept dropping by unannounced, bearing gifts and handing out unsolicited advice about child rearing. "It was almost as if our child was their child," he said, "and it was hard for us to set limits, because my father genuinely loved the baby." It took some doing, Matt said, but finally he persuaded his parents to back off and play a less intrusive role in the new family's life. There are tactful and tactless ways to separate, but all include tears and anger. Separation hurts, but it is necessary to protect the marriage.

The flip side of separating from the family of origin is building new ties with the two sets of parents — ties appropriate to adults rather than to parents and children. Both the young couple and their parents must participate in defining the new relationship. The nature of the relationship doesn't depend on how close the families live or how often they get together. In some cases the two generations feel closer after the new marriage is established, while in others the young couple go out of their way to increase the distance. One happily married woman had been brought up in a socially prominent family in New York. Her parents held formal dinners almost every night. Wanting the opposite, she and her husband created an informal California oasis in which they and their children thrived with three dogs, shabby furniture, and almost no social demands. Despite this difference in style, the couple maintained close connections with the wife's family.

The degree of intimacy between the generations varies from family to family and country to country. Western tradition gives priority to the nuclear family, but in many parts of the world priority is given to the extended family. Men and women who marry into a different culture need to be aware of its traditions and to discuss them beforehand. A young husband may think it's perfectly normal to spend every Friday night playing cards with his siblings at their mother's house; a young wife may expect to spend every weekend shopping with her mother. Such close ties can become a problem if the partner feels shut out. And because people tend to return to the cultural norms of their upbringing when children are born, such stresses can intensify at that stage. This issue is especially important in America, where people from a variety of nations and backgrounds intermarry; the need for separating from one's parents and redefining the connection are nowhere more important.

It is common for family ties to be mended, come apart, and be mended again. Maintaining relationships is a lifelong task for both generations. And it doesn't always succeed. The birth of a child creates new roles for each family member and can ease or complicate the ties between them. Tyrannical parents may mellow in old age, allowing grown children to care for them with compassion and forgiveness. Divorce, illness, aging, or the death of one parent all necessitate renegotiation of the levels of connectedness and responsibility. The most radical but predictable change, however, is the one that must occur during the early years of the marriage.

Many marriages fail because the husband or wife is unable to separate from the original family. A man complains that his wife participates in making decisions only after going over the issues with her parents. He mentions the hours that his wife spends on the telephone with her mother. As one divorced man said, "She was never mine, all through the marriage." A wife may also complain about the unbroken ties between her husband and his family; she may feel that their own marriage is a satellite to that of his parents, in which he is still the son.

One of the most poignant stories in my divorce work was that of a young Russian couple in Fresno whose marriage broke even though they were very fond of each other. At issue was his inability to separate from his family. Both husband and wife told me that he and his brothers worked at their father's restaurant every day and every night without pay on the promise of someday inheriting the business. Though the husband worked hard, he never brought home a paycheck. And each night, when the restaurant closed, he and his brothers played cards and had dinner together. He came home late every night.

The woman, who married him at eighteen, worked outside the home to support the family and raised their two girls almost single-handed. She begged her husband to get another job, move to another town — anything that would give her a sense of having a real marriage. He was kind to her, he expressed his love for her, but he consistently refused her request. Finally, when the girls reached adolescence, in an act of desperation she took them and drove to another city and a new job. She hoped he would follow her, but the attempt failed. The man became acutely depressed and cried for two weeks, then hired an attorney and sued for divorce and custody of his daughters, which he won.

When I saw them together, he said of her, "She is the most beautiful woman I have ever known." She said of him, "He's a kind and decent man. But I can't play house any longer." The marriage dissolved. One child did very well; the other suffered for many years. The man married a woman who was willing to live within the extended family. The woman also remarried. She later said of her second husband, "He loves me, and it's very important to him that I do the things that make both of us happy, but I lost my children."

The man's failure to separate led to a serious tragedy for this family.

# 5

## The Second Task

*Building Togetherness and Creating Autonomy*

THE FIRST STEP IN MARRIAGE, separating, occurs alongside the second task, creating both togetherness and autonomy. This task begins in the early years but continues throughout the marriage.

In thinking about togetherness and autonomy, I recall the early days of my own marriage, when Robert and I began building the structure that has now lasted for nearly fifty years. We had known each other very well, having met in college, where we engaged in both a passionate love affair and radical politics. But our relationship changed dramatically when we got married. Suddenly our free and easy lives ended, and the rigid roles of husband and wife took over.

Breakfast said it all. Instead of asking him what he would like for breakfast (I had never really learned to cook and was ashamed to admit it), I rose gallantly each morning to rustle up bacon and eggs. I was convinced, perhaps through radio shows and magazine articles of the era, that this was what a good wife did. Finally Bob felt secure enough to tell me that he hated bacon and eggs. So did I. It took two smart people a whole year to arrive at this candid confrontation.

Gradually we realized there was no set formula for marriage, that we could just be ourselves. And soon we found the courage to build not Marriage with a capital M but *our* marriage. We began to feel like adults with control over our lives — control that extended far beyond the breakfast table to include our friends, our social interests, our politics, and our intimate lives. We spent a lot of time observing the marriages around us, talking about the couples we met. Although this felt like delicious gossip, it served the more serious purpose of educating ourselves about the best way to plan our lives and shape our interactions.

During this early phase we learned what we needed from each other and, equally important, what we did not want. Much of our education occurred when we tried to anticipate what would please or displease the other, learning from the response whether we were right or dead wrong.

I found out that Bob did not want a daily dose of encouragement. He did not take criticism as an affront and did not need to be right. There was nothing about his home or his mom that he missed; he wanted adult friendship. He needed to talk a lot about his work, ideas, and the people he worked with, and he wanted not a sounding board but intelligent opinions. I soon learned that this need for close friendship was very important, because I was his sole confidant in these matters. He also needed from me a sense of lightness, humor, and irreverence for the establishment to help keep things in perspective.

What he learned about me in those early years, he tells me now, is that no matter what my moods sounded like, they never threatened the marriage. Although his career came first in those days, he began to realize that a good marriage requires a quid pro quo, and my interests should get equal consideration in the future. He also overcame his early anxieties and grew confident that he would be able to meet the full range of my emotional and intellectual needs.

I was happily aware that Bob found me very attractive, and this was entirely unrelated to how I looked at breakfast or to what I wore. He needed to feel loved and to be told so a lot. Most of all, he needed very much to feel that I was happy in the marriage. If I was unhappy, things came to a halt. He could not stand my disappointment or my anger. So I soon learned that what I said or the mood I reflected was serious and that I should not invoke distress lightly. I also learned that being married was fun. I loved his attentiveness. I loved being loved. I became fascinated with his world at work and felt very involved with his career. I was delighted to have him so concerned with my contentment, and I returned his attentiveness in full measure. The rewards were enormous.

We began to generate our own rules. The first was to never go to bed angry at each other, a decision that turned out to be a godsend. We agreed, with some reluctance, always to call home if one of us was delayed, even though it felt like a throwback to the onerous reporting-in of our adolescence. Gradually, and in ways that were almost imperceptible, we each began to change to suit the other.

I learned a lot about myself by contrasting myself with my husband. I was much less organized and never knew how much money was in my wallet. More volatile than he, I did not always understand what upset me. This made things difficult, since I could not communicate to him problems I was only dimly aware of. We both learned to live with our differences and with a certain amount of ambiguity. We relied a lot on humor and intuition. He stopped being so anxious, became much looser, and loved it. I became better organized once I got over my anger at having to do so. His work schedule and my inner life were often unpredictable, but we gradually stabilized and began to manage well.

By building togetherness and autonomy, I mean putting together a shared vision of how you want to spend your lives together — constructing the psychological identity of the marriage as an entity in itself. The adolescent and the young adult are fundamentally "me"-centered, for a person at this stage is chiefly engaged in establishing his or her identity separate from the family of origin. Building the new, shared identity of marriage requires a shift from the "I" of the emancipated adolescent and young adult to a solid and lasting "we." At the same time the sense of we-ness has to include room for the autonomy of each partner. In couples who divorce this we-ness is often weak or absent altogether.

The sense of being part of a couple is what consolidates modern marriage. It is the strongest rampart against the relentless threat of our divorce culture. We-ness gives marriage its staying power in the face of life's inevitable frustrations and temptations to run away or stray. It also gives the partners a sense that they constitute a sovereign country in which they make all the rules. People cannot usually choose what time to go to work or school, but they can determine what goes on inside their marriage. Within the civilization they create, they can exert true control.

A marriage that commands loyalty and is worth defending requires each partner to relinquish self-centeredness and to sacrifice a portion of his or her autonomy. In the past, marriage meant the subservience of women, who were absorbed into the identity of the husband. Girls were raised to avoid developing a strong sense of self, because they were preparing to be someone's wife. This worked for marriage and society as long as women were willing to sacrifice their autonomy for marriage. One of the primary functions of the women's movement was to revolutionize this ancient pattern, which still predominates in most of the world, and to substitute coequal roles — a genuine we-ness in place of a culturally imposed "we" that was really "he."

In a good marriage the new identity is built on a solid foundation of love and empathy. Each partner must learn to identify with the other, and both together to identify with the marriage. Metaphorically, the marriage as superordinate identity is the first child they produce together, and like a real baby it brings real joy, as the couples in this book reported.

As part of this task, each person experiences a concomitant change in conscience and moral sense. What is good and what is fair within the relationship is no longer formulated in terms of "what is best for me." Henceforth, the couple's decisions reflect consideration of what is best for him, what is best for her, and what is best, on balance, for the marriage.

Among the couples I studied in all types of happy marriages, men and women alike talked about what would be "good for the marriage" or "harmful to the marriage" as well as what might be "good for me." They seemed to carry an image of the marriage as a separate presence that required continuing attention and nurture, like a healthy garden. They said things like, "What we both need and what the marriage needs is more time together." A pregnant wife and her husband worried about how the baby would affect the marriage. Couples considered the consequences for their marriage of a geographic move or a new job. One man, reeling after the death of a child, said, "We are both on edge all the time. We need to get back to the early time of the marriage and take care of it, to restore it so we can each heal."

One woman told me, "My husband wants another child, and I decided to do this for him and for the marriage. I don't think he wants it just for him. It's really for the marriage, because it's a chance to undo the trauma of the first pregnancy, when he was absent and angry — because he was so worried about money." She paused and said, "I'm forty. I'm no longer young. But we both agree that one child is not a family. Two children is a family."

Another woman said, "This marriage is the peak experience of our lives as adults. And just now I have to be careful to protect the marriage. I'm pushing ahead in my career, and he's on a plateau. We both try to address it, and we try to spend a lot of time together, feeding the marriage."

A man explained, "What makes this marriage happy is that you're part of something larger than yourself. I see so many people who fail to see problems. We tend the marriage."

Many marriages fail because the couple has not built a sense of togetherness. The reasons are many. Some people think that marriage just happens, with no need to give up part of themselves. They are reluctant to stop focusing only on their own careers, their own talents, their own social interests. Some people are unable to empathize with others; they have a stunted capacity for viewing another person as a full human being. Some people are so needy that they cannot see the partner's needs. In such circumstances the marriage does not evolve into a strong structure that encompasses and supports two people, so it crumbles in times of crisis.

How does mutual empathy come about? It flowers along with the couple's growing intimacy. For intimacy is rooted in love and in the risks and rewards of self-disclosure. It grows through learning to hear what the other person says and to use this information to understand the other and shape one's own behavior accordingly.

Sara Turner did return to Matt after visiting her family. "After I got back, we had a wonderful reunion," she told me, "and then we had our first blowup. What a relief! That's when I began to learn something very important about marriage."

"After the fight or after the leaving?"

"Both. I didn't know you could get angry — certainly not with people you love. I never learned how to be angry, and being angry frightened me very much. And I can't tell you how important it was to learn that I could tell him exactly how I felt — how lonely I was, and how angry I was at being left alone."

"How did he take it?"

"That's the other thing I learned — or, to be truthful, that I began slowly to learn. That what drove him crazy and what scared him to death were my silences. That if I could talk to him, he could deal with almost anything. I also learned about a side of him I hadn't seen — that he was a very reasonable, civilized man, really a wonderful man."

Sara paused solemnly. "We learned to listen to each other. That's what I learned during that first couple of years. We have loved each other our whole lives. When I got fat, he said he loved fat women. And when I lost the weight, he said he loved thin women. Finally I understood that he loved *me* and that I pleased him all the time. It's been very good between us. It's been the best."

Sara's voice took on an urgent tone as she continued, "I learned that marriage doesn't happen all at once. You see, I had this notion — I know it sounds quaint, but a lot of young women had it — that once you got married it filled every space, every moment of your time." She laughed. "Of course, I learned otherwise."

Matt's words echoed hers. "In the early years I didn't know how to express my feelings. She used to threaten me with leaving, and it would absolutely panic me. It took me a long time to learn that she didn't really mean it. And it took me a long time to understand that there was often a discrepancy between what she said and what she meant. Then things became easier."

The happily married partners I interviewed not only learned the other person's life story, they kept it in mind at all times. This was living information that they used in their everyday interactions. Each was truly able to identify with the other. One husband said, "So many men, beginning with her father, treated her cruelly. Knowing this gives me the opportunity to do it differently." A wife said, "His first wife always denied him sex. I go out of my way to show my interest in him sexually. This has been a problem for me since menopause because of my own waning sexual desires, but I always try to keep his earlier experience in mind."

Although few of these people had any training in psychology, most were remarkably tuned in not only to each other's history but also to each other's moods and body language. Their connections extended far beyond the popular notion that communication is merely telling the other person what is on your mind. Moreover, they tried to modify their demands according to what the other could tolerate rather than insisting on something the other could not do. This is often a delicate judgment call. One woman told of taking on the sole responsibility for caring for their child, who had cancer. "We came through it," she said.

"These things don't make you stronger. They don't do anything good. They just scare the shit out of you. I was too frightened to ask for help for myself. My husband couldn't hear about it or function with it. It was a daily fear. I dreamt about it for years. But we did it." Note her protectiveness toward her husband combined with her use of the pronoun "we."

One very distressed young man, whose business was in bankruptcy, refrained from telling his wife about daily confrontations with angry creditors, opting instead to carry the full burden alone. He told me, "She just got too frightened. It reminded her of her crazy childhood and her dad never paying child support." He, too, said, "We made it." It's not true that in a good marriage both partners help equally to deal with every crisis. Rather, each does what he or she can.

The process of reaching intimacy through disclosure and attentiveness, of broadening ego boundaries to include the other, is sometimes more gradual for men. I'm not talking about love, as I have no evidence that men and women differ in their need or ability to love. But unlike love, which can be quietly contained and deeply felt, intimacy requires having access to a host of tender, gentle feelings. For a man to gain access to these feelings requires lifting the repression and isolation of many years, daring to undo the conscious and unconscious defenses established in boyhood to protect himself from being dominated by the powerful mother of his early years. To fail at this separation is to risk being a mama's boy. To succeed at it, the boy places his inner emotional life in a box, which he later must open if he is to achieve intimacy.

Matt told me how he carefully kept his feelings in reserve as he grew up, to the point that he was almost not in touch with them. This is a common reaction in our society. He also emphasized how much he appreciated Sara for helping him regain access to his own feelings.

I like to explain how this process works by describing a scene from the French surrealist movie *Blood of a Poet*. A man and a woman are seated across from each other at a table, playing cards. The woman says imperiously, "You need the queen of hearts," indicating that in this game he has to show his capacity for love. The man goes into a panic because he realizes that the queen of hearts is not among the cards in his hand. The woman sits, demanding the card. Underneath the table is the prone body of a little boy — obviously the child he was many years ago. With fear and trembling, the man reaches down slowly under the table into the child's left vest pocket and produces the queen of hearts, which he then plays.

The men I interviewed, who were all able to regain access to their feelings early in the marriage, fully acknowledged the value and singularity of the resulting intimate relationship. Many men gave full credit to their wives for this newfound access to their own feelings; they felt as if they had recaptured a lost part of themselves. One man said, "Because of her, I'm sure of how I feel. With her, I feel whole. I love about her the fact that she taught me to say 'I love you.'"

Some scholars have complained that women are unfairly expected to carry the emotional work of the marriage. I find that often women do carry the emotional work of freeing the man to gain access to a wide range of his long-buried, powerful feelings. In these marriages the women who did so felt well rewarded.

Because it requires parting with self-centeredness, the shared marital identity is always achieved against enormous inner resistance. Closeness inevitably evokes anxiety and reawakens fears of being laughed at, rejected, abandoned, or not loved. A process that calls for taking two steps forward and one step back, it requires a good measure of courage.

The growth of the self and of conscience and morality yields part of each partner's autonomy to the we-ness of marriage — and this is inevitably accompanied by pain and disappointment. Each person is angry about having to yield, about having to share, about having to give up earlier freedoms. Each is angry because of the new responsibilities of adulthood and the terrible burden of the permanent and demanding presence of the other. There is always great danger — particularly early in the marriage — that the partner's demands will be perceived as voracious, dangerous, exploitative, or demeaning. There is danger that the requirements of adulthood will be confused with the partner's demands and blamed on the partner. In some divorces the partner is unjustly accused of being a nag or a tyrant who insists on the importance of getting to work on time or keeping the house in reasonable order.

Creating the supra-identity of the marriage is only half the task. The other half is maintaining autonomy and establishing distance between husband and wife, allowing each a space that is private and protected from intrusion by the other and even from intrusion by the marriage.

Differences must be acknowledged, allowed for, and even welcomed. Togetherness has its counterpart in individuation. Closeness has its necessary counterpoint in flexible distance.

Carving out autonomy within the shared concept of the marriage is far different from maintaining the individual lifestyle that each partner brings into the marriage. A marriage in which two people live separately side by side, without an overall sense of belonging to something together, is more like a business relationship.

As the roles of women have changed in recent years, these issues have become more complex. In traditional marriages, with their clearly marked spheres for husbands and wives, the culture defined the function of the family, marital roles, and the separate and conjoined agendas of each partner. As one man who married in 1954 told me, "In those days, if the couple did not produce a baby by the third year of marriage, it was assumed that the man was either homosexual or impotent." But in today's marriages choices abound. It is a truly formidable task to negotiate who does what and when and how decisions will be made with due regard for the changing priorities of both partners together and separately.

Throughout the marriage husband and wife must make room — even if reluctantly — for change and for difference, for altering values, tastes, needs, and careers. Husband and wife continually confront the issue of how to reshape their shared identity so it continues to express what they want as a couple and what they need as individuals. Given the vast number of choices and trajectories, this challenge creates a never-ending tension in marriage.

Paradoxically, it is out of this push-pull of autonomy and togetherness that the couple acquires a sense of good emotional, moral, and cognitive fit. To reach the conclusion that the relationship is uniquely gratifying requires the meshing of both partners' conscious and unconscious wishes and needs and the acceptance of compromise as reasonably fair or at least temporarily necessary. To achieve this state, not only must each person feel free to make his or her wishes known but both must agree on what is fair. This agreement allows each one to accept disappointments without rage and take a fair portion in lieu of everything. It works only if the couple regards the well-being of the marriage as more important than the separate desires of either partner. The sense of what is fair is heavily influenced by the family of origin and the social milieu, but the final definition and modifications have to be worked out repeatedly in each marriage. In today's world each couple negotiates its own code of justice.

Building mutual empathy and we-ness while respecting difference and autonomy is critical in preparing for the rewards and strains of parenthood. If pregnancy occurs before the work on these tasks has progressed significantly, parenthood begins at a grave disadvantage for the child and for the married couple. The parents bring the baby home to a house made not of bricks but of straw or twigs — a house that may collapse. The issues of togetherness and autonomy have to be reexamined when the children leave home and again at retirement.

This central task of giving and taking as you build the marriage has never been harder. Nowadays men and women tend to marry later and are reluctant to relinquish their personal lifestyles. It would help people contemplating marriage to understand that it is necessary to give up some of the rewards of being single. Marriage demands that you meet the other person halfway, that you accept part rather than demand the whole. Before marrying, couples should also beware: some compromises demand too much; the price can be too high. No one should give away his or her heart's desire.

Whatever the calculation that goes into the decision, you cannot be married and single at the same time. Balancing togetherness with autonomy is one of the major keys to a successful marriage.

6

# The Third Task

## *Becoming Parents*

CHILDREN BROUGHT SPECIAL MEANING to the lives of the happily married couples I talked to. When I asked them to describe what it meant to be a parent and how parenthood affected their marriage, men and women spoke movingly and sometimes eloquently.

"Having our first child together was one of the high points of our lives. It was a passage of some sort. I felt an unambivalent commitment to the relationship, to marriage, to the family. And that is still the way I feel. I never think about it, but I know I won't ever leave this relationship or want to get out of it, and being a father is a very deep part of that."

"Marriage needs children. That's what makes it a marriage. Otherwise it's just a date."

A man said, "I remember the ecstasy when I held our child for the first time. It was the peak experience of my life."

"He's the first person I ever wanted to have a child with," said one woman. "I knew a lot of men, but I'd never felt that way about a man before."

"I feel sorry for people who don't have children; they don't know what they've missed."

For the couples in this study, parenthood was one of life's peak experiences. It helped define the marriage, promoted psychological growth, and provided countless joyful experiences, along with wrenching problems. Each person said that life would have been less rich without the shared experience of parenthood. Each said that life would have been easier without the children but that the difficulties were worth it. Children provided a sense of stability and purpose. For many, children gave the marriage ethical meaning and a sense of generational continuity. All believed that children helped keep the couple together.

The arrival of children changes a marriage forever, bringing laughter, pleasure, worry, and nonstop excitement to the household. Kids quicken life's tempo and brighten its colors; the decibel level gets higher and higher through the years. They evoke in parents a special tenderness and protectiveness as well as powerful feelings of responsibility and concern. Parents often say they are bowled over by the strength of these feelings.

Children these days come with accoutrements that take over the home — teddy bears, strollers, changing tables, mobiles, baby monitors — and the landscape is soon crowded with Mother Goose, dinosaurs, the original knights of the Round Table and the new knights — Batman, Superman, Megaman-X, the Ninja Turtles, GI Joe, and Transformers, plus their accessories.

The children's schedules, bedtimes, and food habits set the tone for the household. The questions they ask as they discover the world — What does January do? Where does the dark go in the morning? — become part of the family story. Caring for these developing people involves countless worries. When will this child sleep through the night? Will he ever be toilet-trained? Will she need orthodontia? And the biggest worry — how am I doing as a parent?

Parents talk about all of these issues all of the time. They laugh and cry, comfort and blame each other in a child-centered discussion that takes over much of the marital dialogue. During the early school years the conversational content changes, but the focus on children does not. The questions become: Will she have an accident on her bike? Is he behind in math? Could she be really gifted in music? Should I talk to his teachers?

This hectic drama takes place against a backdrop of immense psychological change and growth in both husband and wife. As the children grow up, parents relive their own childhood experiences, fears, early conflicts, and joys; doing so enables them to connect emotionally with the child. "I remember," says the mother, "that I, too, believed a wolf lived in the basement." "I remember," says the father, "how scared I used to be on the playground when the bully threatened me." As each parent encompasses the child and the child's experiences in a newly reworked sense of self, he or she grows psychologically. The parent is challenged by the new generation to consider and, if necessary, redefine the values to be passed on.

The marriage also changes during this period. Some find child rearing too great a burden, and they run from the responsibility. But in a good marriage the man and woman share new feelings of tenderness and pride and willingly make sacrifices for their children. They also share their resentment and fatigue. Most parents most of the time accept the sacrifices as necessary, fervently hoping that it will be worthwhile in the long run. The adults' partnership is reinforced by the funny, poignant antics of the children and by their shared concern. The memories of these years will sustain the couple when the children have grown and left home.

Each spouse now regards the other differently — as a mother or father and also as a friend and lover. But it is the lover and friend that need replenishing at this time. The children's love for mom and dad is often passionate and can do wonders for parental self-esteem, but it does not fill either parent's need for adult love and friendship.

Pregnancy and childbirth usher in the third major task of marriage: expanding the cozy circle created by two people to make room — psychologically and physically — for the baby and the growing child while safeguarding their privacy as a couple. This task requires taking on the new identity of parent and subordinating one's own needs to those of the infant. Amazingly, our culture takes it as a given that this process will go smoothly, even automatically. Nothing could be more misleading.

The wish to be a parent springs from powerful identifications with one's parents and one's childhood fantasies. The little girl who holds a doll in her arms and the little boy who learns to his sorrow that he will never carry a baby in his tummy find, upon becoming parents, that the real baby requires a level of care and devotion their fantasies could never anticipate. The baby's needs, absolute and imperious as they are, soon yield to the noisy demands of toddlerhood and the elementary school years; then parents must guide their teens through the crises of adolescence and the shaky back-and-forth phase of young adulthood. Carrying out these complex tasks inevitably has an impact on the marriage, either weakening or strengthening the marital bond.

"Nothing prepared me for how I felt," said Sara, frowning. "Don't misunderstand me. The baby was wonderful. But it seemed like the roof fell in. I was totally knocked out by the baby and shocked by what infancy did to me. I'm embarrassed to tell you, I didn't realize what a baby was. I just thought I'd put her in a basket and carry on with my life. It floored me that she required all of my time."

"And Matt?" I asked.

"I don't think we communicated very well. We tried to uphold the illusion of romance and happiness, as if nothing had changed. It was only several years later that we could look back and see what had been going on. You see, when we got together we really created our own world. We fused our lives. We moved into the same place because we had to get to know each other. We were making this huge commitment, but we didn't have a long history together, and so we pushed the 'coupleness' to the limit. But with the baby we had to change all that."

Sara sighed deeply, then got right to the crux of the problem. "I just didn't realize that even a wonderful baby would break this bubble, that Matt and I had to break the bubble of our relationship without damaging what we had created. To be perfectly honest, I was shocked by the changes the baby brought into my feelings about my husband. I was much less interested in sex, whereas he was more interested."

She looked me in the eye, as if to assess whether I would be shocked. Feeling reassured, she went on. "How can I put this?" she said. "Our sex life during the pregnancy was fantastic. I don't know why, but I felt very sexual. It was some of the best sex we've ever had. Then, when the baby came and I was nursing, I changed. There were periods of time when we were focused on everything but each other. And then the idea of making love with someone you haven't related to all day becomes like a routine and loses its specialness. I mean, that's in addition to the incredible fatigue." She glanced at a family photograph nearby. "It isn't only that I was taken up with the baby. I think Matt also felt more responsible, more worried about supporting a family. And that doesn't translate into great lovemaking. I'm sure that although I tried to include him all the time, he must have felt that the real unit was me and the baby. Even during our lovemaking I felt that my breasts belonged to the baby — as if Matt were poaching."

Unlike the other marriage tasks, parenting is launched at a time of perilous transition. The first weeks and months after birth are a period of major readjustment, and I am sad to report that many couples don't weather it successfully. I have seen repeatedly how the birth of a child can trigger the failure of the marriage. And many marriages that hold together lose the closeness and passion they had before. That is why it is so important that the couple protect themselves when becoming parents. So before discussing the task of parenthood in its positive light, and the intense joy that it brings to so many marriages, I want to look at the darker side.

> *Rock-a-bye-baby, on the treetop,*
> *When the wind blows, the cradle will rock.*
> *When the bough breaks, the cradle will fall,*
> *And down will come baby, cradle and all.*

If people really listened to the words of our best-known lullaby, they'd be shocked. The song tells of perching the baby in its cradle at the top of a tree, where it is sure to be buffeted by gusty winds. The cradle will come crashing to the ground with nothing to break its fall. What's more, the mother and father are unconcerned about this, because they have a barely disguised wish to destroy the baby even as it sleeps. The song accurately conveys their ambivalent feelings — loving the baby and resenting it at the same time.

Many lullabies and folktales around the world convey a similar mixed message. The baby is welcomed and rejected, raised high and dashed to the ground, covered tenderly and given to a black-robed horseman.

The birth of the baby transforms the parents' inner psychological and emotional lives and forever changes the dynamic between husband and wife. The dyad becomes a triad. And at no other time are the ghostly and living presences of the families of origin more powerful. Old wounds may open just when the warm, wonderful fantasies of having a child of one's own are fulfilled.

At this stage a woman is challenged as never before. Becoming a mother requires making an enormous psychological change, one that is even greater than the move from daughter to wife. Although she is proud to have achieved this major milestone, she may find the demands of motherhood utterly exhausting. And it is precisely at this time that unconscious conflicts about her relationship with her own mother percolate to the surface. It's as if her mother is in the room with her as she nurses the baby, which can be deeply rewarding for women who identify closely with their mothers but painful for many, whose feelings are more conflicted.

No one anticipates the changes; no expectant parent can realize how completely the baby takes over. The mother feels overwhelmed by the nonstop demands, yet she is tied to the baby by a thousand and one biological and psychological strands. Feeling physically and emotionally drained, she needs support, praise, rest, and devoted care. In other words, she needs mothering — not necessarily from her real mother but from the universe of mothers and sisters so that she can give her full attention to the baby and conserve her strength.

In many Third World countries, motherly and sisterly care for the new mother is part of the culture. But in our society of nuclear families, she seldom receives this kind of help. If she turns to her husband to meet these needs, she may be frustrated by his lack of understanding. Many men like the nurturing role, but they need to feel nurtured in return. And when his wife is lavishing her attention on the baby, a husband may feel left out — at a time when his sexual and emotional needs for her have been powerfully stimulated.

A young woman may envy her husband at this time because he has not had to undergo the discomforts of pregnancy, the ordeal of labor and recovery, and the intense demands that the nursing mother necessarily experiences. The husband may become the object of his wife's angry feelings about the baby, while the baby receives the good feelings. This often gets translated into the ubiquitous complaint "You don't do your share" or, on a conscious or unconscious level, "You had the fun and I have the burdens." While the amount of ambivalence varies for different couples, it's perfectly normal to have such feelings.

On the other hand, creating room for a baby is also difficult for a man. A woman has biology to help her make this change. From the moment she finds out she is pregnant, through all the tiredness, morning sickness, quickening, thump of fetal feet, swelling abdomen and breasts, and finally the birth itself, her sense of self expands to include the baby. When she suckles the infant, pats it on the back, and rocks it to sleep, her inner world is enlarging.

A man's experience is different. He can attend Lamaze classes, rub his wife's back, hold her hand during the birth, feel a surge of ecstasy as the head crowns, and rush to take photographs of his newborn child — but biologically he stands in the wings. Neither his inner world nor his belly automatically expands to include the child. He has to work to encompass the new role of father — a role whose complexity and challenge have been underestimated in our society. Indeed, for some men this unanticipated psychological change, which requires a new empathy, poses a major life crisis.

The new father finds himself suddenly displaced by a demanding infant, who does not yet smile, make eye contact, or reach out and hug him. But the baby does take away his wife, so he may feel jealous of and angry at both mother and baby. For some men this situation revives the early memory of a mother who appeared to reject him in favor of a younger sibling or the father. Unconsciously he sees the baby not as an innocent newborn but as an archrival, and he reads his wife's anxious preoccupation with the new baby as pure rejection. In addition, the husband's sexual drive is often stimulated by the image of his wife nursing the baby. As the folk saying goes, men get frisky when women have babies. A common dilemma is that his sexual excitement often rises steeply just as hers diminishes.

The young father may think, "I really love this baby, and I want to share in its upbringing. But my wife doesn't want me or care about me. She got what she wants, and she doesn't need me, except to take care of her and the baby. Fine — I'm out of here."

What may follow is a scenario I've seen many times. As the young man struggles with his feelings of rage and pride, he may seek solace with another woman. And even if the affair begins as no more than a dalliance or an attempt at revenge, it may, to his surprise, turn sticky. He finds himself more involved than he planned. The outcome can be divorce within a year or two of the child's birth — a tragedy for the whole family. It's so important that new fathers be forewarned of the powerful, difficult emotions they will naturally have about this "intruder." But our society does not offer such advice to men.

Another source of discontent is the sexual deprivation that follows birth. At this juncture sex is often interfered with by the mother's, and sometimes the father's, anticipation of the baby's cry. The baby — psychologically and physically — has entered the marital bed as a serious rival for both parents. Also, some women who have had episiotomies say that sex hurts for as much as a year after childbirth. Although gynecologists assure them that the pain will disappear in six to twelve weeks, it does not always do so, and this surely poses problems for a good sexual relationship.

After the physical changes and stresses of pregnancy and childbirth, a woman needs to be reassured that she is still desirable and beautiful. If the husband does not provide this reassurance, the wife may be vulnerable to the attentions of another man, someone who makes her feel attractive, not as a mommy but as a woman.

All of these changes in the dynamics of the marriage can jeopardize it. In the past the birth of a child did not threaten the marriage, in spite of the problems it raised, but it surely does today. A significant number of divorces occur because the couple is not ready to integrate a child. Moreover, feelings of rage and jealousy run deep, drawing from the most primitive roots, and may even be expressed violently. My professional experience has shown me time and again that violence can begin after the birth of a child. I recall one husband who cared for his wife with great solicitude during her pregnancy, but afterward, as she stood with the baby in her arms, he took an open can of sardines from the kitchen table and threw it at her. The jagged edges of the can barely missed the mother and infant.

Or the scenario may follow another script. The father may whole-heartedly identify with the mother's urge to give the baby total priority. He may back away from his sexual and emotional demands on her. The result is a glorification of the child within an emotionally impoverished marriage. This kind of marriage, in which a couple's needs are given short shrift, can go on indefinitely or can explode suddenly, to everyone's surprise.

The good news is that in a successful marriage, both husband and wife are able to face their internal conflicts and make room for the child. But at the same time they do not allow the child to take over the marriage. It helps greatly to know ahead of time that the post-birth period is stressful. The woman needs to apportion her attention between husband and child, recognizing the importance of her role as wife and sexual partner. She needs to be aware that her sexual interest may diminish, especially if she is breastfeeding. As one woman said, "I felt that my body belonged to the baby." But she should not ignore her husband's aroused sexual needs and treat them as one more demand on her fatigued condition. He cannot stand to feel rejected by her.

Both husband and wife are at their most vulnerable to feeling rejected, hurt, and unappreciated for their heroic efforts. Ultimately both parents need to appreciate that restoring their life as a couple is vital to the child as well as to the marriage. Needless to say, the same issues come up at the birth of each child, and the problems are more acute if the children are close in age.

How people resolve these conflicts depends very much on whether they have built a marriage structure that can hold against the on-slaught of the baby and be enlarged to include the child. The woman who before pregnancy had empathy for her husband will usually find it again, recognizing his feelings and the justness of his claims on her. She will want to be responsive to him. Similarly, a man who was sensitive and responsive to his wife will realize that the deprivations are temporary. He will identify with her in a flowering of mutual love for and pride in the baby.

The resolution of these complicated issues varies also with the baby. If the infant is appealing and easy to handle, if he or she reaches out to the parents and smiles, it is undoubtedly easier for both parents — and for the father especially — to respond happily. If the baby is colicky and interferes with the parents' sleep for months, if she re-quires a great deal of care and patience, both parents are exhausted and resentful of the child's intrusion. The baby herself contributes, albeit unintentionally, to the new family that is in formation. At this time the potential for child abuse can arise because of the parents' physical and emotional deprivation and their anger at the intruder.

The young mother needs to help the new father feel competent and important with the baby. For many men, learning to take care of an infant is a difficult task. The father's response to the baby is influenced by his sense that he and his child have succeeded in forming a rela-tionship independent of the mother. Matt said, "There was one special moment several weeks after my daughter was born when I looked at her and she smiled at me. I said to myself, 'Hey, I can recognize my daughter Karen from every other baby in the country, from every other baby in the world.' And I felt great because we were finally father and daughter. Until that time, I have to tell you that our connection was shaky, but I never would have admitted it."

The task of parenting requires conquering the primitive fear, anger, and jealousy that come into the family with the baby. This involves getting to know the baby as an individual and learning to love and cherish the child as he grows at his own pace and becomes a full-fledged person. But parenting also involves maintaining the marriage and setting aside the parental role at regular intervals so that husband and wife can continue to be friends and lovers.

There are various ways to do this. One couple meets for dinner once a week and follows this rule — they cannot discuss the children. Others go away for a weekend to hike, shack up in a motel, or pursue shared hobbies, leaving the children home with a sitter. Others have a late dinner together nightly to catch up with each other's lives. The details of the plans are unimportant. What matters is holding to the recognition that parenting is only part of marriage, not the whole of it. There is a close emotional link between how a man and a woman feel about each other and how they respond to their children. A good marriage enhances the connection between each parent and the child. And children feel more secure when they are aware of the love between their parents.

It is all too easy for the marital relationship to erode when children take center stage. The couple's sex life may decline for several years after the birth of a child. But parents who become entirely absorbed in child rearing have emotionally abandoned each other and the marriage, leaving two hungry people whose adult needs are not being met. At the other end of the spectrum is the couple who are so absorbed in each other or their individual interests that they emotionally abandon their children — leaving two hungry children.

It is possible to strike a balance, so that the couple's life together replenishes parenting and parenting enriches the marriage. Obviously the needs of the parents are sacrificed to the needs of children at certain critical times; this is what parenting is about. But when one parent or the marriage itself needs attention, the children's needs can be put on hold; this is part of what marriage is about. The balance shifts over time as the children grow and as family crises occur. Husband and wife can help each other keep their perspective and point out when the other is veering too much in one direction. As one woman said, "It takes two to create a child and two to create a marriage. The children bring us together, and we love them. But we also love each other." A marriage involves not only sharing in conception and parenting but also helping each other and the marriage to recover from these transforming events.

When I asked Sara and Matt to tell me about their children, Matt replied, "They're both adults in their thirties. Karen is married. She and her husband and our only grandchild live in Denver. They are both architects in practice together. They met in grad school. Bill is still unmarried. He's in television in L.A. in the operation end. He wanted to write music but decided he couldn't make a go of it. We're pretty excited because he called yesterday to say there's a lady he wants us to meet. So we may see some big changes pretty soon. We talk on the telephone a lot, and we try to see the kids about every two months."

Sara said, "Being parents to young children was lovely, and compared to their teenage years it was easy. I did much of it, but with a lot of help from Matt, especially when things got hectic. Most of the crises when they were young had to do with illness. I'll never forget when Karen ran a very high, undiagnosed fever when she was three years old. Matt stayed home from work for six days. We spelled each other every two hours around the clock. When the fever broke, we collapsed in each other's arms."

"And the teenage years?" I said.

"Raising teenagers in the Bay Area was terrible at that time," said Sara. "A lot of our friends' children got into serious trouble with drugs. There was at least one suicide and an accidental death we knew about. But I always felt that our kids would come through, and they did. Karen was my greatest concern. She was always pushing herself to get A's. She was very bright, and school was easy, but no matter how well she did she drove herself mercilessly. We tried to get her to relax, but I'm afraid we failed. Bill is more laid-back. When he was sixteen, he got involved in one marijuana episode and was picked up by the police. Fortunately he was very young, and no one pressed charges. But Matt and I took it seriously. Anyway, we got through adolescence and survived."

People change in unanticipated ways when they become parents. One man in the study told me with amusement that he never imagined he could change a diaper. But he not only diapered, he ended up feeding, burping, and rocking the baby and doing many other things that surprised both him and his wife. Men and women discovered deep reservoirs of love for the child beyond their expectations. Some who had spoken candidly of their fears and misgivings about having children, their concerns about being good enough parents, told me with excitement of their newfound joy.

They also confessed that they were surprised at how easily they could become enraged over a child's behavior and how much they needed to spell each other and to invoke new controls over their suddenly reinforced tendencies to let fly with anger. Almost everyone had lived through periods of worry, sometimes sheer terror, as when Matt and Sara's daughter was so desperately ill.

The children of the romantic marriages I studied enjoyed a close relationship with both parents. Most were cared for largely by their mothers, many of whom worked part-time when the kids were young. In many cases these children were treasured as a symbol of the parents' passionate union, the result of a particular night of exciting lovemaking. This sense of specialness was an advantage; however, the children of some romantic marriages felt peripheral to the parents' very close relationship. They were less likely than children in traditional or companionate marriages to vacation with their parents. The children's departure for college was less wrenching for the parents, who looked forward to being together again.

I asked Matt and Sara to tell me about their adult children's relationships.

Matt said, "Karen is crystal clear. She's always said what she thinks. She and her husband have a very different kind of marriage than ours. She has told us many times that she prefers a greater reserve and more formality in their relationship with each other. I think she found our style a little too close for her comfort."

Sara chimed in, "Bill feels the opposite. He keeps telling us and his friends that he wants a marriage just like ours. He thinks that what we have is ideal."

I was interested that Bill and Karen had such different takes on their parents' marriage and had decided on different paths for their own relationships. Throughout this study I found that children did not necessarily opt to follow their parents' choice in marriage, although they recognized that their parents were happy. Differences among the siblings were very common. In most of the families I studied, the children were raised to value their own decisions, even if they ran counter to the parents' preferences.

Many people find it shocking to think that the needs of the children and of parents can clash. After all, we like to believe that children strengthen marital bonds by their gifts of love and joy. And they do. Nevertheless, it is also true that children can threaten a marriage by coming between the couple. With the baby drawing away so much love and attention, one or both parents may be left sexually and emotionally hungry. Ultimately this imbalance does the children little good and harms the marriage. Married people need each other, and they want and need contented children. Balancing the two needs is one of the most important and difficult tasks of marriage.

It's encouraging to find that the couples in the study weathered this passage successfully. Their marriages were happy, and their children were developmentally on target and doing well in the various domains of their lives. What these couples accomplished required constant effort and vigilance in nurturing the marriage and children.

# 7 &

# Matt and Sara Turner Revisited

THE TURNERS' LIVING ROOM was suffused with somber light from the heavy fog enveloping the Oakland hills. Sara flicked on two lamps, and suddenly the room felt warm and safe. In their individual interviews, both Matt and Sara had described their marriage as romantic and passionate, but I wondered if they had been recounting a shared myth that both believed to be true but perhaps was not. I very much wanted to see them together to observe for myself the interaction between them.

The two sat side by side on the sofa, arms touching lightly. As I set my tape recorder on the table and tested it, I noticed that they were fumbling with some unseen object behind their backs. And then I saw Sara take a bite from a banana, put it behind her back, and pass it to Matt. He took a bite and passed it back unselfconsciously, as if this were the way anyone would eat a banana. There was a large fruit bowl on the table, and it would have been easy for each of them to take a banana, but this was not their style. They had transformed eating into an intimate game that spoke volumes about their way of interacting.

I was touched by their sweetness and the connection between them. It was a visceral bond, a special closeness that was not evident in many of the other good marriages. I also enjoyed their light bantering, and I was impressed with how openly they expressed their feelings for each another.

We talked informally for several hours, reviewing the history of their marriage. They told me how their values had shifted, how despite many opportunities both in Washington and Sacramento they had gradually shed their active political careers and concentrated more on family and friends. They talked with affection about their close circle of friends, some of whom they had known since college.

In response to my questions, they described the crises in their lives, mainly the deaths of their parents, their daughter's serious illness, which required surgery, and Sara's near-fatal car accident. Sara said, "We've enjoyed the good times and tried to transform the bad ones. That's a chance life gives you. I know there are going to be more crises, and things are going to get harder because we're getting older and I'm aware of it." She described in some detail her concern about a recent illness of Matt's, which had frightened her.

As Sara was talking, Matt looked at her in a sweet way, and when she was finished, he reassured her. "My life has never been better, and it's never been better between us." His eyes became moist as he put his hand under her chin and stroked it.

"I love you," she said.

I felt like an intruder on their privacy, but they didn't seem to notice.

Taking a cue from Sara's conversation, I asked about the future and their feelings on aging. Sara said, "I've been having a hard time lately with getting old. I've been feeling old for the first time. I mean, when you start looking in the mirror and you look like your mother, it starts to get scary."

"What do you think is going to happen?" I asked. "How is this going to affect you?"

"I'll probably drive Matt crazy, my asking all the time if he still loves me and if I'm still attractive," she said.

Matt laughed. "You've already done that." He added, "It drove me crazy early on, but it felt more like I wasn't doing what you needed from me."

"I guess it depends," she said, "on how bad I start to look."

"No," he said. "I can live with the changes you go through. I have no doubt about that."

Like every other relationship, marriage draws on a wide range of each partner's potentialities, selecting some and, in so doing, closing off others — and that process continues through life. Matt and Sara's story shows us what happened and also what *might* have happened in this romantic marriage.

Sara started the marriage as an immature young woman — bright and engaging but still an adolescent in many ways. She had led a protected life and was closely tied to her family and her small town. She never worked or lived independently but went from high school to college, which was a major step, and right on to marriage.

Sara completed her growing up and began to mature in the early years of the marriage. "The marriage helped me to explore the parts of myself that I had to hide before," she told me. "There was tremendous relief in knowing that I was acceptable for who I really was. It was a relief that I could be who I am. I could get angry. I could be smart. I could know the answers. I could rely on my initiative, on my imagination, on my own sense of right and wrong.

"Before my father died, we went on a vacation together where we talked and talked. We told each other how much we loved each other. His death was a great loss for me, but it was complete. It was final. Matt was there with me and for me, always, to get through these terrible things, as I was with him when his parents died. So, having learned about life and faced death, I knew what was important. I gave up feeling sorry for myself and grew up."

Sara discovered in her marriage that she no longer needed to be the little girl who had to please. She felt genuinely loved and protected by the discipline and sense of order that Matt brought to their lives. Their meeting confirmed her childhood expectations that a man's love would envelop her and that she would love him passionately in return. Matt treated her as a full partner and an adult in matters of sex, decision-making, and money. And she began to act accordingly. Eventually she expanded to enjoy her freedom, sexuality, and full adulthood.

In return, Sara demanded that Matt do what he enjoyed, that he have the courage to follow his interests. She supported him in this, accepted the economic losses involved, and met him halfway. She also demanded that he be a father in a true sense, not like his own father, who only got to know his children when they became adolescents. And she demanded full fidelity and performance as a skilled lover over all the years of their marriage.

Matt, the scion of a prominent, wealthy family, started out accepting the values of his social class without examining whether they fit him. Until he fell in love with Sara, his relationships had consisted only of brief flings with married women and visits to prostitutes with his fraternity brothers. Not only had he repressed his early childhood, he had damped down his emotional life. He had been an unhappy, lonely little boy, but he never acknowledged that.

When he met Sara, he was able to move out of his conventional mold. He fell in love with her "spirit," saying, "I love the way that she is with the world." Sara represented the inner freedom, expressiveness, and imaginative playfulness that had eluded Matt. Most of all, he found in her a woman with a passion for loving who needed his love, support, and encouragement. She helped him break out of his three-piece suit so he could "feel whole for the first time." Matt added, "When Sara came into my life, she taught me to be different. I love that about her."

The scenario could have been different. Given her long-lasting relationship with her father as an adored little girl, Sara could have played lifelong baby to Big Daddy Matt. She might have sulked, gone through life frigid, blamed him, and been angry at him without being able to express her anger. She could have transferred to him her feelings of being unloved by her mother and demanded from him the same adulation she had gotten from her father.

Matt, too, could have lived out the conventional role for which he had been primed. He could have taken care of the fragile little girl in place of his fragile mother and spent his life in international trade, hating it but eventually getting used to it and deciding that boredom was an inevitable part of life. In response to her continued frigidity, he could have become involved in extramarital affairs. And he could have remained a constricted man with little access to his feelings.

But those scenarios did not come about. The remarkable fit of the marriage transformed them both and enabled them to grow to adulthood together. As the curtain rose on the fourth decade of their marriage, Matt and Sara had weathered many crises while maintaining a strong romantic connection. Their early love had been strengthened over the years by their immense gratitude to each other for the enhanced sense of themselves and for the pleasures they had found in adulthood. She was grateful for the help he gave her in becoming a passionate, sexual woman and for the shared rewards and sense of achievement in motherhood and parenting. He was grateful to her for helping him to achieve independence from his family in choosing his life's work and to attain far more than he had ever dared hope for in his relationship with her and his children.

Like Sara and Matt, the other couples in this study were profoundly grateful to each other for the changes they had experienced over the years — psychological transformations they attributed to the marriage. The couples in romantic marriages were particularly grateful to their partner for helping them achieve confidence in their capacity to love and be loved with passion. They felt that because of the marriage they had found a major part of themselves that was lost or unavailable before they met.

PART THREE

*Rescue Marriage*

# 8 ❦

# Helen Buckley

LIKE MOST PEOPLE in the mental health field, I believed that a wretched childhood diminished one's chances of achieving a happy marriage. Certainly this assumption was bolstered by the childhood histories of many of the divorced people I had seen over the years.

I was therefore surprised and elated to discover through this study a group of long-term happy marriages in which one or both partners had suffered terrible, cruel childhoods, including early abandonment, sexual and physical abuse, severe mental illness in one or both parents, and other serious traumas. Remarkably, the tragedies these people experienced as children did not spell doom for their marriages. Eventually a fifth of the couples in the study fell into the category I call rescue marriage. Despite their difficult beginnings, these people were able to establish happy and loving relationships with their spouse and with their children. The chosen partner and the marriage itself, as it flourished over the years, helped them overcome the pain of their early traumas.

The discovery of these lasting, successful rescue marriages is one of the major findings of this work, one that should bring hope to countless people. I know many young men and women today who have grown up fearing that because they were abused as children, they were doomed to repeat that suffering in their closest adult relationships. Here is direct evidence that people who have suffered great pain can put it behind them and have a stable, rewarding marriage.

Actually, I had long been uneasy with the notion that an unhappy childhood inevitably leads to a tragic adulthood. I'm keenly aware that the only people therapists know about are those who come for treatment. And yet we all know people who have risen above childhood tragedy and forged a satisfying life.

Every good marriage provides healing. We marry with the hope that our sadnesses will be comforted, that a loving partner will redress the loneliness, rejections, and disappointments of life. As children we had to share our parents with siblings, but now we have an exclusive relationship, and we fully expect that it will protect us and help us weather the crises of life. And indeed a good marriage does deliver in these ways.

But in the marriages I am about to describe, rescue lies at the core of the relationship and is manifest in the couple's daily interactions. Like the story of the ugly duckling, the rescue marriage fulfills the child's fantasy that early miseries will be canceled by the happiness of adult life. In the fairy tale the little duck, who doesn't look like the others, grows up feeling rejected, unloved, mocked, and demeaned. One day, from an appropriate fairy-tale distance, he spies a flock of swans, which seem to him the most beautiful of God's creatures. Looking into the mirror of the lake, he discovers suddenly that *he* is a swan; he never was a duck. He joyfully joins the other swans, who welcome him to their group with love. In a somewhat similar biblical story, the stone rejected by the builders becomes the cornerstone of the temple. The people in successful rescue marriages experience the enormous relief and pleasure in acceptance that the ugly duckling felt; they feel grateful for their rescue every day of their lives.

All close relationships have the power to bring about psychological change. In a parent-child relationship, a love affair, a close friendship, an important student-teacher relationship, each person influences the other to think, feel, and behave in particular ways. In all of our important relationships we play one part, and we draw the other person into playing a counterpart. In the physical and emotional closeness of marriage, these reciprocal influences take center stage. Husbands and wives change each other to fit the mixed scenario of hopes and fears that each one brings.

When two people with happy early experiences marry, the relationship can bring about change toward even greater harmony. If one person conveys the message "I perceive you to be a loving, considerate, kind person, as I expect and need," the other is moved, often unconsciously, to approach that ideal. Each person moves closer to thinking, feeling, and behaving in accord with the partner's projected ego ideal. With this bounty at the core, a good marriage can promote unselfishness, togetherness, and, to use an old-fashioned word, virtue. And psychological growth can indeed continue to transform the individuals in a good marriage throughout their life together. In the rescue marriage these psychological changes stand out dramatically because of their magnitude.

The idea that mutual rescue can lie at the core of a marriage was first suggested by my interviews with Helen and Keith Buckley. I met Helen at a meeting she chaired of a community advocacy group concerned with the unmet health needs of California's children. I spoke to the group about my research on the long-term effects of divorce on children. I also spoke briefly about the happy-marriage project, which was just getting under way. Helen called the next day to say that she had spoken with her husband, Keith, and that they would like to participate in the study. They had been married since 1954.

Not long afterward I was sitting in Helen's home office in San Mateo, California, sipping Earl Grey tea on a rainy afternoon. Seated behind a mahogany desk, she wore a charcoal-gray wool dress with amber beads, her thick graying hair held in place with old-fashioned silver combs. At fifty-nine, Helen was very much a successful businesswoman of commanding presence and charm. She has a steady gaze and speaks in clear, confident tones. Helen runs a chain of Yamaha music schools that teach violin to children as young as three and four. Although we could have met downtown, she asked me to come to her home office because we would be able to talk without interruption.

I began with my usual opening. "What's good about your marriage?"

"It's friendship and love, love in a very sharing way," said Helen with great assurance. She paused a moment, mulling the question, and continued, "So many things hold us together. It's hard to know where to begin. My husband and I are very different, which has been a positive force through the years."

She described how she and her husband think about the world. "He's a meticulous, mathematical type. As a certified public accountant, he's a neatnik who keeps everything in order. I'm more outgoing. I think conceptually and more intuitively, more daringly."

She ventured further. "I need him to keep me on track. And he needs me to add a little risk to his life," she said, smiling.

"What would happen if he didn't keep you on track?"

A shadow seemed to fall across her face. "He keeps me from falling into abysses which I otherwise might fall into."

Abysses? That is a powerful word. Obviously this marriage was different from the romantic marriages I had seen. The image of dark, dangerous, bottomless places was so potent that I decided not to plumb its depths right away. We needed to build a relationship of trust before moving into more difficult terrain.

I asked, "How did you and your husband meet?"

"We were good friends for two years before we became romantically involved in college," she said, resuming her confident tone. I noticed that she didn't say they were lovers. "We belonged to a church group in the early fifties with lots of people our age. It was a whole bunch of fellows and only two girls, but we all felt like one big group of guys. I had just come to Chapel Hill from central North Carolina, and they all seemed very worldly to me and wanted to protect me, which was fine with me. Keith was the first person I dated in the group, but then we went our separate ways for a while. I attended the University of North Carolina at Chapel Hill, and Keith went to Duke over in Durham."

"So he was the first man in your life."

"He's the only man I've known. Not long after we started dating, Keith told me he loved me and wanted to marry me when we graduated. And I was shocked. I was genuinely shocked. I was so insecure about everything, especially about getting married, that I wouldn't accept his ring. And so for nine months, from September, when he proposed, to the following May, I insisted that we have philosophical discussions. And only then did I accept his ring."

I was intrigued by the dignity of this nineteen-year-old with her delaying tactics. How, I wondered, did she manage to carry on "philosophical discussions" for nine months with a young man in love? I gathered they weren't having sex during that time. Somewhat cautiously, I asked, "What did you talk about?"

"We talked about our goals and values, about our philosophy of raising children . . ." Her voice trailed off for a second, and then in a rush she said, "You see, Judy, I come from a poorly educated family. His family was highly educated. I came from poor farm country, a broken home, and neglect. I was worried about whether I was stable. But we had certain things in common. We were both raised as strict Lutherans and started with many of the same beliefs. Then I told him the biggest fear of my life — that I would be promiscuous like my mother and grandmother and abandon my husband and my children."

Helen's voice, expression, and gestures had changed. Her temples throbbed, and she swallowed hard as the words spilled out. "My mother abandoned me when I was two years old. The whole time I was growing up, she only came to visit me a few times. I never knew when she'd come because she never called ahead." Tears glistened in her eyes at a particular memory. "She did once, though. She called and said she'd come see me on my tenth birthday. I got all dressed up and waited for her all day. But she didn't come . . ." Helen's voice trailed off, and she swallowed again.

"I was not quite two when she left. She was an alcoholic, just like my grandmother. She just walked out one day and never looked back. She divorced my dad — it was her first marriage — and got married and divorced two more times." Helen wiped tears away with a tissue. "My father also married three times."

Her sadness in recalling these experiences remained powerful even all these years later. "But who took care of you?" I asked. "You were only two."

"My dad put me with a foster family. He had just lost his business. He always said he was going to take me back, but by the time he got back on his feet I was five or six, and by then he was planning to get remarried and didn't want me around. His new wife hated little kids. I would have liked to move in with him, but I was powerless to do anything about it. He said I'd be better off with my foster parents because they were the only parents I'd ever known."

I asked about her foster home.

"Well, my foster parents lived on a farm thirty miles outside of Durham." Helen grasped the arms of her sturdy chair, as if seeking stability in a shaky world. "My foster mother was fifty-seven years old when she took me in, and my foster father was sixty-two."

She cleared her throat. "My foster mother was paranoid. She used to say she was an old ghost, and when she'd get mad at me she'd say, 'If you don't shape up I'm going to send you to an orphanage where they'll beat you black-and-blue.' My foster father ignored me most of the time. He was crippled by a tractor accident and lost part of one leg, but that didn't stop him from using his talents. He built beautiful stringed instruments in his workshop out back."

Helen fingered an antique flute on her desk. "That's where I learned to love music. I taught myself to play the hammered dulcimer. That is, when I wasn't walking in the woods, which was most of the time. I spent a lot of time alone." She coughed lightly, regaining her composure. "I grew up on my own from a very early age.

"I remember taking my lunch and going for all-day walks. From the time I was ten until I turned sixteen, I roamed the deep backcountry for miles around. Nowadays people would be very nervous about a child walking alone. But no one ever said anything or tried to protect me. I learned a lot about silence as a child."

Helen was squeezing the flute hard but was still in control. I could see the courageous little girl she had been, roaming the countryside alone. Her poignant remark about silence may be a clue to her survival. Many abused children grow numb, but perhaps she had protected her inner emotional life by keeping her own company.

"I remember climbing a fence that ran through the back orchard," she said. "I don't remember being forbidden to do that, but I must have been. My foster mother put me in my bed, which was a crib. It seems strange, doesn't it, to put a four-year-old in a crib? She grabbed me by the hair, pulled me up a flight of stairs, and washed my mouth out with soap."

"What for?"

"I don't know," she said. "I don't remember doing anything wrong."

"You were a very good child."

"Yes, I was. But I do remember the soap. It was Lava soap. Awful and gritty. I couldn't get the taste out of my mouth. When I tell my children about my early life, they cry for me. But I don't know, maybe there's a silver lining. Because my foster mother was paranoid, she shook up my sense of security. But that probably made me rely all the more on myself."

I did not actively encourage Helen to continue this story, because the memories were so painful, but she seemed eager to get it all out, including this terrifying portrait of her foster mother. "She always thought someone was trying to do her in. She kept a shotgun in the kitchen and sometimes fired it out the door at night, at noises in the dark. I was scared to death she'd kill someone or maybe some night shoot me if I was late coming home. One night she did fire at me, although she said she aimed the gun in another direction."

"Did she ever hurt you?"

"As far as physical punishment goes," she said, "I would be hit, not spanked. I remember once she smacked me across the face with a fly swatter. And another time she threw a brick at me and barely missed my head. She told me I was sassing her, but I don't remember doing that. I was a teenager, so maybe I was being a smart aleck. One thing she did that was probably not good was that she told me I was big and fat and that I looked like a wart hog. She said I had stringy blond hair and a fat behind and nose and lips like blubber."

Helen laughed. "I grew up thinking I was grossly fat even though I was thin. In fact, my children found a picture of me standing in front of the house when I was fifteen and said, 'Look, you're tall and skinny just like us.' But my foster mother always pointed out how unlike my mother I was. As you've probably figured out, my mother was a very attractive woman, especially to men. They flocked to her. My mother was very promiscuous. But I vowed growing up that I would marry only one man and would have sex only after marriage."

One meaning of the abyss was now clear. Helen was deathly afraid, as she had said, of repeating her mother's behavior. I asked, "How much do you know about your mother now?"

"My mother is a survivor and so am I. She's got some serious problems but has accomplished great things in her life," said Helen. "Yes, she's an alcoholic and has had three husbands. But she was also an officer in a local chapter of the DAR and got heavily involved in some celebrity golf tournaments sponsored by RJR Nabisco."

She continued, "Sometimes I think I'm a lot like my mother, even though she left when I was so little. We're both active in the community. But my value system is from my Lutheran upbringing."

"How often do you see her?"

She said calmly, "I haven't heard from her in years. I really don't know if she's alive or dead."

If one were to design an environment antithetical to the development of self-esteem and the sense that people are trustworthy and the world is a benign and rational place, one might come up with Helen's history. A child who is abandoned by her parents through divorce, death, or negligence before she is old enough to understand it suffers terribly.

Not only does she feel wretchedly alone and frightened, but almost inevitably she concludes, "I'm not lovable. I wasn't worth sticking around for," or "If I had been good, my mommy and daddy would still be here. I don't deserve anything. I'm bad." No amount of reassurance that the child is not responsible for the abandonment can fully wipe away these feelings. Early abandonment can have a crippling effect on development. But Helen, besides being abandoned by her parents, grew up in a foster home that repeated the earlier rejection; she was severely mistreated and lived in fear for many years.

For a person whose childhood was traumatic, the move into adulthood is often excruciatingly painful. Some suffer lifelong depression and a feeling of being starved for affection, unloved and unlovable. Believing that nothing will work out, they miss opportunity after opportunity, compounding their sense of failure. Many get caught in relationships that replay the feared themes of their childhood. Others, afraid to risk rejection, turn away from all offers of intimacy.

But when Keith proposed, Helen did not send him away. She stood her ground with dignity and great sweetness, saying, "Let's wait. Let's talk about what we want for the future. And let's see what we have in common. Let's decide carefully whether this is the right choice for both of us."

This nine-month conversation — a courtship that seemed almost out of the age of chivalry in its purity — soon included stories of their past suffering and hopes for a brighter future. Given her sad, deprived history and fearful expectations, Helen's ability to ask, "Do we really belong together?" and to create the answer in the process of asking was a heroic achievement, and it set the foundation for their marriage.

How did the people in these successful marriages find each other? We cannot choose our parents or our children, but we do choose the person we marry. Yet so many people make the wrong choice. In many of the happily married couples I talked to, the two partners came from widely different backgrounds; only one couple grew up together in the same community. Yet they all made good choices. How did they pick their mates?

Aside from physical attraction, which is of course very important in choosing a life partner, at a deeper level one is searching for the best conscious and unconscious psychological fit with another person. People often come together through a common interest — shared hobbies or enthusiasms, work, or political, ethical, and religious values. Helen and Keith were members of the same church group and shared a conservative view of marriage and family. And, as they gradually learned, both had had unhappy childhoods. As one man in the study said, "We share interests and disinterests." Two people may have a common past or background: "We both came out of terrible first marriages and are both survivors," or a shared vision of the future: "We both wanted to live in a small community and raise our children." Or "We both wanted to rescue the world," or "We both needed an oasis."

What is shared may be loneliness. All of us look for another person out of loneliness and the wish for intimacy, companionship, and sex. But some find it impossible to live alone after leaving home; they want to be sure someone is waiting in the wings. Some people come together out of shared anxiety: this may be my last, my only chance. I had better grab it and not look too carefully.

People are attracted to each other because of internal images, or transference, related to parents and other important figures. By young adulthood these transferences have been woven into a general set of internal instructions governing what we expect from ourselves and from others. As I have described, these images are very influential in the kind of marriage that people expect to create. My father's death when I was eight has been a lifelong influence and is probably closely linked to my professional work, helping children cope with loss. But my choice of Robert as my husband was certainly influenced by warm memories of my relationship with my father. My absolute conviction as a child that I was a very important and loved person surely influenced my adult expectation that I would have choices and find a man who loved me. For similar reasons Sara Turner had the same expectations.

People are also attracted to each other because of differences: we look for someone who has a quality we lack. As Matt said, "With Sara I feel whole." Thus the search for the right fit involves filling a void we feel in ourselves. This fitting together of psychological differences in ourself and the other person in order to feel more complete is called complementarity.

Some of the most famous couples in literature represent this complementarity. Don Quixote, the mystical, delusional visionary, is drawn to Sancho Panza, who concerns himself with where their next meal is coming from. The crude soldier Othello is drawn to the gentle modesty and sweetness of Desdemona; she finds in him the heroic adventures and boldness that are denied her.

In real life people look for someone with the right fit, but this involves more than filling obvious gaps. The mechanism of complementarity enables us to find in our mate parts of ourselves that we have repressed or denied through fear or disapproval but that we are eagerly seeking to express.

Each of us scans the available pool of partners for what we need. Thus one dependent woman runs to guys in black leather jackets to gratify her need for danger and rebelliousness while remaining meek and dependent. An impulsive woman may prefer men in three-piece suits because she is looking for predictability and safety; the relationship may strengthen her inner controls. For similar reasons, a shy young man may be drawn to a woman in leather miniskirts and spike heels, someone who will live out the wish for danger that he cannot allow himself, while another prefers girls in Laura Ashley dresses because they reassure him that the world is neat and predictable.

We read into external cues what a person is likely to provide. Some choices are conscious and crass: I am poor and want to marry someone rich; I am a nobody so I'll look for someone powerful. But other choices are unconscious and subtle: I am scared to speak up, so I will find someone who is not afraid to fight. I am afraid to express my feelings, so I will join forces with an expressive person. The combinations are many.

Complementarity is a powerful psychological mechanism that can work to good or bad ends. In a happy marriage the fitting together of psychological differences has the power to heal, as the Turners' marriage illustrated. Feelings came naturally for Sara. She made quick decisions, rarely looked back, and was easily swept away by strong passions. Matt, brought up in a reserved household where feelings were not expressed, was an eminently rational man. The marriage afforded greater inner freedom for him and a feeling of safety for her. Together they enhanced each other.

But complementarity can also lead to a collusive marriage in which the couple remains together for neurotic or childish reasons. For example, a man may choose a wife who encourages him to play the indulged and pampered little boy. In exchange, as mother and manager, she allows her husband periodic naughty escapades so she can magnanimously forgive him. Some couples reinforce each other's adolescent stance against the world, refusing to take responsibility for themselves or others long after they have reached adulthood.

To choose wisely in marriage a person first has to be able to stand alone, as Helen did when she initiated the nine-month conversation with her young suitor. To stand alone, you must feel that you have a choice and that you merit a choice, that somebody will choose you and that you will have the opportunity to choose in return.

Standing alone does not just mean living in your own apartment after college. It does mean having a sense of self that allows you to go home alone from a party. It means being able to get through the night by yourself. It means not being driven by loneliness to make bad decisions about who you invite into your apartment. In my experience, many wretched marriages have resulted from the fear of being alone even briefly. Standing alone also requires honing your scanning skills so that you have an accurate early warning system that keeps you from getting hurt. Despite her painful early history and her fears, Helen bravely stood still, neither accepting nor rejecting Keith's proposal as they, at her insistence, explored together whether they should marry.

# 9 ❧

# Keith Buckley

I RETURNED TO SAN MATEO two weeks later to meet Helen's husband, Keith. He met me at the door and quickly made me feel comfortable. Keith is a friendly, good-humored man with a florid complexion, a fringe of gray hair, and surprisingly delicate hands. I imagined those long fingers flying over the well-worn calculator on his desk as he prepared tax and payroll forms for his clients.

Helen had told me a lot, but at that point I knew only half the story. I knew that she and Keith shared moral and religious values. I could picture the internal images that led Helen to search for a loving, trustworthy man who would keep her from falling into the abyss. But what was her role in his life? Why did he did choose her? What made the marriage work?

When I asked what was good about his marriage, Keith teased me by saying, "Well now, how do you know my marriage is good?" He chuckled and shook his head, but I sensed that his humor stemmed from diffidence, not confidence. His style was laconic and reserved. This was not a man who expressed his feelings or thoughts easily.

He laughed again and said, "You certainly like to ask difficult, open-ended questions." Then he began. "My marriage *is* good. We have a lot of fun together." He thought some more. "I miss her when she's gone. We are very different people."

"Can you describe the differences?"

"Well you might call me quite conservative. But I like her challenging ideas. I'm a detail-oriented man, and she's a conceptual, problem-solving person. She's somewhat Pollyanna-like." It took me a few moments to realize he didn't mean that as a criticism. "She's upbeat and optimistic," he explained. "She sees the doughnut while I see the hole." And then, getting to the crux, "She's a very strong person. She had a very difficult childhood. It could have gone either way with her when she was two years old. And she went a positive way instead of a negative way."

I sensed that Keith carried Helen's memories along with his own, even though he hadn't known her in childhood. He seemed on familiar ground in talking about her experiences, and he launched into a detailed description of her background rather than his own. He retold the stories about her foster parents, adding a detail Helen had omitted: throughout her childhood she had had a recurrent dream of being chained to a post. Keith talked with feeling about Helen's rejection by her mother. He knew that Helen had cried when her mother didn't come for her birthday. He then said proudly, "She surmounted all that."

"How do you account for this?" I asked.

"It's just in the genes, I guess."

When I asked about his own childhood, he began, "My mother was a librarian and what they called a spinster. She didn't get married until her mid-thirties, and my father was a few years younger. I was born a year later. I remember they bickered and fought all the time. You see, my father was a very caustic person who liked to hurt people. My mother was a very gentle person who would never hurt a fly."

As Keith spoke, he moved his hands from an open position on his desk into loose fists. His voice rose as he said, "My dad never gave her credit for anything. He was a penny-pinching miser who made her life and mine miserable." He looked down at his hands, which were trembling. He stared for a moment, as if willing them to be still, but they wouldn't stop shaking. I was amazed at the force of his anger. After a moment he regained control and looked at me earnestly.

"I adored my mother. She was very good to me. I wouldn't have done nearly as well as I have in life if it weren't for her. But my relationship with my dad was terrible. Eventually my mother developed somatic symptoms — she had a kind of colitis that made her life miserable — and so when I was twelve I tried to get my father to ease up on her, to help her out. But he was out to control her and wasn't going to give her an inch. He was ornery, mean, and brutal."

Keith looked back down at his clenched hands and said, "I hated my dad. I left home when I got drafted, and when I came back I tried to get along with him, but it still was no good. He always said mean things to me, that I'd never get a job. He was always, always putting me down. He was always negative and hurtful."

When Keith said he had no memories before age ten, I asked if there was truly nothing he could recall.

"I remember once my parents taking a vacation. I was sitting in the back seat of the car, and the whole time they were bickering. I remember my mother crying and saying, 'Maybe we should get a divorce,' and my father saying angrily, 'Yes, maybe we should.'"

"How did you feel?"

"Terrible," said Keith, his fists again clenched on the desk. "And I hated him, but I was scared about divorce."

"Did she want you on her side?"

He drew a deep breath. "My mother was an extraordinary person. She spent a lot of time trying to make me feel good about myself. I remember going on walks with her when I would be full of doubts and fears and things. But she would never talk about what my father did to her or anything else like that. She was a very moral person and active in the Lutheran church."

Keith relaxed as he talked more about his mother. "All my growing-up days I wanted to help her."

"Did you?"

"I never got that wish. She died when I was seventeen."

Like Helen, Keith entered adulthood burdened by unhappiness; his father was cruel and tyrannical toward him and pitiless toward his mother. Unlike Helen, he did have one loving, moral parent, for whom he felt love, respect, and compassion. But he suffered greatly because he was unable to alleviate her pain. His love for Helen and his empathic understanding of her suffering were rooted in his love and pity for his mother.

How did Keith avoid being the failure that his father had predicted he would be? How did he avoid becoming a cruel man like his father? Most of all, how did Helen and Keith create a marriage that was happy for both of them?

People who have been severely deprived and traumatized as children do not give up all hope for love and happiness in adulthood. They do anticipate that new relationships will repeat past disappointments. After all, life has always been thus; why should it change? There's even some comfort in living out a painful scenario simply because the misery is familiar: at least some part of life is predictable, even if predictably sad. But everyone, including those who have suffered terribly, hold on to the contrary hope that the future will *not* mirror the past. They swing back and forth, believing that old scenarios will endlessly repeat and hoping they will not. This hope for change is what brings troubled people into psychotherapy.

Many children in unhappy surroundings hold steadfastly to a different vision of life. One woman in the study whose parents quarreled violently throughout her childhood said, "As a little girl I walked a lot in strange neighborhoods looking for stately and serene houses. I'd stand in front, wishing with all my might that I belonged there." She had no idea what went on behind those closed doors, but the fantasy sustained her.

It is possible for youngsters to maintain rich mental images amid unbearable suffering. Early in my career I worked with Jewish children orphaned by the Holocaust. Many had witnessed the murder of both parents. One boy who lived for many years in refugee camps held on to a tattered chemistry textbook that he could not read, a talisman that kept alive his hope and dream of becoming a scientist like his dead father. And Helen, during her long, solitary walks, was probably comforting herself with images of a far happier life, free of abuse and rejection.

From this study of rescue marriages I have come to appreciate the power of relationships, especially in young adulthood, to reawaken these hidden hopes. When the aroused hope coincides with a good psychological fit of mutual needs and yearnings — as was the case for Helen and Keith — some people can surmount the past and build a future with good expectations. Clearly the danger of falling into old patterns always exists, but these happy rescue marriages point to a phenomenon that has not been explored in the psychological literature — namely, the healing power of a good marriage.

I am not suggesting that marriage is a good substitute for psychotherapy for people who have suffered severely in childhood. Unlike Helen and Keith, many traumatized people cannot take even the first steps toward changing their lives without good treatment, and even then the outcome is not assured. Many people today, including those in rescue marriages, undertake therapy at particular turning points with specific agendas in mind. What distinguishes the rescue marriage is not that the people have done it entirely on their own, as Helen and Keith did, but that they have recovered successfully, with the marriage itself playing a major role.

In a rescue marriage, the psychological transformation begins when two people with severely troubled backgrounds are attracted to one another despite deep-seated fears of being hurt once again. If their hopes are strong enough, they may trust each other enough to create a shared future vision. Each supports the other in working to prevent a repetition of old scenarios. They calm each other and gain a feeling of confidence they have never known before. Their relationship teaches them that they can close the door on the past and affirm their deepest hopes. The effect can be electrifying.

Keith and Helen began their marriage with a remarkably good psychological fit in terms of what they hoped for and needed from each other. Helen, projecting onto this gentle and virtuous man the frightening images of her past and fears of being hurt once again, was frightened by Keith's proposal. But she also brought strong images representing her search for love and kindness, which may have been based in part on the teachings of her church. Feeling safe with Keith, she found the courage to express her most cherished secret hopes. Her long-held wish that she could outrun her fears and become a loving, faithful, and virtuous wife evoked a fervent response from Keith, who desired nothing more than to be a virtuous, loving, and faithful husband who would stay by her and protect her from falling into the abyss.

Similarly, Keith was afraid of failure and expected rejection when he approached Helen, because of the poor self-image imposed by his tyrannical father. But he gathered his courage and defied that pessimistic inner voice. He also projected onto Helen his need for a strong, lively woman who would help him achieve the confidence to be the good man he wanted desperately to be. In helping him overcome his guilt at not being able to rescue his mother, Helen responded to his need and became that encouraging person in his life.

Helen and Keith lovingly helped each other change without consciously understanding or even thinking about the powerful psychological forces affecting them. For both, a major task was to keep at bay the people they feared becoming. They worked throughout the marriage at the task of separating themselves from the internalized images of their parents. As we shall see, at certain junctures the need to work on this task reemerged with a fury, challenging them anew.

Although the ghosts from the past gradually lost their power over the years, the transforming power of Keith and Helen's relationship needed continued reinforcement. Helen and Keith began this process intuitively soon after the marriage began, as if they realized that separating from frightening role models, building trust, allowing intimacy, and creating a sense of togetherness would be especially difficult for them. The devils were strong and the dangers great. They took special measures to strengthen their marriage.

As Helen described the early years of their marriage, she folded her hands primly. "After all the planning that went into getting married, being married was duck soup. You realize I was determined not to repeat all the divorces and all the troubles that everyone in our family had. I thought I would focus on communication. We'd talk things over.

"You see, I had to figure out everything for myself because I had no good models. So for the first five years of our marriage, we had weekly sessions where we'd sit down and Keith would tell me everything that bothered him and I would tell him what bothered me. I made him do it. Most of the time I had nothing to say because he didn't have any bad habits. I was the one with the bad habits. But after our first baby, we couldn't do it on a regimented basis and gave it up. By then we had already learned to deal with most of it. Talking together was built into the pattern of our marriage."

I was impressed that such a young woman could create a forum for talking that encouraged her shy husband to meet her halfway. Their planned conversations, begun during the courtship, continued during the marriage until, in Helen's words, "the pattern of communication got established." In these sessions she encouraged Keith to criticize her, while she told him he could do no wrong.

Keith, however, saw these sessions in an entirely different light, not at all as an opportunity to scold his wife for her bad habits. "We spent hours and hours talking about our relationship," he said. "We discussed what was happening and what we should do about this or that. You see, Helen worried there were so many divorces in her own family, and would it happen to her? She even convinced me to do some talking."

He paused and looked out the window. "It's difficult for me to talk," he said, "especially about myself. I don't normally do it. We went over and over these things on many nights. My wife needed to feel sure that she wouldn't end up like her mother and aunts. She got me to be more open and to think how I felt about things, and I wasn't used to doing that. I got to the point that I really understood why I felt the way I did about her, and I could tell her. That was a big change for me. I wasn't really used to knowing how I felt or thinking about it."

"And you were able to tell her?"

"Yes, I try," he said candidly.

Keith chose his words slowly. "You know, when we first got married, my father had so often told me I would fail that I was sure I'd mess up my job and my marriage. But she never doubted. She never lost confidence in me." He smiled broadly.

Whether a rescue marriage succeeds or fails depends on its specific inner dynamics. In the meshing of mutual needs, husband and wife transform each other in ways that neither can predict. And in fact we do not have the knowledge at this time to predict success or failure. This duet can play out to happy or tragic ends.

To succeed, the marriage must enable each partner to undo the long-lasting effects of a wretched childhood by supporting hopes for a close, loving relationship. This support is rooted in the partners' strong mutual identification as survivors and in the complementarity of their conscious and unconscious needs. Feeling strengthened and relieved within the safety of the new relationship, each partner gathers the courage to draw on hopeful, benevolent visions. Although anxieties don't vanish, they no longer dominate.

In this form of marriage the concept of the man and the woman is different from the concept at the core of a romantic marriage. The rescue marriage depends first on the partners' strong identification with each other, an identification so close they may seem to share the same history. When I asked Keith about his childhood, he began by talking about Helen's. These partners have an intense awareness not only of their own past suffering but of the other's difficulties, as if their togetherness had put down roots into the past. Each one's identity has expanded to truly include the other, almost as if they were one person. Many couples said, "We are both survivors." "We were both depressed during our entire adolescence." "Who else would have us? We both come from really crazy families."

The rescue marriage also rests on the fact that each person becomes an important symbol for the other, standing in marked, specific contrast to an early childhood figure. "He has the kindest eyes in the world," said a woman who had been beaten by her father throughout her childhood. "Clarity, absolute clarity is what you get," said a man, contrasting his wife's rationality with his mother's crazy defense of her husband's right to beat her.

In this complex interaction each projects onto the other a virtuous, benevolent figure that is the opposite of the feared transference figure from childhood. And each evokes behaviors in the other that are quite different from those of the cruel figure and in accord with their hopes for remedy and rescue. Clinical theory tells us to expect that Helen would look for a man who would act toward her the way her cold, abandoning father did. That experience is still an active source of great pain for her. Her strong memories of mistreatment by her foster mother are evident not only in her words but in the movements of her face and throat muscles when she describes the abuse. Certainly she could have become involved with a man who would fall easily into the "love them and leave them" role, who would reinforce her tragic expectation.

In these rescue marriages each partner was for the other an inspiring figure that was both real and iconic. Helen was for Keith a symbol of courage, of successfully battling the odds. Although his own tragic mother went under, Helen could overcome. He was for her a steadfast figure who, unlike her parents, could be counted on to be there. In some marriages, one partner set the moral guidelines for both. "My husband always knows right from wrong," said a woman whose father went to jail for political corruption.

An important part of the mutual rescue was having children and raising them well together. These couples worked extra hard at parenting to avoid following the poor role models from their childhoods. Having happy children who loved and respected them had special meaning for all people who felt rejected by their own parents. It was as if the bad karma was broken by their accomplishment.

By recasting old roles, reshaping expectations, and pushing toward complementarity, people are able to emerge from their terrible past and create a hopeful relationship for themselves. We come to adulthood unfinished, and marriage, as the central relationship of adult life, provides the axis around which people can change and grow.

But attempted rescue marriages may fail. One example that I see frequently is the "gimme shelter" marriage, in which two young people are running away from their parents and from the onerous responsibilities of adulthood, such as jobs, school, and paying bills on time. Typically, after the first glow dissipates, each sees the other as responsible for the demands of reality. They then push each other into behaving like the parent from whom they were escaping. "She nagged all the time, just like my mom," says the young man. "He expects me to have everything ready, while he watches TV," says the young woman. As they re-create their own parents in each other, they want to run away from their own creation, and the marriage breaks.

Even more tragically, soon after the wedding the partner may be perceived as representing someone from the past — myself as victim, my hated sibling, my abusive or incestuous parent. In that case, instead of healing there is an unhappy reliving of early scenarios. Or a partner who wants to be rescued by the marriage may lack the reciprocal desire to take care of the other. The partner may be blamed for early injuries, punished for the abuses of childhood, expected to make up for all the deprivations. This is a dance from hell. There is no end to the misery that people can reenact without realizing that the experiences driving them to attack occurred long before they met. Such a marriage can last a lifetime, held together by the powerful glue of misplaced vengeance, guilt, and fear. Or it may break. But even when the marriage ends, the rage continues.

A rescue marriage can also fail by becoming codependent, reinforcing the original problem. Typically, in a codependent relationship one partner's serious symptoms are consciously or unconsciously maintained by the other. In the classic example the spouse of an alcoholic, despite well-meaning intentions, reinforces the behavior and subverts her own needs. There is no mutual rescue in codependence. There is no growth, no breaking out of early unhappiness. Instead there is collusion, which results in a regression or freezing of symptoms rather than resolution of the problems and alleviation of suffering.

In the successful rescue marriages I studied, each partner was careful not to play martyr or to merge with the other. They did not sacrifice themselves to rescue the other, play a role that maintained the other's symptoms, or simply sit admiringly at the feet of the loved one.

In the tenth year of their marriage, Helen and Keith confronted a powerful ghost from Helen's past that threatened to destroy the marriage and damage the children. When the abyss Helen feared most yawned in front of her unexpectedly, Keith rescued her from herself and the legacy of her tragic history. But it was their marriage that made the rescue possible.

"It was the funniest thing," said Helen. "After we'd been married ten years, we didn't have a fight or anything, but for some reason I thought we should get a divorce. It came right out of the blue, for no reason at all."

"No reason? How do you explain that?"

"I have no idea. My son was six and my daughter was two."

Helen's powerful impulse to leave the marriage occurred when her daughter was two — the very age when she herself had been abandoned by her mother. Helen did not make the connection between these two events.

"Suddenly I had this powerful impulse out of nowhere that I was going to leave him, get a divorce, and leave my children."

"What happened?"

"I talked to my husband about it," she said. "He said it wouldn't be a good thing to do."

Keith's response to what must have been a bombshell was remarkably restrained.

"I insisted that I had to go. He spoke to me in his calm, logical way and then suggested that if I had to, I should go away for a few days, that together we would make arrangements for the care of the children when he was at work. I have trouble remembering the exact circumstances, but I left for three days. I'm a little hazy about where I went. But I returned as planned."

"And that was it?" I realized that the reenactment of her abandonment had been blocked both by her going to her husband and by his measured response.

"Yes. And the impulse to leave my husband and children went away." Helen blinked. "My daughter, who was two, says she remembers being left and not knowing where I had gone. Although Keith was home every day after work, I'm sure he was very upset. She was really insecure after I came back from those three days, really clingy. Keith helped with both kids, but after that she wouldn't let him change her diapers or do anything for her. I had to do everything myself. She had problems after that, and we got some professional consultation about what to do. For over a year, she was afraid that I would disappear suddenly. After that she recovered."

* * *

Helen's story is an excellent example of what is termed the anniversary effect. Many people who have sustained severe losses seem to have an unconscious clock ticking inside them, and the alarm goes off on an anniversary of the date of the loss. The person may have no conscious awareness of the day but feel very sad without knowing why. He or she may be driven to dangerous and destructive behavior that is symbolically linked to the original trauma. Sometimes the person feels impelled to reenact the early experience in the role of aggressor rather than victim. That was the powerful unconscious force behind Helen's wish "out of the blue" to leave her two-year-old daughter and her husband.

But instead of telling her husband angrily that the marriage was finished and she was leaving, she turned to him and in so doing asked for his help. Instead of accusing her of having a secret love affair or of behaving like her wanton mother, Keith gently and rationally helped her overcome her need to leave. Without at all understanding what prompted her sudden impulse, he was able to keep her from ending the marriage. He very wisely encouraged her to leave but to do so under safe conditions and within limits that they both could control. Together they planned for the care of the children during the three-day absence. His love for her and his expectation that she would return on time never wavered.

This poignant example of traumatic childhood events resurfacing dramatically and unexpectedly years later shows how a rescue marriage can prevent the reenactment of destructive and self-destructive behavior. I doubt that either Helen or Keith realized how narrowly they escaped disaster.

Somewhat later I asked Helen how sex was in her marriage.

"Fine," she said. "But I've always been less sexual than Keith." She shrugged. "In fact, as I've gotten older, I could do without it entirely. I enjoy it, but I don't have the same drive he does. It's more important for me to be hugged and cuddled."

"When you were younger, and sex was going well, how important was it for you?"

"Not as important for me as for him. I've had orgasms but certainly not all the time."

"Was sex harder because of all your concerns about your mom, following your mom's footsteps?"

Instead of answering, she said, "The repression was always there. I remember I slept in the same room with my foster parents until I was twelve years old, when I finally got my own room."

Later, when I asked Keith about sex, he answered slowly. "It's been very important for me, but not as important for her, especially lately. I hear this is fairly typical in women as they get older. We don't talk much about sex, which is fine with me. We always dress privately. It keeps a little of the mystery going, you know? And by not talking about it, it keeps it from becoming commonplace."

"Am I right in guessing it's been a little bit of a problem between you?" I suspected that dressing privately and not talking about sex were efforts to mask an unresolved issue.

Keith rushed to defend his wife. "She has to run a business, do all her volunteer work, take care of the house and me and umpteen other things."

The we-ness created here was very different from that of Sara and Matt's romantic marriage, where sexuality and passion were central. For Helen and Keith, we-ness was based more on stability, morality, and kindness. They both recognized the importance of sex in nurturing their relationship, but Helen preferred cuddling to intercourse.

Keith and Helen's marriage did not completely banish the past, nor did it resolve all of the psychological issues they brought to adulthood. Helen's fear of following the path of her sexually promiscuous mother made it hard for her to enjoy the full sexual gratifications of adulthood. And despite Keith's appreciation of his wife's liveliness and access to feelings, he remained reserved and inhibited.

For many years psychologists have thought about the differences in children's resiliency. What makes some children able to survive terrible experiences while others suffer permanent psychological scars? What allows some to hold on to a sense of integrity and a vision of hope and trust while others live in depression or die in despair?

Good rescue marriages shed light on this important issue, for the people in them share some important characteristics. All realized at an early age, sometimes as young as six or seven, that their parents or caregivers were very troubled people. Intuitively they began to distance themselves and to spend much of their childhood alone. Helen took long walks alone in the country and learned to live with silence. Another woman, Robin, told how, when she was eight, her psychotic mother said to her, "Robin is dead and you are Joan." When Robin objected to being declared dead, her mother responded by holding her head under water in the bathtub. Robin learned very quickly to present herself as "Joan," but she never believed it. Thus, at an early age Robin and Helen, like many other youngsters, made a conscious effort to cooperate with their caretakers as needed to stay alive. But they held on to a keen sense of reality, keeping their perceptions and feelings in quiet reserve. They did not relinquish their separate inner world; they were able, physically and emotionally, to be alone.

By adolescence most concluded that the situation at home would not change, but they were determined that their lives would follow a different course. Sometimes they were helped in this realization by a parent. One father said to his daughter when she returned home as a college freshman, "Don't come back. I can't protect you from your mother." But most decided on their own that they would leave home as soon as possible. They spent a great deal of time and energy making coherent sense of their lives and dreaming about their plans and hopes for the future. This self-contained time was an important part of the process of breaking away from identification with their parents.

These intelligent children, with their clear view of reality, were able to recognize bizarre behavior in their parents or caregivers and not identify with it. They were observant about what happened to them and about what happened between their parents, and they made a clear decision to do things differently. One woman recalls saying to herself at age six, "I will never let anyone treat me the way my dad treated my mom." It is remarkable and very important that she didn't wait until she was twenty-one to recognize the problem. She began to distance herself emotionally from her family at an age when most children still identify closely with their parents.

These people also held on to their capacity to feel. Although they were angry at how they were treated, they were also compassionate, appreciative, and grateful for help they received from any quarter. This continued access to feelings, especially angry feelings, is unusual and important. In many case histories of childhood abuse, victims report a sense of numbness, not the rich emotional response that these people showed. "My mother?" said one young woman. "My mother is Saddam Hussein." Such an expression of anger, bitterness, and humor is surely the opposite of numbing. One young woman, whose father used her as a child to carry messages between him and his various mistresses, left home at sixteen and never returned. Although she was a strong feminist, she took her husband's name "so I would have no connection at all with my parents."

Not all of these people who did well in adulthood had a supportive, caring figure in childhood. Keith had a loving mother, but Helen had no comparable person to turn to. Although she identified with her foster father's interest in music, he was not a protective parent or mentor. In fact, none of the people I talked with mentioned a mentor. For some, institutions were important. The church and its values were very important to Helen and Keith. But neither spoke of a special relationship with someone in the church.

Most of these people had depended on their own resources as children. They seem to have taken the mildest encouragement from adults and responded warmly. It is remarkable that they were able to nourish themselves from so little. Their ability to recognize that not all adults were their persecutors allowed them to rekindle and maintain hope for a different kind of relationship and a different kind of life.

At the end of my interview with Helen, I said, "It's amazing what you've done. I can't tell you how impressed I am with what you've been able to build in your life and how grateful I am for your willingness to tell me all these things. I'd like to know what you feel you've learned that would be helpful to others."

She responded, "I've learned that I need balance, to be cautious. Otherwise I'll get into a lot of trouble. And he provides that. Keith is not a risk taker. I add spice to his life. I want quick solutions and I tend to jump ahead. He's slower to act and react. I've learned to be patient, to wait for him to decide things. This is the way it is in our marriage.

"I know many people who are divorcing, and I've noticed two things," she continued. "One is that people expect more from their partner than they're willing to give themselves. The other is, they haven't talked to each other. I really believe that if you give more than you expect to get, you will reap all the benefits you can possibly imagine."

"What would you lose if you lost Keith?"

Her eyes teared. "My best friend. Only death could break our marriage."

When I asked Keith to summarize what he had learned in the marriage, he began, "You see, she made me realize that I'm not alone. That means sometimes I have to do things even if I don't want to. I have to give something of myself. My initial orientation was always to withdraw into me. The biggest challenge I think was to realize there are other people in the world aside from my mother, father, and me. I don't think I became less self-absorbed until college, when I was courting Helen."

"And she changed you?"

"She changed everything. If I'd had my way I wouldn't have done things this way. The joys, frustrations, and angers were not anticipated. Everything is unexpected. The best part of the marriage has been realizing I'm never alone. If she didn't push me, I'd live in a world of silence."

"What would happen if you lost Helen?"

"Oh boy," he said, looking pained. "I've thought about that, and I would lose a lot. What I'd miss most are the challenges and new ideas she brings. She's always suggesting new things, saying why not go there, try that, do this."

A quiet sadness fell over Keith. "Without her I would have to struggle not to be a recluse. Without her I would feel old."

# 10 ❧

# The Fourth Task

*Coping with Crises*

It's tempting to think that people in long-term happy marriages are merely lucky. Perhaps their marriages are never tested by the nasty vicissitudes of life — car accidents, breast cancer, job loss, the death of a child. But that is not the case. Every couple in the study had lived through at least one major tragedy, and some had experienced several traumatic events. No one escaped the wolves at the door.

The fourth task of marriage, coping with crises, is more varied than the other tasks because each stressful event evokes different anxieties and touches off different emotional chords. Every crisis has the potential to strengthen the marriage, weaken it, or bring it down altogether. An ongoing stress such as poverty is very different from an acute stress such as sudden unemployment; a diagnosis of diabetes is not the same threat as a diagnosis of breast cancer. The impact of a community disaster is very different from that of a family tragedy. A child's death is vastly more difficult to assimilate than the timely death of an aged parent. Moreover, a couple that handles a stress in isolation has a different experience from one that is surrounded by friends and family.

In general, crises fall into two major categories. The first result from the foreseeable changes that occur in life, such as the move into middle age, which is often accompanied by the children's adolescence. Certain birthdays, midlife, menopause, aging, and retirement can produce crises, as can pregnancy, childbirth, and particular developmental stages of childhood and adolescence. Although such crises can be anticipated, their shape, passion, explosiveness, and tempo are not predictable.

In the second category are the unexpected twists of fate that may occur at any point in life. Some can be anticipated, like the death of a parent, and some are never foreseen, like the death of a child. The happily married couples in this study endured a wide range of serious misfortunes, including serious illnesses, geographic moves, and job losses. Even a strong marriage can be profoundly shaken by an external disaster such as earthquake, fire, or war.

Crises that appear to originate in the marriage, such as a rise in the level of conflict between spouses or a decline in one partner's sexual interest or even infidelity, often have their roots in stressful events outside the marriage. Unemployment, the death of a close friend or parent, or a natural disaster — all have the power to cause dissension and unhappiness in the marriage. The tragedy is that most frequently the man and woman have no awareness of the real cause of their difficulties. The visible anger may mask deep sorrow or mourning; nagging may be a cover for profound concern and worry. Typically the partners are unaware of the relationship between their changed behavior and its source and therefore are unable to deal with the issues.

The crises that I describe here present serious threats to a marriage because they change the partners' feelings and behaviors toward each other. They have the power to break the relationship. A couple can protect their marriage only if they understand how the external trigger is affecting their relationship. The ways in which some couples have handled crises successfully reveals the general principles involved in this task.

Two and a half years after I first spoke with Helen and Keith, I returned for a follow-up visit on a balmy July evening. The air smelled of honeysuckle and mown grass as Keith led me to a lawn chair in the back yard. When Helen joined us, I asked, "How are things? Have there been any major changes since we last met?"

Helen looked at Keith and took a deep breath. Slowly and soberly she began, "Well, you came at a good time. It's mostly over now, but for a while it was touch-and-go. A year ago I was diagnosed with breast cancer."

"How awful," I said, looking closely at both of them.

Helen picked up my phrase. "Yes, it's as awful as they say."

"How are you feeling?"

In her usual reassuring tone, she said, "I have a checkup tomorrow, and so far I'm doing fine. But I had a dream the other night. I dreamed the cancer was recurring. Within the past few weeks I've dreamed that a lot. In the dream I walk into the hospital and they say, 'You're going to have chemotherapy for the next year.'"

"What do you make of the dream?"

Reassuring herself as well as me, Helen responded, "Well, I think it has to do with the answer to a question that's bugging me. I've been trying to decide whether to expand my music schools. The dream seems to be saying no, don't do it. Take it easy."

"So have you decided?"

"I decided to listen to the dream. I'm not going to expand, at least for the time being."

Once again I was impressed with Helen's courage and pragmatism, her ability to turn even a foreboding dream to good use.

She continued, "The breast cancer changed my perspective and Keith's. It makes clear what things are really important and what is minor." I noted that she was not afraid to use the words "breast cancer" instead of a euphemism like "my illness." Helen smiled at her husband. "He was marvelous. He was there every step of the way."

"Were you surprised?"

"Of course not." She smiled. "You know, the doctor told me that many times husbands are unable to stay for the chemotherapy treatments. Most women come in with a female relative or friend. But Keith came with me."

Looking at me closely, she said, "I think I know what you want to ask. Did my illness affect our relationship?" She looked back at Keith. "And the answer is no, I never questioned that it would affect the relationship. I never questioned that he'd be there for me, be reliable." She reached across the table and touched his arm as he looked at her lovingly.

Keith said, "It was awful. They discovered the lump in her breast right after we went to my aunt's funeral. She died of breast cancer because they caught it too late. The doctors were scared, and we were scared. And we needed to have it operated on right away. I was devastated. I was afraid I was going to lose her. I changed my whole schedule so I could stay home with her. But now it's all back to normal. And it really hasn't changed things here in the long run." He paused and added, "This is the only major illness we've ever faced, and we did it together."

"Was this the worst crisis of your marriage?"

"Absolutely," he said, glancing at his wife.

"Of our adult life," said Helen.

"Losing you would be the worst for me. Even thinking about it . . ." His voice trailed off.

"Tell me what you did."

Keith replied. "It was a joint project. We approached it very logically, one step at a time. I was always involved. I felt that I should be, and I didn't want to be cut out of it."

The people I talked to in happy marriages used the pronoun "we" more often than most, but it's unusual for someone to speak of cancer as a "joint project." He almost seemed to be saying, "We have cancer." Cancer is different from a child's fever or an economic crisis because it is a death threat. Thus the extension of the "we" speaks movingly of the couple's physical and emotional bonding.

When Keith walked me to my car later, he said, "I didn't want to say this in front of Helen, but I must say I've been worried about her, that she has too much to do at work and in her other activities and in coping with the disease. I'm always afraid she'll get burned out, that she'll spread herself too thin, that she'll be physically overextended. This is one of the major sore spots in our marriage. She's a caring and giving person who overcommits, who wants to do lots of things, always wants to be there when asked. I feel that she's way overcommitted, especially with her volunteer work. I worry about her being burned out, and I worry about her health now that she's in recovery from the mastectomy. We talk about this a lot. I try not to show her how worried I really am."

We know quite a lot about how a crisis can significantly change a person's inner and outer worlds; afterward things can never be the same. We must absorb the shock of the change and master the losses: mourn the death, deal with the cancer, rebuild the destroyed house, get on with life. Some crises have a relatively brief impact, but others change a person forever. A person who loses a job may find new employment. But a child with cystic fibrosis will never get better. The loss of a breast is permanent.

But far less attention has been paid to the fact that crises ricochet within a marriage. When a crisis hits, a husband or wife is not just a kindly bystander or good friend. He or she is a direct player in the unfolding drama. When a partner who is grieving a death looks for support or someone to blame, the bereavement enters the marriage. A crisis may redefine the couple's relationships, with parents, other family members, and children. It may either solidify or weaken the sense of we-ness that has been built through the years. People may cling to each other for support, or they may fly apart in different directions because every time they look at each other they experience the tragedy again.

What influences the outcome?

When one partner loses a job or some other economic problem occurs, every family member is affected to some degree. If the individual becomes more anxious, worried, frightened, guilty, or angry, he or she turns to the partner with a range of new needs and anxieties, which in turn bring up new needs in other family members. Any crisis can set off a chain reaction in the marriage and in the family, sometimes even in the extended family and the community at large. Each partner's self-image and the image of the other person, the marriage, and the world may change. Core questions are asked anew: Will you love me if I can't take care of you economically? Will you consider me less of a man now that I've lost my job? Will you pity me? Will you love me if my body is mutilated? Will you comfort me? Will you consider me less of a woman?

Each crisis poses different threats to the marital interaction and offers different opportunities for redefining togetherness and autonomy, recasting each partner's role. A crisis requires renegotiating the tasks of marriage. And because people today live longer, a couple in a lasting marriage will inevitably face many crises together. No one leads a charmed life.

In marriages that break under the strain of a crisis, I have observed several themes. One is the anxiety, often expressed as anger, that people feel during and after the crisis. One partner may project all this anger on the other — a readily available target. The accusation "You always fail me when I need you" is a familiar one. Scapegoating makes the blamer feel better, but it removes support when it is most needed.

One couple I know divorced within six months of a terrible accident that occurred when the father, momentarily distracted, lost control of the car. One of their three children was killed. Although both parents were devastated, as were the surviving children, the mother's grief turned to anger at the father. She openly blamed her husband for the child's death, even though he shared her grief and suffered in blaming himself. When she filed for divorce, the tragedy of the child's death was compounded for the children, who lost not only their sister but their intact family. The father's loss and grief were compounded by his wife's accusations, and he became chronically depressed.

After such a tragedy a partner may feel unbearable guilt: how can I permit myself to have a happy marriage when I am the wicked person who failed to prevent the accident? Or, more commonly, how can my husband and I enjoy sex when our child has been killed in a car crash? This is a universal human reaction, which we call survivor guilt. Some people seem to follow the old Bedouin adage "Change your place, change your luck" after a crisis. They think, usually irrationally, that if they flee the marriage they will leave the problems and stresses behind.

People in marriages that survive and become stronger after a crisis experience just as much anxiety and guilt as everyone else. They are just as distressed and angry, but instead of scapegoating, they help each other bear the new burden. And they fully acknowledge the importance of the help they give and receive. One man, who was diagnosed with colon cancer not long after our first interview, told me at the two-year follow-up talk, "My illness brought us closer together. It either makes or breaks a couple. The current challenge for me is survival. My body has let me down, and I'm worried about my wife and sons." His wife said, "I've encouraged him to rely on me so he won't become depressed. I don't know how people go through these major crises alone."

The task of coping with crises involves several steps that the people in the marriages I studied seemed to carry out instinctively. First, they tried their best to realistically acknowledge and think about the consequences of the crisis. They worked at maintaining a perspective that did not attribute all their problems to what had just happened. By constraining their view of the crisis they managed to keep its effects from spreading. And they tried to distinguish their fears of the worst-case scenario from what was likely to happen. For example, even though the parents of a child who had cancer feared the worst, they knew he might benefit from treatment.

Those in strong marriages also tried to see how the crisis would affect not only the marriage and the victim but other family members.

They thought realistically about the extent and duration of the crisis, searching out whatever information they could find about the potential range of effects. By planning realistically as much as possible, they avoided the extremes of freezing into helplessness or rushing around in meaningless activity.

Second, they protected each other by not blaming, in spite of the great temptation to do so. In fact, they went further by trying to protect each other from inappropriate self-blame. The woman did not say to her husband who had just lost his job, "If you had done what I told you, you'd still be employed." Or "If you'd taken the child to the right doctor, we would have had a correct diagnosis six months ago." Or "If you'd kept your eyes on the road, we'd all be fine today." They protected each other against self-reproach and shame.

Third, they took steps to allow some degree of pleasure and humor back into their lives by keeping things in proper perspective. "Let's do something for us that's fun. Let's do something for the children. We can't be all doom and gloom." They tried their best not to let the tragedy totally dominate their world.

Fourth, they didn't play martyr or pretend to be saintly. Fear makes everyone cranky and difficult, and these couples surely fought with each other. They were as tempted as anyone else to do destructive and self-destructive things, like driving away the people they needed and loved the most. But they were usually able to block these impulses and stay in control because they saw the connection between the crisis and the inappropriate hurtful response. They recognized that anxiety about illness and death can lead to helpless rage, that despair over a loss can lead to the feeling of being singled out for persecution ("Why me?"), that worry can lead to profound disorganization. They made a great effort to keep destructive tendencies from getting out of control and harming the marriage.

Fifth, they blocked the crises that they could see coming. Rather than waiting until a spouse's drinking or acting out or depression was overwhelming, they intervened at an earlier stage. One woman, whose husband started to drink and come home late because his job was in trouble, told him firmly, "I'm not going to tell our daughter that I don't know where her father is. Stop drinking." She put her demand in terms of the daughter he loved, and the man did indeed stop drinking. Later he praised his wife for her foresight in preventing disaster.

\*    \*    \*

Consider Helen's illness. Beyond the shock of a diagnosis of breast cancer, with the terror of perhaps facing death and certainly facing suffering from surgery, chemotherapy, and radiation, such a crisis forever changes the marriage. A woman's self-image, at least from puberty on, is linked to having two breasts. If she loses one or both, she feels mutilated, robbed of her sexual attractiveness and her very identity as a woman. She feels ashamed, disfigured, and disoriented as well as frightened. Most of all, she fears rejection by the man in her life.

In Helen's case the loss of a breast was inevitably linked to her early childhood experiences of rejection and abandonment. These were the major themes of her early life, and cancer rode on top of them.

Keith had to deal not only with her pain and fear but with his own fears of losing her: his adult life depended on Helen's presence. And inevitably he feared his own death. The connection is unavoidable, because cancer often strikes in middle or old age, when people are concerned about their own mortality, potency, aging, and sexual attractiveness. A man may be afraid to touch his wife or be unable to look at her scar. He may feel that she is fragile and he might hurt her. He may think at some primitive level, as we all tend to do despite our sophistication, that her illness is contagious.

If the husband is a sensitive person and the relationship is strong, he will realize how anxious she is, how afraid of rejection, how enraged she feels at the curve ball life has thrown her. He will know how vulnerable and in need of love she is and will reassure her that she is attractive and beautiful to him.

Keith and other husbands in good marriages move closer to their wives when serious illness strikes. It is not easy. Keith worked part-time when Helen was undergoing chemotherapy so he could accompany her to the treatment sessions. He showed empathy and sensitive understanding, literally identifying with his wife's agony. Rather than she alone having breast cancer, it was Helen and Keith together who were hit by this misfortune. As he said, "It's a joint venture."

This crisis required renegotiating the task of building we-ness in their marriage. Keith and Helen closed ranks and faced the crisis together. This capacity for mutual identification is a hallmark of a high-quality marriage.

Helen's illness wrought changes in her sense of autonomy and independence. She responded to her fear of becoming an invalid by becoming even more active in her volunteer activities. Keith worried about that, but he recognized that her need to be busy might be a way of recovering from the illness. In this situation the task of maintaining autonomy takes on a new dimension. His solicitude might make her irritable and angry or make her retreat into silent unhappiness. Or she might come to appreciate his concern. His worries about her level of activity might be groundless. Whatever the outcome, cancer introduced new strains to a task that had been resolved in this marriage.

Although the death of an aging parent is usually thought of as a crisis only for the adult son or daughter, it can put serious stress on a marriage. The death of a parent very often shakes up a person's psychological balance in surprising and unpredictable ways. At the simplest level the bereaved person may turn to his or her partner for comfort. Even if the spouse gives that comfort willingly and lovingly, the partner may feel that it is insufficient. Hurt feelings add to the ongoing pain.

But the situation can be more complex. The survivor may feel more and more bedeviled and sink into deep melancholy. She may feel very angry at the dead parent for having abandoned her or, on the contrary, relieved to be rid of the all-consuming worry that preceded the death. He may feel guilty that he failed to take all the right steps in the treatment of the illness or did not visit the dying parent often enough. She may rejoice that she is alive and surviving but feel very guilty about this sense of relief. If the parent who died was a central figure in his life, he may feel that the world has become a desolate place.

These varied reactions to the death may occur at the time of death or much later. One man described feeling numb when his father died. But on a visit to Hiroshima ten months later, as he sat on the grass outside the museum, he broke into uncontrollable sobbing. He recognized his tears as those he had been unable to shed at his father's funeral. The individual may keep these powerful feelings locked inside or allow them to spill into the marriage. She may become withdrawn and melancholy or may rage at her spouse, accusing him of being callow, unloving, inattentive, or emotionally abandoning. All kinds of feelings may be projected onto the other person in a fit of towering rage.

Although a connection between the death of a parent and divorce has not been reported, I have noted a number of divorces that occurred after a parent's death, especially if the parent had a commanding position in the adult child's life. In some cases the survivor seemed to feel so guilty about the death that she believed she was not entitled to a good marriage because the dead parent had never had that.

In some cases a loss precipitates anger and conflict and accusations that get completely out of control. Sometimes a survivor may succumb to severe depression that is not recognized. In one such instance the husband in a twenty-year marriage lost a lifelong friend in a tragic industrial accident. For the next two years the man went to work, then came home and lay on his bed for hours. Often he slept in his clothing. His wife, an intelligent, educated woman, saw his severe depression as a stubborn rejection of her rather than as his reaction to the tragic loss of his closest friend. She angrily filed for divorce without recognizing that her husband urgently needed treatment.

Those people in good marriages were better able to stave off anger and guilt and to support a partner in mourning without seeing the withdrawal or anger as directed at them personally. They recognized signs of depression and actively sought treatment. Even when the reaction was severe, it was contained by recognizing that the source was in the death that had occurred.

Many couples took steps to ease the emotional impact of an impending death in the family; they acted out of compassion rather than calculation of the impact death would have on the marriage. One wife with a new baby to take care of encouraged her husband to spend three months with his dying mother in a distant city. She recognized that it would be very helpful to the mother and would greatly relieve the pressure on her husband. Several couples took a dying parent into their homes for the last few months of life, allowing some long-delayed reconciliations as well as very good care for the dying person. In some cases the initiative was taken by the partner of the son or daughter, who recognized or anticipated the other's need.

Some spouses devoted themselves to an ill parent even when doing so deprived the family of attention. One wife went off every weekend for four months to attend to her dying mother, who lived several hundred miles away. Her husband, who worked very long hours at his job, took over full care of the home and the children without complaint. The woman was very concerned about the burden that her absence had placed on her husband and young children. When I asked him how he felt about this period, he said, "It was her finest hour," referring to his wife's capacity for devotion and sacrifice, not to him and the children, but to her mother.

Even an external disaster, such as a hurricane, flood, fire, or earthquake, can take its toll on a marriage. People in a community often work together very closely at the height of the crisis, acting with courage and compassion. But afterward, when they confront the inevitable dislocations in their lives, their guard is down and they are swallowed up by the panic they have suppressed. A range of feelings from irritability to rage can bubble to the surface. These feelings, augmented by the dislocations of daily life, can easily result in scapegoating within the marriage.

A friend told me that after a devastating earthquake in which she and her family almost lost their lives, she was barely conscious for several days. Then she got up one day with the obsessive notion that she had to bake cookies. Her husband had cared for her tenderly when she lay in bed after the earthquake, but the cookie baking unleashed in him a fierce rage. For the first time in his life he struck her. People often exhibit very bizarre symptoms after their lives have been severely dislocated. And these individual ways of coping, which help them get back to functioning normally, are likely to be incomprehensible to the other person and to arouse great anger.

Often several crises occur together, or a crisis may bring up other problems, revealing the inevitable seams within a marriage in bold relief. One family in the study lost their house in a devastating fire at a time when they were struggling with a marital crisis because of the wife's anger at the husband's long hours at work. She said, "The marriage was in trouble at that time, and then the house burned down. And we just dealt with the crisis so differently. Our styles were so different. It was impossible for either of us to see the sanity in the other person's behavior. It was the straw that broke the camel's back.

"It was horrible, because I felt my husband's way of getting control over the fire was to deal with insurance claims and become pathological about receipts and filing systems. And I just wanted to make a nest. I wanted to have some soup simmering on the stove and have a place where the kids could play with some toys, and some flowers on the table. He was so ornery that he got real verbally abusive, which he had never been before."

In her anxiety she became incensed at his filling out the insurance forms, which she saw as pathological. He in turn thought her need for flowers on the table was "pathological." They became very angry at each other. But the wife saw that their very different ways of coping with the fire were driving them apart. The couple became frightened when they realized that their behavior was out of control and took steps to fortify their marriage.

The woman later reflected, "I was afraid that the marriage was going to be a casualty of this whole thing. We re-etched our values at this time when we needed to do so. I don't recommend a fire as a means to an end, but the low point in our lives clarified that we're really important to each other and that family is important." She laughed. "And it gave us the opportunity to realize that many people give up on a marriage too soon and don't see how these troubled times can really forge a very strong bond as well as a passionate, exhilarating time. If there is a theme to my marriage, I said to myself, it would be that a marriage should give you someone you can count on, particularly through hard times."

Her husband remembered his first reaction to the disaster. "The entire house was burning, and I watched, simply stunned by it all. The fire, though, was pivotal in pressing me to reevaluate the facets of my life. I somehow had the object lesson that if we could get through the fire, we could get through anything. And when I had to replace what we owned, I realized how constricted my life had become with respect to interests outside of work. The fire was a catalyst in our getting closer, in our whole relationship."

The fire made this couple feel as if their entire history had been wiped out. The house, with its mementos, photographs, and furnishings, represented the bonds that held them together. It truly symbolized their marriage. As the husband told me, "It's like we were groping in the dark to find out who we were and what we were." They had to rethink what they valued and agree on what they wanted to restore and what they could let go. And in so doing, they literally renegotiated the goals of the marriage.

Couples who experience the loss of their home are drawn almost inevitably to assess what they have lost, what is worth saving, and how they should rebuild their lives. In mourning the house, they mourn the loss of their past, but they are also able to look at some flaws they would like to correct. This couple reported that the experience, however traumatic, ultimately brought them closer. They rekindled their investment in the marriage and shaped it more to their liking.

I have seen many instances where disaster has the opposite effect. The angry feelings between the couple mount, and each one finds the other's behavior bizarre and unacceptable. The problems appear insurmountable, and one or the other walks away. This couple had the imagination to sort out the issues and use the tragedy to make a new and better start.

Marital difficulties and unemployment rates are linked. Domestic violence rises sharply during a recession, an example of how external crises resound in a family's life. In addition to the serious economic concerns, for most men and an increasing number of woman in our society a job is central to their self-image, and its loss is a devastating blow.

Satisfaction in other areas of life doesn't make up for the loss of a job. It's a black hole. The man feels like a terrible failure and fears that his wife will reject him and his children will be ashamed of him. He may feel he has no place to go but down, or to the local bar. Violent behavior often has its roots in shame, in his feeling that he is not fully a man, in his fear of her silent or nagging accusations, and, strangely enough, in his inability to tolerate her sympathy or pity. So he establishes a pseudomanhood by lashing out in a very primitive way at the person he needs most at this time.

Needless to say, she may not look beyond his violent behavior to understand these complicated motivations. Her patience is low. She's worried to death. And the household soon becomes a battlefield rather than a place of comfort, sympathy, and encouragement, which they both need desperately. Tragically, when people need support the most, they often destroy the compassion that might have been available.

Moreover, the age-old practice of finding a scapegoat works on some level. People who face intolerable worry or pain look for a scapegoat because it's easier to be angry than guilty, easier to feel rage than helplessness. As one woman said, "We want to blame someone, something. In a disaster you look around and you're tempted to blame each other." Laying the blame on a spouse doesn't solve the problem, but it temporarily relieves that individual's guilt and worry. But when each person accuses the other of failing, the marriage may be destroyed.

How did the people in these good marriages deal with this problem? Some of the men in the study who had had high-level management positions in banking, advertising, aerospace, or architecture lost their jobs in the recession of the early 1990s. This was especially difficult because they knew that they would never regain jobs with the same income and status. As one man explained to me, "In advertising, you're over the hill at thirty-five. Clients have the illusion that new ideas come from young people." He added sadly, "After twenty-five years in the company, I got twenty-four hours' notice. I got a lead parachute."

One man, a stockbroker, could not find work for a year. He car-pooled, shopped, painted the garage, feeling miserable and depressed as the crisis reverberated throughout the family. Although his wife continued to work full-time as a nurse, her job could not support the family. When their twelve-year-old son's grades plummeted from A's to D's, his wife, despite their bad economic situation, insisted that the family go into counseling together.

I asked what her husband had said to that. "I insisted it was for me," she replied, "although it was really for him and our son. It was very helpful, and we made it."

"What do you think helped the most?"

"I think what helped a lot was my saying to him, 'Don't take the first job that comes along.' I really meant it. I said, 'I don't want you to do something you don't like. That's very important to me.' I also kept saying, 'Let's not panic.' And I kept him from rushing into things too soon and from coming apart."

I was interested in how intuitively this woman, and other wives, held the man's shame at bay and vigorously counteracted his sense of humiliation. All of them told their husbands not to waste themselves. They set out to protect the men as much as possible from self-accusation and feelings of failure. Additionally, they responded sensitively to the man's anxiety about the wife taking over the role of breadwinner. They tried very hard to maintain the household routine and keep the children from acting out. Obviously, such measures cannot provide a job, but they protect the family and the marriage, and keep the husband from feeling victimized.

Sometimes people took extraordinary steps to head off what they saw as a major threat to the marriage. One husband lost his job and became severely depressed shortly after their first baby was born.

Although the wife had a good job, she felt anguished at seeing her husband lying on the bed staring at the ceiling, behaving as his father had. He was not the kind of man who could be happy staying at home and raising the children while she worked. She realized that he would eventually resent her heroism, detest her strength, and, in rage at his own inadequacy, leave the marriage.

So, in a desperate act of courage, she quit her job and told him that if the family was to survive, he had to get a job. Within two weeks he found work. Within a year his self-esteem was restored, and two years later she was able to resume her own career. Obviously, such a drastic strategy would not work for everyone. Some men would not rally and find that job. Others might remain depressed for other reasons. But in this case it worked. She knew the marriage was in trouble, and she took a courageous, risky step to save it.

Nowhere are the tasks of marriage more salient than in coping with a crisis. A couple can't handle a crisis well unless the foundation of the marriage is solidly in place. Only if the structure is strong will they be able to protect each other from their own vulnerabilities and accurately assess the threat. But even if the marriage is strong, it will need to be reinforced to meet the crisis that threatens to blow the house down.

# 11 🙟

# Marty and Tina Delgado

## *A Different Kind of Rescue*

I WAS INTRODUCED to Marty and Tina Delgado by a couple participating in the study. Close friends of the Delgados, they had attended Marty and Tina's twenty-fifth wedding anniversary and were moved by the way the two had talked about their "marriage made in heaven."

But when I met Marty and Tina, I discovered a marriage in which fighting and yelling occurred fairly often. It was very different from Keith and Helen's relationship, yet it soon became clear to me that Marty and Tina had a rescue marriage of a different sort.

Their turbulent way of interacting was on display when I interviewed them together. Marty was pacing the living room like a lion in a cage. He was angry at Tina for saying something to me that had infuriated him, namely that his illness two years earlier had not changed her or the marriage.

"How could you say that about my illness," he shrieked. "How could you ignore it?" Marty's arm flew up in the air as he raged. "How could you ignore something so important?" He was pacing, pacing, pacing, unable to control himself.

"But it didn't change my career or the marriage," said Tina, sitting straight on the couch, calm and courteous. "I didn't say it wasn't serious."

She turned to me with rising excitement and said, "Judy, you see? This goes on all my life. Look at me, Marty. Look at me. He never looks at me. Look at me!"

Marty kept pacing and glared straight ahead, shutting her out.

I had the sense that I was witnessing a typical scenario in this marriage. So as not to lose the chance, I spoke up. "Marty, why don't you look at her?"

He stopped cold and said in an entirely changed tone, "Because if I looked at her, I would see the face of the woman I love." Realizing he'd told me more than he intended, he sat down. "If my guard weren't down," he said, "if I hadn't just driven in from Portland, I wouldn't have told you or her."

Marty's words told me that his pacing up and down and screaming had little to do with the woman sitting on the couch — and what's more, he knew it. But how to explain the rage, the anger, the acting out, alongside of his acknowledgment of love?

I first met Marty on a blustery day in March in his office at the San Francisco marina. He imports seafood from Asia, Australia, and New Zealand and ships it to restaurants throughout the country. As I entered, Marty was talking on the phone to a colleague and jabbing his fingers in the air. He talked in an avuncular way, but the message was clear — this is a dirty business, and you gotta play dirty pool or you're not going to get anywhere. He waved me to a comfortable-looking chair across from his desk and wrapped up the call. He smiled and said, "That guy is just too nice."

Marty, who was about fifty, was short, balding, and very charming, very bright. He greeted me with some apprehensiveness, but he warmed to the interview and ended up talking to me for most of the morning. He is a very forceful and opinionated man, quick to laughter and probably extremely quick to anger. He considers himself an expert in the ways of the world, by which he means the world of competition.

"What's good about my marriage is my wife," he said expansively, in answer to my question. "She has been a source of strength. She's my best friend. She's someone I totally respect."

"Tell me about her."

"She's a woman with a great love of life. She loves living. She loves animals. I'm not even allowed to kill a spider in our house." He grinned and said, "Let me tell you a story about my wife. When we were married twenty years, we threw a big party. We invited five, six, seven couples. It was a very wonderful party, and we asked people to not bring gifts but to come prepared to do or say something. One friend came with eight pages written about our marriage. It was just hilarious.

"We were having a wonderful time, and then at midnight someone said to me, 'Say something about Tina.' And so I said I wanted everyone to know how much I love her. And if the marriage were ever to end, if something happened and the marriage went down the tubes, I would want her as my best friend, because she is such a great person. After that, our friends asked her to say a few words about me, which she did, and she said some very lovely things.

"And so after a while everyone went home and we both went to bed. I woke up in the morning, and I looked over to the other side of the bed, and there was my wife sitting bolt upright and looking straight ahead. I said, 'What's the matter?' And she said, 'Listen up. Make no mistake about it. If you and I were to separate, if we were divorced, I would take you for everything you have in the world. You would be lucky to have underwear left on you, after I was through with you.'" Marty beamed with pride. "That's my wife," he said. "Clarity, absolute clarity. Clarity is no issue. You know exactly what it is."

"What's the advantage of clarity?" I asked.

"It's simple. You don't have to wonder. You don't have to worry. What you see is what you get. What she says is what she means. She meant what she said when she was raising our children. I'd say, 'You touch that and I'll break your arm.' But my threats were empty. She'd say, 'If you touch this, you will have a problem.' And they had a problem. Just very simple. I have trouble knowing what I think, what I feel. She always knows. She's absolutely clear."

"Tell me what's disappointing about your marriage."

"The first years of our marriage were a nightmare. We fought, we threw things. For five years we threw things. You can still see the marks on the furniture where we threw things. In fact, even now, five years ago, I threw something and smashed it into the wall, and you can still see the damage. It's only become muted recently. Usually she would stop. She tore the shirt off my back. She screamed. I screamed. We screamed through that entire period. She started and I would finish. And we would keep going. It isn't like we would reconcile. We would keep going."

"And someone got hurt?" I asked.

"No, we didn't get hurt. She would go after me, and I would defend myself. But I never hit her, never. I never touched her. She tore the shirt off my back, but she never hit me." He smiled as if this were a gift.

I said tentatively, "You were careful not to hurt each other physically."

"Yes, we were very, very careful. We screamed. We howled. We threw everything. Once I threw a whole dustpan all over the room. And then gradually we calmed down."

Marty and Tina were clearly different from the other couples I'd visited. I said, "Marty, you mean you have fought throughout most of your married life, yet you're telling me that this is a good marriage? What is good here?"

He gave me a happy look. "Affection, respect, a great sense of humor. And love. What is good is that we love each other. I learned a lot of things from her. When I married her, I'd never heard about different kinds of music or about art or about culture. And she taught me all of that, and I like it very much. I value it. And she learned from me how to take care of herself. She doesn't take crap from anybody."

"Marty, that doesn't explain it. What kept you guys together?"

"What kept us together?" He thought and said, "Let me answer that. Who else would want us? Let me tell you how we met. I was twenty-two, she was twenty. Looking into her eyes, I saw something that said to me, This person and I belong together. So I said, 'Lady, I'm going to love you like no man will ever love you.' And I meant it. I was scared. But this is how I felt. And this is still how I feel. Every time I think of her, I think of her surrounded by her three dogs. They adore her, and she takes wonderful care of them. If I come back in another life, I would like to be her pet. She is a wonderful, generous, loving woman. She is all anybody could ask for."

Later I said, "Tell me about your family."

"You got all day? Let me tell you the key thing. My father was a brute, and he beat my mother all the time. I figured when I was little that I would stop it. And when I got to be a teenager, I took a coat hanger and stood between him and my mom. And she screamed at me for attacking my father. That was my home."

"And Tina?"

"She came from a great family too," he said with a snort. "Her father lusted after her. And her mom was totally ineffectual. That's it in a nutshell."

I asked, "What were you and Tina fighting about?"

"It was about sex," admitted Marty. "There was a lot of fighting. She would get excited, and then at the last minute she would pull back. You have no idea what this did to me. I felt terrible. She treated me as if I was exploiting her, as if I was going to rape her. That was the last thing on my mind. I had no clue as to what was happening. Finally I realized she had no clue. I felt that she did not like me, that she thought of me as a braggart. It wasn't until years later, when she was in therapy, that she realized she had been sexually abused as a child. But she stayed with me. It wasn't until nine or ten years into the marriage that she was able to enjoy sex. We both had some sex therapy, and after that she allowed herself pleasure."

"So what were you fighting about?"

"That's what I do when I feel bad," said Marty.

"How much of the marriage has been taken up fighting?" I asked.

"A lot," said Marty.

"Was there pleasure in the fighting?"

He answered instantly, "There was relief. Probably the marriage would have broken up without it."

"How so?"

"Because we were able to get so much out of our gut — it maintained the marriage."

"After the fighting, was there sweet reconciliation?"

"There were no sweet reconciliations."

Looking to see if the conflict were an overture to sex, I asked, "Were there sexy reconciliations?"

He said insistently, "There were no sexy reconciliations. We wore our anger like a badge of honor."

With utter honesty and eloquence, Marty had captured the human condition in all its complexity. He added, "You should know that the fighting also slowed down a lot when we moved to California and got away from our families. And she got her own career going."

Jumping ahead, he said, "Another thing that held us together was the children. We adore our children. I was a great father. I diapered my children. I bathed my children. I got up at night. Always our children knew how much we loved them. She was a fabulous mother."

Unlike Helen's early trauma, which resurfaced with her own daughter, Marty and Tina's childhood problems did not seem to extend to their own children. But I wanted to know for sure. I asked, "How are the kids?"

He talked about his son and daughter with great affection. John and his wife were living in Seattle, where his son and some friends were trying to start a new computer business. "We speak twice a week. I have to say I admire his nerve. But I think he might make it. I wish I knew more that would be useful to them. I try, but he's way ahead of anything I ever learned," he said proudly.

"Ellen is very different. She and her husband are expecting a baby in three months, and Tina is so excited you'd think it's the only baby going to be born in California. I feel the same way, but I try not to show it. Ellen is a musician. She's artistic and sensitive. She's been a delight to have around. She and her mother have always been very close."

I left Marty feeling shaken. I had not expected to find a marriage like the Delgados' in this study. They had found each other almost by chance, and their life together had begun as a runaway "gimme shelter" marriage. Both felt enraged at their families and helpless to change what had happened to them. They both felt unloved and exploited. What bound them together was love, mutual identification, and profound compassion for each other's suffering.

In Tina, Marty found a woman whom he could admire and respect, in contrast to his parents. As a child and a teenager he fantasized about helping his mother, but when he actually tried to protect her, she threatened him for daring to criticize his father. Marty felt betrayed by both of his parents. Subsequently, when his father hit him, he hit back. And he gave up on helping his mother.

The adult Marty lived out his childhood feelings of helplessness and anguish by yelling, beating the walls, and destroying property — but he never hurt his wife. Over and over he howled at the moon, expressing his rage, not at Tina but at the ghosts of his parents, ghosts he could not lay to rest. In terms of the tasks of marriage, he could neither separate from nor connect with them. He was haunted. But unlike many men who feel uncontrollable rage, Marty was absolutely aware that he was not angry at his wife. His love for her was constant, and his admiration for her boundless, even though she bore the brunt of his tantrums.

To Marty, who felt he had been emotionally starved all his life, Tina was a symbol of nurturance and life. She was a strong woman who stood firm and was not afraid of him. She was not fragile, and she could not be beaten. She refused to be drawn into his aggression, and her poise both provoked and calmed him. Her rules were absolutely clear, and he loved that clarity. The firm boundaries meant he could scream and be safe. She rescued him from his sense of starvation and his fear of running amok with his rage.

I spoke with Tina the next day in her office. Petite, with red hair and freckles, Tina was an orthodontist with a growing practice in San Mateo.

I began by asking what was happy about her marriage.

"That's an interesting question," she said, brightening. "What's happy is that we're finally in harmony. The angst is past. We're no longer struggling for power. We've been together now for ages. Really, our entire adult life. And we're extremely appreciative that we're together and we've been able to make it."

She recalled their courtship. "I've always liked compact men. He was short and muscular. He'll deny this when you talk to him, but he decided on our first date that he would marry me, and he said to me, 'We should be together. No one will ever love you the way I do.'"

"What happened?"

"He pursued me. He was very aggressive and came on very strong. And I was a virgin." Tina glowed with the memory. "I must have had some existential knowing, something that attracted me to this rough man. I found it exciting. It had to happen. I had to do this. I remember vividly the night before I went to bed with him. I said to my close friend, 'I don't know that I want to marry him, but I have to do this.' It was like it was a fait accompli. It had to happen."

"Tina, this is fascinating. What was it that had to happen, and why?"

She stopped cold and said hesitantly, "I had to leave my home. I had to depart from all the comforts that I had been brought up with."

"I don't understand."

"Well," said Tina, "I might as well tell you. I was overinvolved with my father. You might say it was an incestuous relationship. It ended by the time I was six."

"How incestuous?"

"I don't think there ever was intercourse. I'm not sure. I don't remember very well. I knew there was something wrong. I don't really know what went on, but I knew that I was in his bed and I knew that he was naked. I was my father's favorite. I was the one who carried messages from my mother to him, like if she wanted to go out to dinner, she would send me to ask my father. I was my father's favorite over her."

"Did your mother know?"

Tina's answer was barely audible. "She knew. She knew."

She went on, "The other part that drew me to leave my home was that he, too, my husband, was seeking to leave his home. We were brought together by abuse in our families of origin. And we came into tumultuous years together. It's like all the ugliness was dumped into our marriage. What has kept us together is the hurt and sadness of our childhoods, and that allowed us to sustain the marriage on a totally unconscious level."

"And how did it affect your marriage?"

"Every which way. But in part, being married allowed my memory of it to come out. My husband didn't stand in the way of my discovering my childhood. You see, he loved me. As crazy as he was — and he was crazy — I never had to wonder if I was alone. Sometimes I felt alone, but I knew I wasn't alone. Because I wasn't alone, I could feel how lonely I used to be. I felt safe and protected and loved. And by my mid-thirties I could finally begin to face that I had been unsafe, unprotected, and unloved throughout my whole childhood and adolescence. It wasn't until my father died that I began to understand my rage."

I asked about the early years of the marriage.

"It was a nightmare," she said. "You have no idea. We were fighting constantly."

"About what?"

"About everything. He was intensely jealous. He flew off the handle at nothing. We fought over who would make dinner. And we fought over the fact that I was going back to school. We fought because he nagged at me because he didn't like the way I ran the house. It was a nightmare. What saved my life was that I went back to school to study biology. You see, I'd quit college before I got my B.A., and the only thing that kept my head, kept me in any kind of mental health, was that I went back to school. I became a student. I understood about being a student. I understood about exams. I understood about deadlines and things like that. And that's what kept me going to dental school. Otherwise it was chaos."

"And somehow you made it."

"Yes, he was always there for me. And I never doubted that he was faithful to me. What kept us together was hope, love, and tenacity. I was not going home. There was no home to go to. He and I lived in this terrible place. Do you know what the slums of Philadelphia look like? It was terrible. It was the ugliest place in the world. It was a hostile world. All the dirt and all the grit of all the factories was everywhere.

"And then, miraculously, we came to California. You have no idea what that move did to us. It was spiritually like being shot out of a cannon. My husband was offered a job here, and he jumped at it. I jumped at it. We came west and never looked back. We never had a moment's regret. The few years after that were among the happiest years of our lives and our marriage. Living here was like being reborn. We came out of that dark, ugly, overcast world, and coming here was like a fantasy we could hardly dare dream about. It was a wish come true."

When she spoke of California, she was also referring to the marriage she and Marty had created. Philadelphia and California symbolized their terrible childhoods and the happy marriage. By saying she felt shot out of a cannon, she was describing the unexpected transformation of her life and herself.

"Do you love him?" I asked.

"Yes, very much. He is a very good husband. He's devoted to me. He loves me, and he feels and tells me that I'm beautiful." She stopped as if it was hard to go on, as if she suddenly saw herself through his eyes in a way she hadn't expected. "I remember in the first years of the marriage that one day I came home a total wreck after a hard day. I dragged myself up the stairs. There was a full-length mirror near the entry, and I looked at myself and said, 'Oh, my God, what a mess.' Then behind me I saw Marty looking at me, and his eyes lit up with pleasure. And I realized I looked like a princess to him, and it was wonderful."

Tina continued, "It took me fifteen years of marriage to see his kindness and his gentleness, to get past the facade and see underneath. It took all these years, and then I fell in love with him."

Tina also gained by this marriage. She found a man who loved and respected her but who also insisted on an adult sexual relationship, whatever her past. Though he was furious when she rejected him, he would never rape her. Some men might have had affairs, hit her, or left her. He may have bashed the wall, but he did not harm her. He always saw her as a lovely woman. He was profoundly sympathetic. His love for and pride in her helped her feel like a woman who was lovable; she no longer retreated into frigidity or fear of sex.

Tina said, "It's very important that we shared our children. They were born the fifth and the seventh year of the marriage. And from the minute they arrived on the scene we loved them. They brought us together. Whatever my husband was in relation to me, to his children he was the kind, loving parent. He never hesitated to get up in the middle of the night, to be kind, to be gentle. He never in any way took out his turmoil on the children. He was himself tormented, but the children got us both on course. We did a great job with them. We just loved them."

"How was it, with all the trouble you had in your families, that it didn't carry over to your children?"

"I have no idea," she said. "All I know is that it didn't. Both of us were nurturant. I was the disciplinarian, but we both protected them. I was the one who was reading all those child psychology books.

"My daughter is expecting her first child, and we're both very excited. We're very pleased with her marriage. Thank God she didn't have the kind of parenting that we had. My son also has a good marriage. He has a strong sense of himself. He has a good relationship with his father. Essentially, they both love us."

Marty and Tina were joined in a high-conflict mutual rescue marriage that was rich in humanity, passion, and love, though it was punctuated by intense fighting for many years. Yet love held them together. They understood each other's painful history and empathized with each other's unfilled and unfillable needs. Their marriage was better than either of them had ever expected. This was a cathartic relationship in which the partners never hurt each other; they were able to yell and scream and relieve their pain in a safe place. Their past trauma was part of the we-ness of this rescue marriage. Survivors, they both needed to work lifelong at separating from the internal images of their parents. Like Keith and Helen, they needed to work at reinventing themselves and keeping those persecutory figures at bay.

After talking to Marty and Tina and other couples, I concluded that a stable family of origin is not a prerequisite for a happy marriage and that a couple can engage in high conflict and still have a good relationship. They can triumph over their own anger and rescue themselves and each other from repeating the miseries of their past. They can also, it appears, protect their children and bring them up with full cooperation and love.

By understanding a successful rescue marriage we learn about the complex internal workings of all good marriages. Marriages that work well bring about psychological changes in each partner. The man and woman change and grow to accommodate to each other, expanding to encompass another human being. Each partner learns to really understand how the other feels and thinks so that he can judge what will distress her and she knows what will make him happy. They both learn what will cause anger, what the relationship can tolerate without breaking. This experience enlarges and significantly changes each of them.

But far more than this, the rescue marriage shows us how a good marriage can help to heal early traumas and repair a person's shattered self-esteem. When people with painful childhoods take a chance on a new relationship, they may find that the devils they feared have been left behind. As each feels loved and respected, and not rejected, abused, or humiliated, their hope and courage are strengthened. Their sense of themselves and their view of the world change. This we saw very dramatically in the marriage of Helen and Keith, who became entirely different people than they were before their marriage.

The rescue marriage confirms that adult relationships have the power to bring about profound psychological change and that adults have an enormous capacity to continue to grow. This is encouraging evidence that although the major elements of personality are laid down in childhood, people have the potential to change throughout their adult lives.

I also conclude, from Helen's anniversary reaction, from Marty's explosive rages, which continue sporadically, and from the experiences of many others, that the old devils do not die. Dangers remain, and the remedy that the marriage provides depends on continuing love and vigilance.

# 12 🙧

# The Fifth Task

*Making a Safe Place for Conflict*

THE FIFTH TASK OF MARRIAGE is to build a relationship that is safe for the expression of difference, conflict, and anger. The appealing notions that a good marriage is conflict-free and that good communication can avoid anger have gained popularity. But every married person knows that "conflict-free marriage" is an oxymoron. In reality it is neither possible nor desirable. Marriage can inhibit conflict or forbid its expression. People can and do maintain a facade of sweet accord, especially in public. When I was growing up, it was not considered proper for a wife to express a view in public that differed from her husband's. But in a contemporary marriage it is expected that husbands and wives will have different opinions. More important, they can't avoid having serious collisions on big issues that defy compromise.

There is no way, for example, to have half a child or one and a half children. One couple in the study had their only fight that came close to violence over whether to have a second child. She wanted the child desperately, and he felt they could not financially support a larger family. There is no way to live in the city *and* in the country or to live near his family and her family and at the same time live far from both. One partner cannot take a job in California and the other a job in New York without radically changing the nature of the couple's relationship. Communication and negotiation and compromise are surely desirable, but they do not banish serious conflicts, nor do they help people deal with the sacrifices entailed or the serious disappointments that individuals sometimes suffer, whichever way the decision falls.

Living closely with another person while bringing up children and making way for the needs, wishes, and even whims of other family members inevitably creates frustrations. And who among us is able to give up independence and selfishness without a struggle?

As Tina and Marty and others in the study have shown us, powerful, primitive angers stemming from early childhood are revivified by the very closeness of the marital relationship. These angers often figure prominently in the rescue marriage, but they occur in all marriages, although less dramatically. One woman in a romantic marriage told me that when her husband got discouraged about his work, it reminded her of her father's many depressions. She said, "I get freaked out at the thought that my husband is just like my father, and I start to attack him. When this coincides with my menstrual period, it can get out of control." Powerful feelings rooted in early-life traumas often do not respond to mediation or compromise.

The conflicts of marriage have many sources. One source is the financial conflicts of marriage as a business partnership in which two people are pulling sometimes together and sometimes in different directions. And clashing agendas are inherent in the intense emotional relationship between a man and a woman, which inevitably evokes passionate feelings from long ago.

Conflict goes with the territory of marriage. Happy and unhappy marriages alike face the same demons, but in a poor marriage they tear at the fabric of the relationship and may destroy it. In a good marriage the demons are carefully contained. What is the difference? What prevents anger from breaking the marriage apart? What makes it a zone of safety that the couple finds so reassuring?

The happily married couples I spoke with were frank in acknowledging their serious differences over the years. Many described vividly remembered stormy episodes. They spoke thoughtfully about the serious differences that divided them and discussed how they had kept these conflicts from disrupting the marriage. Their advice was realistic and pragmatic. As one husband said, "You don't need brakes until you're in danger of going out of control."

What emerged from these interviews was not only that conflict was ubiquitous but that these couples considered learning to disagree and to stand one's ground one of the gifts of a good marriage. Submissiveness by one partner and unthinking conformity were not valued. In fact, many couples spoke of their first quarrel as a cornerstone of the marriage, a chance to see each other in a new light. Conflict taught them a lot about the fears each had about expressing anger and about being the victim of the other's aggression. Those who were frightened of aggression were vastly relieved when the expected catastrophe did not occur. Everyone survived.

We fear conflict because we fear retaliation. We fear our own anger and our partner's anger for its destructive potential. We are afraid that if we lose our temper or disagree strongly, we will be rejected or abandoned by our partner. The high incidence of divorce gives people good reason to be frightened by intense disagreements and anger; the men and women in these happy marriages learned not to threaten to leave in the heat of an argument. It was understood that the quarrel did not signify the end of the marriage.

One woman explained this very well. "Whenever I said, 'That's it, I've had it,' he would take it seriously and think, Oh, my God, she's leaving. Finally I had to say to him, 'Look here. I'm going to get really mad, very, very upset, but I'm not going anywhere.' I had to reassure him that I could get really angry and say all sorts of things, but I was not going to leave. That gave him a safe environment to be able to fight back."

Thus the first step in establishing a safety zone where strong anger can be expressed freely is to make it clear that the fighting will not breach the walls of the marriage. Both partners have to feel sure that their relationship is secure. If one or both partners have experienced abandonment, either as a child or as an adult, this message needs to be reiterated many times.

A good marriage provides a holding environment for aggression. Broadly speaking, the couple's love and friendship, the togetherness they have built, their shared interests and history, including the children, all combine to provide the overall structure that contains the aggression. The ties that unite them are far stronger than the forces that divide them. Their awareness of this strength acts as a powerful deterrent to letting things fly out of control. It enables one person to interrupt the anger out of concern for the other and for the marriage. As one woman described it, "When things get too hot between us, I say to him, 'We don't want to do this to each other.' That stops us both."

Conflict in a good marriage occurs within a context of connectedness and caring. An important part of the structure that protects the couple is the rules they devise together. All of the couples in the study had a clear, inviolable rule that physical violence was unacceptable. It was understood that a physical attack would break the marriage. Even when someone was carried away by a tantrum, he or she stopped short of violence. Marty described vividly how he curbed his rage. But the loss of temper and regaining of control just in time was mentioned in all of the kinds of marriages.

One husband said, "Sometimes I get angry at her, and we get into a shouting match. Sometimes I just don't say anything and walk out of the room. Other times I've taken one of her hats and put my foot through it. Once I threw her birthday cake down the stairs. Once I threw a chair off the balcony. But we have never touched each other in anger. She has never pushed me, and I have never pushed her. We've never done anything physically harmful to each other in twenty-nine years."

The recognition of absolute boundaries is very useful, not only as protection from harm but as a constraint that must be observed. In these marriages everyone understood that some remarks, once said, cannot be unsaid. Some actions, once done, cannot be undone. All understood that rules, while providing safety, did not forbid heated argument. One of the satisfactions of a strong marriage is being able to state your mind without fear of dire consequences. But even in a tantrum, restraint is required.

The rules about physical violence were especially reassuring to former victims of abuse. One woman said, "It was very nice to learn to fight and to know that no one was going to hurt me ever. This has never been an issue. I've always felt safe fighting with him. There is a basic trust that we have for each other." This woman made it very clear that the goal was not to eliminate fighting but to make it safe for both partners.

Each couple had their own rules to contain conflict. One couple decided that a problem had to be brought up within forty-eight hours of the upset. Another ruled that it was taboo to bring up old arguments: "Once it's over, it's over," they said emphatically. Several forbade going to bed angry at each other. Some couples did not blanch if property was destroyed in an argument. Marty showed me where he had damaged a wall of their house — behavior that other couples might draw the line at. Some marriages permitted a great deal of anger; others were more constrained.

These couples also used guidelines as to the domains that could be fought about and those that were considered off-limits or areas of continuing agreement. The guidelines varied, but all of the couples had some taboos. In most cases this understanding had evolved slowly, often wordlessly, as they learned each other's vulnerabilities. Fighting about religious differences was out of bounds. In religiously mixed marriages, the issue of which faith to raise the children in was settled early on, though rarely without argument and compromise. They complained to each other about the frequency or infrequency of sex or about lateness or overwork or household chores, but they did not fight about these matters. Nor did they fight about having to take care of aging or ill parents; indeed, they went out of their way to make compassionate plans. They did not fight about personal preferences — the opera versus a baseball game. If the two partners did not share an interest, most would attend functions separately and not impose on the other.

Most of all, the people in these marriages did not fight over non-issues. They recognized that the pressures of life and the defeats of the workplace ricocheted into the marriage. They understood intuitively that a man or woman who was humiliated at work and came home to yell at a spouse or child, kick the dog, or sit incommunicado in front of the TV set was not being deliberately provocative. They knew how worry could lead someone to provoke a quarrel and how satisfying but useless it was to blame everyone but oneself when things went awry. They were realists. As one man said, "We would have the same stresses in our life no matter whom we married."

These couples did fight over autonomy, money, and work. Some men wanted their wives to work, while others wanted them to stay at home. In some cases conflict rose to a crescendo when the children left home and the hard-working husband felt jealous of his wife's new freedom to pursue hobbies or go back to school. Arguments about the intrusiveness of in-laws could be intense, especially after the birth of the first child. One woman told me emphatically, "The only thing that would break this marriage is his busybody mother." Arguments erupted over the best way to handle children, especially teenagers and stepchildren.

Very heated arguments arose about who should handle the money from two incomes, who should pay which bills, and how the money should be allocated. The allocation of funds was an especially sore spot in second marriages because of the need to negotiate the conflicting interests of several families and two or more sets of children.

Fights, usually short-lived but explosive, also arose over suspected infidelity. As one woman told me, "We don't have many fights, but sometimes I go crazy with jealousy for no good reason. Maybe it's in my Spanish background. Once he had a back injury and I thought that he was falling in love with his very attractive nurse. So I stomped out. He got very angry and told me that I had gone mad. But I just couldn't hear him. Then I saw my daughter crying, and I said to myself, what the hell are you doing? And I stopped."

Some of the most distressing arguments arose over smoking and drinking. In one marriage the husband and wife sat in the car to argue, to avoid upsetting the children. She told him that passive smoke was a proven carcinogen, and while the children were young he could not smoke in their home. He could do what he wanted outside. The man admitted that the request was reasonable, but he was furious. He punished her by not talking to her except when absolutely necessary for three months. Then he accepted the injunction on his smoking and they resumed their customary relationship.

In several families, drinking became an issue when unemployment threatened. Usually the women were quick to say that the behavior was not acceptable. As one wife said, "I was clear as a bell." When other couples found themselves in similar difficulties, they confronted the situation quickly, clearly defining the consequences for the marriage. The spouses who were called on the carpet later told me that they resented the ultimatums at the time but later forgave their partner.

One of the most interesting mechanisms that these couples used to keep the expression of anger under control was by maintaining their awareness of themselves and the other even when the fighting was stormy. They made a special point of knowing each other's vulnerabilities, and they were very careful to avoid rubbing salt into old wounds. I had the sense that they read imaginary dials in each other's gestures, words, and expressions. Each dial registered the mood, the depth of upset, and the impending approach of the hurricane stage. This awareness helped them regulate their own feelings and behavior. As one woman said, "After all these years, we are both aware of each other's vulnerable spots. That doesn't mean we don't sometimes touch them. We are human. But it does mean that we both have more respect for not treading on them." They also had some awareness of their own danger points. "I have a terrible temper," said one man. "I had to learn to control it; otherwise we would have had a terrible time." A woman said, "The way we fight is that I freak out and he calms me down."

It is a major feat to take responsibility for one's own and one's partner's behavior — and still disagree with passion. I do not know if these couples acquired this ability in the marriage or if each one had it before they met. I am reluctant to conclude that it reflects their mastery of negotiation skills, because there is little evidence that skill played a part. What did contribute was their maturity and sensitivity to the partner's needs, their ability to remain connected even in anger, their sense of fairness, and their internal brakes, which were in good working order. Also they were able to distinguish between little problems and big ones, between minor compromises and those that give away one's heart's desire. They were willing to take an equal part in maintaining the marriage in lieu of "having it all" in solitary splendor.

PART FOUR

# Companionate Marriage

# 13

# Kit Morgan

LIKE MOTHERS EVERYWHERE, I continue to worry about my grown children, even though they are happily married, well established in their careers, and raising — dare I boast? — fine, healthy children. One source of my concern is how incredibly hard they and their spouses are working to do well in their jobs, take care of their children, maintain their marriages, keep their households going, make time for friends, and juggle a zillion other demands.

My son is an academic at a major university. His wife, who is an artist, must be near art centers and galleries. Thus they have chosen to live in a large metropolitan area, which unfortunately has deteriorating public schools. After much soul-searching, they put their children in private schools, and this requires many hours of driving to and fro. My son spends long hours writing research papers, and he travels to conferences all over the world; my daughter-law works part-time to supplement their income. Both take parenting seriously and try to spend uninterrupted hours with their two children. Both husband and wife do the grocery shopping, prepare meals, and clean up — but she does more, especially the driving and housecleaning. Because there is little time left over for her art, which is an essential part of her life, she rises at five A.M. to spend an hour or two in her studio before the rest of the family is up. Fortunately they have boundless energy. I watch them in awe. At the same time I wonder — but do not ask — if they ever have time to be alone together.

My daughter, also an academic, described a dilemma confronting many young marriages today. She called to say that she had visited a major university with a topnotch department in her field. She was thrilled by the people and excited about their programs; it was exactly up her alley. The chairman told her that she was their top choice for a tenured position in the department.

"But —" I began.

"I know the buts," she reproached me. "Ed said he'd be happy to go there for a year. But things are really rolling for him here. His big grant finally came through." Ed is also an academic on a fast track.

"Yes," I said. "But last year, if I recall, he was flying back and forth to the Bay Area for job interviews."

"Mom," she explained, "with all the equality that Ed and I have, some things are more equal than others. When women think of moving the family because of a job they want, they think about how it will disrupt the lives of their children and husband. Women take responsibility for the happiness of everyone in the family and feel guilty about uprooting them." She sighed. "I don't think it's fair, but it's still true. Men expect that the woman and children will adjust to the moves they make. And we do."

"How are you going to decide this one?" I asked, knowing that she had felt isolated professionally for the last year and coveted the job.

She lamented, "The big problem is that there is no right way to resolve these kinds of issues. It's like there are no rules about who goes first or why."

Agreeing to talk again in a few days, we hung up. I thought about my own life. Three years after my husband and I were married, he was offered a job at the Menninger Clinic in Topeka, Kansas. I couldn't even find Topeka on the map, but I never doubted that the decision to move there was the right one. I would simply have to adjust. Those were *our* rules, forged in a very different time. But suppose I had balked or sabotaged the move or refused outright. What would have happened to our marriage?

The third major type of marriage to emerge from this study is the companionate marriage, the newest form and, as my grown children attest, perhaps the most difficult to maintain. Born in the vortex of social change over the past two decades, companionate marriage is the most common type among young people today, reflecting the complex social and moral choices our culture thrusts upon them. None of the couples in this study who married in the 1950s had companionate marriages. But 40 percent of those who married in the 1970s or early 1980s did form this type of marriage. Most of these couples came of age in the 1960s, during the antiwar movement, the civil rights movement, the women's movement, and the era of sexual liberation. Many of the women had been active in consciousness-raising groups, and the men supported the values of the women's movement.

A companionate marriage is founded on the couple's shared belief that men and women are equal partners in all spheres of life and that their roles, including those of marriage, are completely interchangeable. Both husband and wife lead important parts of their lives outside of the home. While one partner, usually the wife, may take time out from her career to devote attention to young children, she remains committed to both work and family.

Although companionate marriages have existed for some time among the aristocracy and the intellectual elite here and abroad, contemporary couples have cast these relationships in a new light, consciously incorporating a modern vision of marriage and the roles of men and women in American society.

I do not mean that all of the people in companionate marriages are trying to make a political statement. Most of them are far too busy raising small children, creating careers, and building families — trying to stay afloat in a hectic culture. Nevertheless, whether they have thought about it or not, the changed social values of the past two decades, including the philosophy of the women's liberation movement, have been incorporated into their daily lives. As a result, the relationship between husband and wife has been transformed.

At the core of a companionate marriage is friendship and trust and the belief that both partners have equal responsibility in all domains of the marriage. They share the economic burdens and child rearing, and they believe that both partners' sexual needs and wishes should be clearly articulated and fulfilled. They also recognize that when the children are young and career issues are pressing, their own needs as individuals have to be placed on the back burner. These couples know that people living side by side experience inevitable conflicts that must be confronted openly. They understand that mutual commitment is what holds the marriage together.

More than any other marital form, companionate marriage is held together from within, rekindled each day through the couple's commitment and shared values. The relationship requires high levels of self-confidence, trust, and self-awareness and the ability to postpone gratification.

We should not underestimate the revolutionary nature of these changes. A companionate marriage demands a redefinition of what it means to be a husband or a wife. The argument is not simply over who cleans the house, does the shopping, pays the mortgage, changes the diapers, or puts out the garbage. Something much larger is at stake in this new kind of marriage, which has turned 180 degrees from the traditional form. Unlike the spouses in romantic, rescue, and traditional marriages, the men and women in companionate marriages have the sense of being pioneers. They are actively rejecting the models they experienced as children and those they see in society at large. They are striving to do it better, to create together something joyful, new, and egalitarian.

The couples in companionate marriages spoke about each other as friends, emphasizing their respect for each other and their independence. "My marriage depends on friendship," said one man. "Sex you can have with anyone. I got married for companionship and respect and most of all for friendship." A woman said, "It was not part of my agenda to get married. I was influenced by feminist thinking about women being chattel in marriage." Another man said of his wife, "She's real hard-assed about her career, she's real serious. No one loves everyone all the time, but that's what marriage is about." And a woman said, "It's very important for me to be my own person. I could never be subservient, like my mom, or dependent the way she was on my father."

The rewards are substantial, but so are the sacrifices. A man gives up the role of sole breadwinner but gets to be a parent much the way a mother is; he is much closer to his children from infancy on. How will this change his expectations and views of life? How will this affect his self-image? Will he be, as some people claim, less attractive sexually than a more traditionally macho man? Will he be more passive? Will he have to forfeit advances in the workplace and limit his social and intellectual contributions to society? Or will he be a better man, a more civilized man, a more evolved man whose self-image includes his feminine side?

Men are talking about these changes. One husband in the study confided, "I'm in love with her, but it sure wasn't love at first sight. She's a feminist, and I had to get rid of my stereotypes. I thought marriage was based on the traditional division of responsibilities because my mom didn't work outside the home. I was an only child and the apple of my mother's eye, and I expected women to treat me the way Mom treated me. She did everything for me. She also did everything for my dad, and it was hard for me to do things differently in my own marriage. I had to give up my assumptions about a lot of things."

Although men have surely been influenced by the changes occurring in society, the real transformation in their views occurs within the relationship. Many women are prepared to lay down certain conditions — "If you want me, darling, you'll have to agree that we're equal in everything" — and expect men to comply. Many men have to actively battle the habits of their upbringing in order to make companionate marriage work. It's easier for the men in my son's generation, but it's not easy.

The mother who chooses to continue in her own career must also redefine her self-image and identity. What is a part-time mother? By surrendering her exclusive role in raising the children, what does she gain? The answer, of course, is a career as well as greater economic independence and new self-esteem. She has a trump that her mother did not possess, for she no longer needs to be subservient or dependent, socially or economically. She also has the opportunity to pursue the work she loves, to contribute to her chosen profession or calling, and to participate actively and sometimes powerfully in shaping her community and the larger society. But she gives up the protection of a husband's financial support. She also relinquishes the opportunity and pleasure of taking full responsibility for her young children and being the unchallenged central figure in their emotional world. This can be a wrenching loss, one that tends to be overlooked in the heat of the debate over women's changing roles.

Both women who work and those who stay home agonize and feel guilty about the choices they make. In many cases, of course, a mother must work outside the home because the family needs the money. But the arguments about staying at home versus going to work have stirred deep inner conflict among women in all walks of life, whether or not they have a choice in the matter. Many working mothers of young children question the wisdom of their decision every single day. They are concerned about the effects of their absence on the children, themselves, and the marriage.

"I love my job, but I worry all the time — am I doing the right thing?" said one woman. Another said sadly, "I feel that I'm missing the best years of my daughter's life. They grow up so fast." Said another, "What I want most is to be there when the children get home from school. But where can you find a job like that? It really breaks my heart."

These feelings — of being deprived of the chance to stay with their young children full-time and of having grave concerns about the people who take care of the kids — are widespread and serious. Large-scale studies can shed light on the potential effects of these choices on children by comparing those cared for at home with those in daycare. But studies cannot say what is best for an individual child. The question of what works for Jimmy at age two or for Ann, who is not yet one, can be answered only by the parents, who know what child-care facilities are available in the community and what their family and the child need and want.

At the same time, many women who stay home wonder if having a career would be more fulfilling. There is concern in both camps. My two daughters have selected different paths; each has reaped benefits from her choice and has wept for what she is missing. Yet neither would change places with the other, and they say so openly.

What's exciting about companionate marriage — the sense of greater freedom and control over one's life and marriage — is also what makes it so hard. Major decisions, like whether or not to have children, require careful deliberation; there are no foregone conclusions, as there were in generations past. Whose career will be given priority? How will we take turns? Who will make the financial decisions? Will we have a joint bank account or separate accounts? Will she keep her maiden name, and if so, what will be the children's last name? All of the questions of contemporary married life are on the table. They are examined closely and resolved in the light of principles — sometimes very abstract principles — of equality and fairness.

One woman said, "There are certain themes in this marriage. We keep talking about intimacy. Every now and then he'll roll his eyes as if to say here we go again. But we work at it each time. It's ongoing and will probably never be resolved."

Although every marriage must bend in response to changing concepts of self and partner, the companionate marriage, with few traditions to rest on, requires more flexibility and some careful exploration of what the relationship will and will not tolerate, what each person can and cannot do. The continuing transformation of the marriage requires unwavering attentiveness and empathy. Certainly not everyone can do this — or wants to.

I found out about Kit Morgan and Beth McNeil from my younger daughter, who had known them for several years. She had been impressed with them, their marriage, and their two children, who were friends of her children. Kit and Beth quickly agreed to participate, saying they would be delighted to be part of a study on happy marriage.

Both are forty-two years old. They've been married for ten years. Kit teaches math at a community college, and Beth is a nurse practitioner in private practice and a staff nurse at a hospice in Oakland. She is also involved in a community AIDS project.

As I parked my car in front of their house, I noticed toys, toys everywhere. The front walk was festooned with bicycles, a Nerf football, a rickety doll carriage, and a huge cardboard box with cutout doors and windows. The front steps were adorned with several pumpkins, and the door was plastered with Halloween decorations, including a spectacular glow-in-the-dark skeleton.

When I rang the doorbell, I wondered if anyone would hear its chime amid all the thumps and giggles emanating from within. Then Kit called out, "Just a minute. I'll be right there." He opened the door, ran a hand through his tousled hair, and vainly tried to smooth his rumpled sweat suit.

"Welcome," he said in a courteous, gentlemanly manner. He introduced me to his children — Martha, seven, and Sam, four — who were still laughing from the game just ended with Daddy on the floor. Kit quickly excused himself to telephone the neighbor across the street, who would take the kids while he and I talked. Beth was out of town on a business trip.

The house, so full of life, settled into temporary calm as Kit ushered the children out the door moments later. With his clean-shaven face, wire-rim glasses, and thinning hair, Kit looked the part of the highly intelligent and analytical math teacher. He offered me a glass of sherry, which I accepted.

His reply to my opening question was pleasantly forthright. "It's hard to know where to begin. I think I would say our marriage is happy on all kinds of levels. Beth is the person I'd have dreamed about in my teenage fantasies, the person I'd imagine wanting to be with when I'm middle-aged. And I got her." He beamed. "We share political views and enjoy the same activities. We support each other in our individual pursuits. We have good sex and we're good parents together. Our marriage roles are well defined, but we have not defined them in traditional ways. We had to discover who is comfortable with what in the marriage."

Like many men in the study, Kit was proud of how well his wife fit his boyhood dreams of the woman he would someday marry. He reported on their gratifying sex life and their shared parenting. But then he struck a new note. Right at the outset of our talk he called attention to the nontraditional nature of their marriage and to the roles he and Beth had designed in accord with their own values. This is new territory, he was telling me.

I said, "Tell me how you define who does what."

"I do the cooking and maintenance around the house because I like it more than she does," he explained. "We only talk about those things that neither of us wants to do." He smiled ruefully. "Like housekeeping. Beth's not compulsive or anything, but she likes a cleaner house than I do. Since she cares so much, I figured she should take care of it." He laughed. "But she doesn't like cleaning all that much, and she would get pissed off at me for not doing more. Eventually I realized I was in a privileged position. I didn't have to live in a filthy house, and I didn't have to do any cleaning. It wasn't fair. So now we share the cleaning."

Kit had recognized what so many men fail to perceive — namely, that just because you are more tolerant of disorder and dirt than your spouse, you are not absolved of responsibility for housework. Kit realized that he couldn't hide behind the notion that if the dirt didn't bother him, he didn't have to clean. Instead he was guided by the wish to do what was fair.

Because roles are regarded as interchangeable in a companionate marriage, the question of who performs which household tasks dominates much of the conversation. A typical exchange might be, "Remember, I washed the kitchen floor last week. Now it's your turn to take Jimmy to the pediatrician."

In all of the companionate marriages in the study — only a handful of which had regular domestic help — the wives took more responsibility for the household. In many cases they were more skilled and efficient at that role, but the most important factor was that they carried in their head a constant awareness of the needs of the household and children. I have seen this at work in the marriages of my children and their friends. As my daughter said clearly, she carries responsibility for the emotional and physical needs of the family. She is never off duty.

The men in companionate marriages try to do their fair share of housework, and some are very adept at shopping, vacuuming, and cooking. But most have had to unlearn old habits and acquire new ones. Even those young men like my son Mike, who did not have a traditional upbringing, never master household duties with the ease that they learn computer skills. And, unlike their wives, they *do* go off duty.

When a husband stays home, however, he becomes the one who is never off duty. In two of the marriages in this study the husband was the primary caretaker. Both men worked in the arts, and their talents had achieved recognition. But because they did not have nine-to-five jobs and steady incomes, their wives were the main breadwinners. These men did most of the child care, meal preparation, and housework. They also resented their wives' long workdays and worried that the women were working too hard, suggesting that work and family conflicts are not gender based but reflect the role that each person takes in the family.

Fairness, the couples in companionate marriages said, was far more important than exactly how the chores were allocated. They did not measure exactly who did what; they just tried to get it all done before dropping into bed at night. But they did weigh the division of labor and measured each one's effort. In many families the women did the bulk of the housework, knowing that their husbands' work schedules prevented them from doing more. This was especially hard for mothers with young children who worked full- or part-time. If the woman felt that her husband was doing all he could to help, she usually regarded his contribution as fair. But if he loafed around while she was stretched to her limit, she felt angry and disappointed.

Problems with the division of labor do add to the tensions in a marriage, but by themselves they do not lead to marital breakup. Arguments about which partner is doing more may lead to unhappiness and quarrels, but they do not result in divorce unless they are reflections of other issues, such as profound bitterness and feelings of exploitation and emotional abandonment. Of the thousands of divorces that I have seen, I have never known of one that hinged on an unequal division of chores. Many women do work a second shift, but that alone does not break up a marriage.

Kit shared in the housework, but I wanted to know what else was up for negotiation between them. I said, "There's a lot you and Beth discuss and make decisions about."

He nodded. "We discuss everything. From the situation in Iraq to our personal problems. We challenge each other and are interested in the other's opinions."

I noticed that again he had mentioned world politics before their personal lives. Reading my thoughts, he said, "What's happy about our marriage is that we are both interested in the world and in each other, so we talk a lot."

"What would Beth say is happy about your marriage?"

"I think she'd say that we love each other and we are each other's best friends. I think she would also say she's happy to be in a relationship where she doesn't have to be a caretaker for the man. She was in other relationships with men very different from herself where she was taking care of them emotionally." Like so many people in happy marriages, Kit had thought a lot about his wife's life experiences.

"What would your children say is happy about the family?"

"Well, Martha is seven, and she's a really happy kid. Sam is only four, so I suppose he's too little to articulate how he feels, but he sure acts like he's happy." Kit chuckled as he recalled "a wonderful dream" his daughter had recently had. As he told it, I suspected that the dream was wonderful not only for the child but also for her father. "In her dream she discovered she could fly. And she was flying around in the back yard, but she had to keep the house in view because the house was the source of her power to fly." He looked at me squarely. "Isn't that a lovely dream?"

"It's a beautiful dream," I said. "What do you make of it?"

"The family is the source of her power, and with that she can fly. That's how I fly too," he said with a broad smile. "It's been an incredibly conflict-free marriage. I mean we fight and all, but what it's usually over is that we're both so incredibly busy. Mostly we flare up over something left undone. You know, it's a fact of life in urban America — there's just so much stuff that has to get done and so little time to do it all. It's extremely frustrating! Especially when you have kids."

"The pressures are relentless."

"Exactly. But the pressures are not a reflection of our marriage. If I was married to someone else, I'd have the same pressures. This is what marriage is about in the 1990s. It's marriage under pressure. Especially with children."

When he said that, it occurred to me that what I had been studying for twenty-five years, as I listened to couples describe their harried relationships, was marriage under pressure.

One of the key differences between people who stay happily married and those who divorce or stagnate in an unhappy marriage is reflected in Kit's statement. He was not looking for easy answers; he knew that maintaining marriage, family, life, and career requires performing a difficult juggling act every single day. By contrast, many people who seek divorce have come to believe that their partner is responsible for life's pressures, and they fantasize that a new person will make the pressures go away or that divorce will provide an escape. This is a pipe dream. One can escape the pressures of a particular relationship, but not the stresses of modern life.

"How soon after you met Beth did you begin to think about marriage?" I asked Kit.

"My folks had a terrible marriage," he replied. "Now this may sound strange to you, but I didn't then and still don't have any use for marriage. The idea of marriage was a real downer. Beth had similar feelings but for different reasons. Neither one of us was into marriage.

"There were not many models of good marriages around me as a kid," he went on. "My view of marriage then, and to a certain extent now, is this whole ridiculous vow about till death do us part. How the hell are you going to know it will last that long? I mean you need to choose someone you know and like. But if it's not working, you should get the hell out. You know, this whole thing about how, when you're twenty years old, you're going to make a vow that holds and makes sense for the rest of your life? To tell you what you're supposed to feel at sixty? Forget it! I don't believe in marriage in that sense."

Anticipating my next question, he said, "I know what you're going to ask. Why the hell did we marry?" He laughed. "It became real clear to both of us that we wanted to spend our lives together and that we wanted the people we cared about to know that."

Kit had answered one of life's most complicated questions with stunning simplicity, although not with convincing logic. In a companionate marriage, all questions are open — not only who does what or whether to have children but whether marriage itself is a valid institution. More and more couples here and in Western Europe are choosing not to marry. Young adults today have to answer each of these questions in their own way and their own good time — usually after they've had several relationships.

Every time I interviewed younger couples for this study, I was stunned by the contrasts with my own life. All of the major steps that my generation took for granted are now open-ended questions. My friends and I never doubted that we would marry and have children. We never considered that our husbands would not take responsibility as best they could for supporting us. We never dreamed of having high-powered careers that might clash with our husbands' careers. We never asked most of the basic questions these couples struggle with all the time. Nor, I must confess, did we have their openness and courage.

Despite his negative sentiments about marriage, Kit ultimately decided to marry because he had found a woman with whom he wanted to spend his life. And he wanted to make a public statement of that momentous decision. Essentially he wanted to distinguish this relationship from the others he had had, and marriage was the vehicle for that. But he wanted a marriage that was very, very different from that of his parents.

"Tell me about your family, Kit. How were you brought up?"

"My parents didn't spend much time together, and when they did it was not fun. It was stormy. My dad was suspicious about everything. They kept getting together and separating, all the years I was growing up. In fact, I can't think of anybody I ever knew who was a good role model for marriage. I can't think of anyone from all my acquaintances, much less anyone I'm related to.

"I grew up feeling like I did in my first memory. I was between two and three, and it was winter. My mother left me in the car to go shopping, and I remember deciding I was no good. My mom was leaving me forever. I was crying, and the windows were fogging up. I remember the feeling I had of total and complete terror and saying to myself at that young age that the world was over. I think I probably felt that many times as my parents came together and apart, that the world was over and I was no place."

Kit leaned forward in his chair and ran a hand through his hair. "Having told you this, it may come as a surprise that our wedding was one of the most powerful days of my life, a day when we brought all our friends together. But it sure wasn't traditional. There was no way in hell I'd get married in a church with some idiotic preacher up there saying some inane stuff that he doesn't know anything about. We wrote our own very simple ceremony and invited only the people who meant a lot to us, plus our parents. And then we danced and danced. I don't think I ever was so happy before in my life — or Beth. We both cried with joy."

He continued, "Somehow, inside myself I definitely had an idea of what I thought a good relationship would be like. It's just the sort of ideal everyone has. And its just that I never saw anybody live up to the ideal. But I suppose I put my own spin on it, because I believe a woman should be allowed to do her own thing, that a man shouldn't dominate the relationship. I guess you could say at heart I'm a feminist. Partly because of my love for my mom and partly because of the women's movement."

"What does being a feminist mean to you?" I asked.

"Two key values: respect and fairness. That's what I wanted for my mom. But my dad, who needed her so much, never treated her with respect. He only thought of himself. And she never fought back. That's what I want for my wife. I think Beth is a fantastic person. And I have a lot of respect for my women colleagues and friends. I think it's fair that we all have the same shot at whatever we like to do. And I want the same for my daughter. I was watching her in the schoolyard a few days ago. Some kid pushed her out of the line. I was very pleased that she pushed her way right back in."

He went on, "My dad didn't believe in divorce, nor did my mom until she just couldn't stand it any longer and realized she had made the wrong choice for herself."

"How long were they married?"

"Twenty-five years. Mom felt guilty about leaving, even though she waited for a year and a half after I finally left home."

"How did it influence your view of divorce?"

"I believe in divorce," said Kit without missing a beat. "I also believe in working on relationships. I know divorce gets more complicated when it involves kids, but I don't believe in prolonging poisonous relationships because of the children or something like that." He paused. "But when I think about the worst models of marriage, my folks would be right up there."

Kit's vehemence about his lack of role models is serious. This kind of anger at one's parents' marriage, which easily translates into anger at the institution of marriage, is dramatic and important, for it is what undergirds the culture of divorce. All of the people in these companionate marriages said they did not want a marriage like their parents'. Born in the 1950s, they didn't see Ozzie and Harriet as ideals; rather they saw through the facade of many suburban families to the carefully hidden turmoil or boredom.

Some eyewitnesses to unhappy marriages reported emotional neglect and cruelty; others saw the frustration and loneliness of one or both of their parents. One woman said, "When I was growing up, I never saw a really happy marriage, where the people were in tune with each other. Sometimes I feel like I was brought up on a desert island. Intimate relationships and intimate sex are foreign languages to me." But somewhere along the line, they decided they could do things differently.

One young woman was amazed that she and her husband had so much in common when they met. She said, "I looked back at the model I had from my parents, and they had nothing in common." Another woman acknowledged, "My mom didn't know then and does not know now what she's interested in, except that she was just interested in taking care of my dad, and he didn't need her."

Many of the men, like Kit, had had poor relationships with their fathers while growing up and did not want to be like them. They painted their fathers as "absent," "remote," "withholding," "cruel," and "demeaning."

In the interviews these couples described how much they talked about divorce. One woman said, "When my first child was born, two of my sisters were going through divorces. To me it was terribly shocking that my older sister, who'd been married fifteen years, had two kids, a car, a house, a truck, a dog — you know, the whole American picture — was getting a divorce. At that time my husband and I talked and talked, and we agreed that we'd never stay together if one of us was unhappy. But if something was going wrong, we would at least have the respect for the other person to tell them."

"Divorce is always possible, but everything in life is a chance. And you have to take a chance," said a woman whose parents divorced when she was thirteen; her husband's parents divorced when he was three. At the same time she wondered aloud if she should consult a lawyer on how to protect her financial interests if she and her husband ever did divorce. "We have a very happy marriage," she assured me, and from everything I could see, it was indeed working well. But this young couple had decided that their children would be raised in the father's religion and would carry the mother's last name. Now the woman was worried about these decisions. "If we get a divorce, will my husband be less willing to support our child because she doesn't have the same last name? I asked my Dad's advice, but he just threw up his hands."

Her story illustrates dramatically how every aspect of a companionate marriage, including very serious issues such as the child's religion, are traded back and forth and settled by negotiation and compromise. Knowing the long-standing religious tradition in this woman's family, I was sure that the grandparents were very distressed that her children were being raised in a different faith. Her story also shows the very high price in anxiety that these young people pay as they strike out in new directions. Being a pioneer is exciting, but it is frightening not to know the far-reaching effects of decisions taken, especially when both sets of grandparents have been divorced.

An inherent danger in companionate marriages, with their emphasis on individual autonomy, is that togetherness may be neglected. What with separate laundry arrangements, separate bank accounts, and assigned household tasks, it is deceptively easy to hold on to the illusion that each person is fully independent. Their schedules are hectic, they are out on different nights, and business travel often takes priority over family time. In many ways husband and wife lead separate lives. Under these circumstances it is especially challenging to create and maintain a strong core of togetherness.

I asked Kit, "With so many decisions up for grabs and such busy schedules, is it hard to stay connected?"

He laughed. "Let me answer that two ways. I think the inside connections of the marriage become even more important when life is so hectic and so unpredictable. I've learned in this relationship how to be intimate with someone, how to resolve differences, how to live with Beth day in and day out. In the world outside she is a super-dynamic person who does everything well. But she shows her vulnerable side to me. I know another Beth than the competent person the world sees. And I love both. I admire her wanting to change the world. But it makes me feel confident about myself as a man and a husband that she needs me in the way that she does.

"As for my other answer, how many couples do you know where the daughter-in-law sends her husband to be with his dying mother? When my mother was approaching death, although Beth had a full-time job and we had the children to take care of, she urged me to stay with my mom in Portland for several months to take care of her, mainly to be with her at the end. She thought it would be important for my mother, for me, and, in some way also important for our marriage. This involved three months of incredibly hard work and sacrifice for Beth. But those were her rules and mine. She was right. We have never been closer."

# 14 ❧

# Beth McNeil

MORE THAN A MONTH PASSED before Beth could find time in her hectic schedule for our interview. Along with two jobs, two children, a house to run, and her AIDS volunteer work, she consulted on several public health programs. It was a challenge for her to find three hours for an interview. But on the phone she sounded pleased and excited about my project. Apparently Kit had told her that our conversation had been very stimulating.

I arrived at their house a few minutes early, and as I sat in the car I had time to glance over Beth's pre-interview questionnaire. Her answer to "Why did you marry?" was succinct: "We were sure the relationship would last." In response to "If you had to select one thing in life you are proudest of, what would it be?" Beth wrote two answers: "My marriage. My career."

A moment later she opened the door with a warm smile and invited me into her home office, a small, cozy space with overstuffed chairs, wicker tables, and leafy plants. Her gracious attitude made me feel as if she had all day to talk, even though I knew how busy she was. Beth had a clear complexion, lovely hazel eyes, and brown hair cut in a no-nonsense style. She looked like the kind of person who could be out of bed, dressed, and ready to leave the house in less than ten minutes.

She began candidly. "Let me describe what makes our marriage work. We like each other. We have mutual respect. We trust each other. That's very important, the basic core of trust. Of course love is important, but love can be, well, sometimes you can love without some of those basics, and that's where love can become a problem. I don't know, I guess there are different definitions of love. But what gives it solidarity is just a basic sense of real trust, of really knowing where that other person is at, and knowing that whatever they're going to do is going to be in your best interest as well as theirs."

She paused briefly. "And values, sharing common values is real essential. One of our strengths is our common world-view. A lot of times people don't think that's important, especially when they first get together. But for us it's real central, and it's also central to our work."

I realized that Beth's views on marriage were very different from Sara's or Helen's. She was describing another kind of relationship altogether, that of a woman and man bound by shared values and commitment and a common world-view — and only later by love. Mutual respect and trust supersede romantic love. Without any prompting, Beth told me how she had arrived at this view of marriage. She confirmed my hunch that her earlier love affairs were an important part of the honing process.

"When Kit and I got together we were both ready. We had both had other relationships and had both made a myriad of mistakes. We had learned from those mistakes, and there was a maturity."

"What kind of mistakes?"

"I was in two long-term relationships that were tumultuous," said Beth. "I made all the possible errors because I wasn't ready to be on my own. I kept falling into relationships that were bad for me, relationships that were too passionate and destructive."

"Can you tell me about these passionate and destructive relationships?"

"Easy," she said, with a self-mocking laugh. "I always fell for the Swedish bookbinder type. You know, the struggling artisan trying to make it in America, the moody genius, the romantic gypsy. I had to have that kind of relationship. Anything tormented." She shrugged and smiled, but she was very serious.

"What drew you to the torment?"

Her smile faded. "I think I sought it out because of how I was raised. My earliest memories have to do with moving over and over during my childhood. We were alternately rich or poor. My father was a first mate in the merchant marine and left home for six months at a time. My mother never stopped feeling sorry for herself. My father never stopped blaming himself for being away and for being responsible for her tears. They loved each other."

Beth sighed. "My job as a child was to take care of my mother when he was away. She would tell me all her problems. We had no boundaries separating us. I didn't have a model of a woman who solved problems, and I had too much responsibility. Anyway, playing the nurturant parent and resenting it at the same time translated into a pattern for me. I was always looking for messed-up guys who were very exciting, guys who came in and out of my life."

"How did that change?"

"My friend Annie and I helped each other halfway through college. Our common word was 'melodrama' — the draw toward the melodrama in relationships, choosing someone who was suffering. Annie and I forced ourselves to face what we really wanted. We talked ourselves out of wanting more melodrama because, quite frankly, we'd had enough.

"We took off on a six-month trip to Europe and India, where we stayed in youth hostels and spent lots of time on buses and trains. We had huge chunks of downtime when we would just hang around and wait, and talk and talk and talk. We laid bare every relationship we'd ever had and would grill each other with questions like 'What did you get out of that relationship?' 'What was in it for you?' 'Why did you do that?'"

The first part of Beth's story was familiar to me. I've known so many young men and women who get involved in passionate, tormented relationships and then, if they marry, ultimately divorce. These are often failed rescue relationships in which the rescuer gets seriously hurt. If they are lucky or get good counseling, many of them eventually realize that they have not separated from the family tragedies that drove them to make a bad choice in the first place. They see that they've been perpetuating their own guilt and agony. What is interesting about Beth's story is how she and her friend exorcised what they called the power of the melodrama, the need to find a tormenting relationship.

"So where did Kit come in?" I asked.

"That was easy. When I got back, I started seeing Kit. My old boyfriend wanted me back, but I knew that was over. Most important, I no longer felt like I was going to hop from one person to the next. I'd gone a year without being in a relationship, and it was okay. I wanted something that was really going to work, and I didn't want to get drawn into more neurotic melodrama. I wanted to avoid my addiction to the tragic flow, but I didn't know if Kit could offer enough excitement. He was always someone I could sit and talk with. He was a reasonable person who understood me."

She was describing a critical point in her development. To make a reasoned choice in a serious relationship, a person must be able to stand alone — psychologically and emotionally. Realizing this intuitively, Beth took a break from relationships in order to examine her own motives and desires. Then, having found a man who was not tormented, she confronted a second major question: would a "reasonable" loving relationship offer enough excitement? Since she had linked sexual excitement with danger and Kit was not dangerous, could she be content with him?

As if to answer my thoughts, Beth described what drew her to Kit and how she came to terms with her choice.

"We just had a lot of similar ways of being. And so our relationship developed. I think what was so refreshing was that the relationship didn't have to suck up all my energy in life — which all my previous relationships did. I had more free time with friends, and more fun. We had fun together without all the tragic undertones. We had a relationship without all the obsessions." She grinned. "We had our ways of finding out if it would work. We lived together for four years before we got married."

It occurred to me that after growing up on storm-tossed seas, Beth had finally reached dry land. She had found a relationship that didn't torment or overwhelm her, one that was safe, loving, and trusting. I wondered, though, about the level of sexual excitement in this calmer relationship. Her frankness made it easy for me to ask, "Were you physically attracted to Kit?"

She answered slowly, sliding her words. "Well, yeah, it was really different, because it was like he'd always been my friend, and then we started relating in a much more intimate way. It's like discovering a whole other aspect of a person. All of a sudden it was, 'Yeah, this makes sense.'

"I had always relied on the initial attraction, and then when I got into the relationship, I'd discover we didn't have anything in common. This time it was the other way around. Kit was a good friend, and then I found attraction and sexual passion. Our sex life is pretty good, in fact very good. I have an orgasm every time. I'd like to have sex more often, maybe three times a week, but it just doesn't happen.

We usually have sex once or twice a week because that's where his interest is."

"People used to think that men were the ones more interested in sex."

Beth laughed at me and said, "I think I've helped him with his sexuality because I was less inhibited. I wanted to get my needs met, and not just his." Beth was contemplative. "I think for sex you need time, time to get in sync, time to know your partner, time to get to know what the other person likes or doesn't like. Sex is one of those things. With some people you can feel incredibly free, and with others you feel more inhibited. What has gotten us to this point in our sexual relationship has to do with other parts of our relationship, how intimate we feel, how honest and open, and how much caring there is, how much concern." She concluded thoughtfully, "The sexual part of marriage is heightened by what takes place in other parts of our relationship."

"How did you manage to loosen Kit up without threatening him?"

"I used to talk to him. I would physically show him what I wanted. I would participate more. I think this was something he wasn't used to. And it gave him permission to accept that I was giving to him, and not to have that performance anxiety. I was used to good sex. I didn't want to settle for anything less. I think I gave him permission to feel, to be in the moment, to explore, to be vulnerable with me, to let himself go and be part of it."

"How does your sex life compare with the melodrama?"

"When I left the melodrama, I knew sex would be less intense, but sex in the melodrama also brought along the unhappy stuff. Generally there is a fantasy element that's missing when you know a person deeply, unlike the early excitement of a relationship."

"Did you find all this out in the marriage or in the years you lived together before the wedding?" I asked.

"Learning to trust him wasn't easy for me. It began when we started to live together. We needed a four-year overture."

Young people today engage in lots of practice before choosing a life partner. They practice choosing and changing their minds throughout high school and into young adulthood, at college and afterward. Painful though it may be, there is no better way to discover oneself and find out how to make informed choices. In the process of making and breaking relationships, we learn to judge ourselves and others. Mostly we learn what attracts us, what we abhor, what is exciting, what is dangerous.

If we are successful, we learn to confront our own failings and to listen to our own inner warnings of danger ahead. We learn to distinguish among love, lust, friendship, and infatuation and to separate truth from falsehood. We understand the terrors of loneliness and the seriousness of a broken heart. And if we have not learned it before, we discover that behavior has consequences, that relationships have great power to heal and great power to hurt, that love and human relationships are serious and make lasting claims.

One way that people practice is by living together before committing to marriage. For many couples in the study, this was a successful strategy. But research has shown that it is not an automatic overture to happy marriage. Several recent studies have demonstrated that the divorce rate is higher among couples who live together before marriage than among those who do not. This is a troublesome finding, because a strong argument for cohabitation has been that it would slow the divorce rate. Presumably, living together would allow a couple to make a more informed decision about marriage.

But I've known many couples who have had a good affair that turned into a bad marriage and then an unhappy divorce because, as they inevitably discover, marriage raises expectations. What's acceptable in a lover won't always do in a husband or wife. As one man said, "An exciting mistress who is always late is tantalizing. But a wife who is never on time is a damned nuisance." The perception of the other and of oneself, the sense of time, and many other aspects of life change radically when two people who have lived together marry. They begin to behave more in accord with traditional expectations. The ghosts of both families of origin are no longer kept at bay by the game "This Is Not for Keeps." Moreover, sex in a rising affair can be very exciting, while sex within marriage is more predictable.

When I got married, in 1947, cohabitation was unthinkable. Although premarital sex was not that uncommon, it certainly wasn't mentioned in public. Among the women in the study who married in the fifties, all were virgins except two, and they were pregnant when they walked down the aisle. None had lived with a man before marriage. The fifties-era men had had more sexual experience, but it was transient — a hot romance with a high school sweetheart or, as in

Matt's case, a fraternity-led visit to a prostitute or a brief affair with a married woman.

The nation's sexual mores began to change in the sixties, and by the seventies and eighties, cohabitation was common. Every couple from that era in the study had lived together for one to nine years before marrying. Without exception, each person had entered the marriage with a range of sexual experiences. Indeed, most had had serious relationships with more than one lover. Living together has become an accepted prelude to marriage in many spheres of American society and is the norm at many universities, although it is still frowned on in some circles.

This trend reflects a total turnaround in people's thinking. In earlier generations a young woman was afraid to live with her boyfriend because, the argument went, if he could have unlimited sex, he had no reason to marry her. She was "damaged goods." The fear of pregnancy out of wedlock was an even more powerful inhibitor. The price of sex with a woman from a respectable family was marriage. When reliable birth control became available in the sixties, the fear of pregnancy diminished, and the external controls on living together weakened overnight.

Now, in our culture of divorce, the fears have undergone a curious reversal. Except for the worry about AIDS, premarital sex and living together are considered safe. But marriage is dangerous! After all, marriage fails half the time and brings misery to those who venture into it. The logic is, if you don't marry, you won't divorce. Like Kit, many young people ask, why marry? They are afraid of marriage because they've seen too many horrible divorces. They think that by avoiding marriage they stand a better chance of maintaining the spontaneity of their love; many have told me that marriage destroys love.

People usually hope that simply by living together they will avoid making a serious mistake. They build elaborate rules to guard against making the wrong decision. One young woman I know told her lover that they had to live together for at least two years before marriage; only then would she consider that they had both passed the test.

But life is more complex than these solutions suggest. The argument that cohabitation enables people to iron out flaws in the relationship or that it promotes more stable marriages has not been proven correct; living together is not a preventive for divorce.

Cohabitation is an individually defined path. It can lead only to the continuation of living together, or it can lead to a reduction of anxiety about commitment, to a good marriage, or to disaster. The path depends on the motivations that have brought the couple together and whether they use the time together to build a relationship that can become a good marriage. If it begins as play, does it remain play or become serious? Does it allow them to learn about themselves and what they do and do not want?

Some couples live together just for the convenience or fun of it. They regard their life together as an extended adolescent moratorium rather than as an overture to anything. They enjoy sex and each other's company, and they don't worry about the future. This is often the situation when people are in their early twenties and feel that they have all the time in the world. They have no need to worry about families, commitment, and ties that bind. But it is not accurate to call this kind of living together a trial marriage, because it postpones the very tasks on which marriage hinges. For these people cohabitation begins as play and ends as play.

"I would meet somebody, fall head over heels, and after one day we would be in bed and going steady," confessed one young woman. "I'd be madly in love, and nine months later I would say, 'Ugh! What am I doing with this person? Get lost!'"

The younger couples in the study had lived together as a real overture to marriage. They had used earlier relationships as practice, but in contrast *their* cohabiting was the beginning of a serious commitment. For many, including Kit and Beth, the decision to marry represented an emotional crossing of the bar, a public statement that their relationship with each other and the world had changed.

I asked one young woman, "Why did you want to marry?"

"Because we are a serious couple. I want the world to know we are a serious couple. I want it acknowledged," she said with great emphasis.

How long had they lived together?

Six years, she said. She had, however, been deeply hurt when they visited her fiancé's parents the evening after deciding to get married. With an insensitivity that cut this young woman to the quick, her future mother-in-law exclaimed, "Why are you getting married? You've been living together for years."

Some couples decided to marry when they agreed it was time to have a child. Some who had already decided to marry set an earlier date when a parent was very ill or on the verge of death. In every case, marriage represented a commitment arrived at thoughtfully, after living together for a time and deciding to stay together for the rest of their lives.

The advantage of cohabitation is that it allows a man and woman to practice having a close relationship, which can be very valuable if they learn from their experience. They can learn more about what they're looking for in a spouse and more about who they are as individuals. But by itself the experience of living together doesn't provide this. The ability to learn and practice constructively requires that each person use the experience and emerge with a better sense of what goes into a relationship. Cohabitation as an overture to marriage is as demanding and as pleasurable as the early years of marriage. Young people can also help each other in the formidable first task of marriage, that of separating psychologically from their families. In this sense, living together can be useful in making the transition to adulthood, a solution that was not readily available to earlier generations.

In describing what she learned from living for three years with a man she chose not to marry, one young woman said, "I learned that you cannot get all your needs met from one person. I learned that I can be terribly difficult to live with and that I can drive somebody crazy. I learned how to stop when I was being difficult, and I learned how to gauge when the other person is on edge and to understand what sets off people in certain moods. I learned a lot about sex, and most of all I learned that the man I was living with was not the right man for me. I needed someone closer to my age than he was, and I wanted someone who had not been married before."

Kit also spoke about what he had learned from a prior relationship. "I had a real problem being angry back then, about expressing it. One of the things I really learned in that relationship is that if you're pissed off, you damn well better say so, because keeping it inside and pretending everything is okay is not where it's at."

For people of Kit's high personal integrity the distinction between extended cohabitation and marriage is easily blurred. Many cohabiting couples expect commitment and fidelity. "I see no differences," he said. "When you're in a live-in relationship, the moral rules are just like marriage."

But cohabitation, like marriage, can fail, and the suffering can be intense. The idea that living together can be a selection process, like trying on a new outfit, is treacherous. Human relationships are not like clothing, where you decide that the cuffs are too long or the hem too short. The lure of cohabitation is that it seems to be a relationship without strings, one that you can enter or leave with ease. But unacknowledged strings can bind very tightly.

Also, because cohabitation does not demand equal responsibility from each partner, it can become a tragic breeding ground for unrealistic rescue fantasies and dependency. It is easy to begin living together — no family involvement, no promises — but it does not follow that the ending will be easy. The breakup of an extended cohabitation can be just as wrenching and as lasting in its impact as a divorce.

Beth had not mentioned wanting to have children, which is one of the major reasons that many people who live together decide to get married. I asked, "Did you plan both your children?"

She looked down at the floor. "It was a serious issue between us for a long time. You see, I wasn't sure I wanted children. I didn't feel ready or interested, whereas Kit wanted them right away. It took me three and a half years to come around to his way of thinking. And remember, I was thirty-two when we got married. For a long time we couldn't even discuss it in a rational way."

She blushed slightly. "We didn't fight about it, not that we avoided fighting about serious issues. It's just that it was a difficult decision for me. I was afraid of having children. I wasn't sure what kind of mother I'd be, and I wasn't sure I could protect a child from all the dangers in the world. I was afraid it would ruin what I had with Kit. And I was afraid of being trapped in a relationship that I couldn't get out of. You can't walk away from a child. I was also afraid that our child would be closer to Kit than to me because he would be the more involved parent, and I was feeling ambivalent. I was just imagining horrible triangles."

Once again I was impressed by how little is taken for granted in a companionate marriage. Motherhood is seen as an option to be considered carefully, one that has consequences that must be examined, whichever way the decision goes.

"I went into therapy for three months, focusing on whether or not to have a child," Beth said. "I couldn't make up my mind. When the therapist suggested that my parents would probably like being grandparents, I suddenly realized that the opposite was true. My mom didn't want me to have a baby. She wanted me to be available for her."

"How did you decide to have a child?"

"Well, I realized that part of me really wanted a child, and I got pregnant. But then I had a miscarriage. Kit was so miserable when I lost the baby that I realized how terribly important this was to him. And I decided to try again, to do it for the part of me that wanted it and the part of me that loved him."

Wondering how her inner conflict about having a baby had affected her, I asked about the pregnancy and the birth itself.

"Kit was a wonderful caretaker," she said. "He came to classes with me and was very attentive. I didn't feel so scared with him at my side. But the birth itself was very difficult. I liken it to crossing the Australian desert and meeting a series of trials along the way. I didn't sleep for three days and was totally exhausted. After the baby was born, I stayed home for a year and felt pretty good about it. Then I went back to work full-time and kept juggling work and family demands. It was exhausting.

"I finally began to realize this is just the way life is. There's a constancy to work and family. Once I got over my misgivings, we were able to go ahead and have a second child. I'm always frustrated that kids don't work at the pace you might want as an adult. And I had doubts that I'd be the mommy type. I want to take care of my children, but I want to maintain everything else in my life — Superwoman." She laughed. "Me and all my women friends."

The question of whether to have children is a particularly thorny one in companionate marriages. Women can now say what many have been reluctant to admit in the past — that they are frightened by the thought of having a baby, that they don't think they will be good mothers, and that they fear losing the close relationship with their husbands. They're free to say that they don't want children, period.

This is new. Traditionally, it has been assumed that all women want babies. And most still do. Motherhood is regarded by many women as the pinnacle of female experience. A man is supposed to want children, too, to carry on his surname and show proof of his virility. Men, however, don't feel as strong a biological need for children and aren't under the same time pressure as women.

But I found very different attitudes in these companionate mar-

riages. Women like Beth felt free to say that they didn't want children
— despite their husbands' wishes to the contrary. They weren't afraid
to make a decision that would be severely disappointing. Men who
wanted children no longer felt it was their prerogative to insist on it.
Some, like Kit, waited more or less patiently, hoping that their wives
would change their minds; others actively pressed their wives to recon-
sider. When Beth saw the disappointment and pain on her husband's
face when she miscarried, she decided to try again — not truly for
herself but for Kit and for the marriage.

"Does Kit do as much of the parenting as you do?" I asked.

"Well, my friends envy me," Beth said. "Kit and I really parent
together. We divide the chores, including carpools and helping out at
the preschool co-op. I'm better at discipline. He's better at explaining
things. We're on the same wavelength about child rearing and schooling, although I probably take the lead more often. I buy the clothes,
make appointments, set up next year's schooling, and so on. He helps
Martha with her piano lessons, and he shows Sam how to ride without
his training wheels. I think the children are happy. I hope they'll have
an easier time than I did."

Beth and Kit consider each aspect of bringing up children, and they
divide the chores and errands that go into it. Beth is frank about her
difficulties with being a "mommy type" and says sharing roles makes
it easier. The only aspects of parenting that cannot be shared or
negotiated are pregnancy and breastfeeding. But Kit and fathers like
him get deeply involved in childbirth classes and help out however
they can in the delivery room. They can change diapers, nurse a sick
child through the night, bake brownies, clean up finger paints, and do
virtually everything that mothers have traditionally done.

But role sharing can raise problems. Since the parents come from
different backgrounds, there's no reason to think they will agree on
every detail of weaning, toilet training, peer relationships, curfews,
manners, television time, handling aggression, and the myriad other
issues that come up in child rearing. With two parents equally in
charge, conflict between them is inevitable. Competition for the child's
affection — did she call for you or me last night? — is a new aspect of
family life.

I was interested to find that although couples discussed major issues
like the child's religious upbringing at length before the birth, the
mundane concerns of everyday life — discipline, food, household rou-

tines, responsibility for chores and caregiving — typically were not discussed ahead of time and sometimes not until there was an emergency. As a result, couples who characteristically thought ahead and planned found themselves confronting problems that they might have avoided. Coparenting in all types of families is still a new arrangement. Each couple is still carefully finding their way and trying to map the territory as they go. It is a challenge to translate an idea like coparenting into the real-life care of real children.

An hour into our interview, I asked Beth, "Would anything break this marriage?"

After reflecting for a moment, she said, "Infidelity would. If he did it, or if I did. It was clear after our first date that we wanted a monogamous relationship. This doesn't mean we can't have friends of the opposite sex, but sexually and romantically we made a strong agreement. We both know there are temptations, but it's a choice. Infidelity is not something you fall into. It's a choice. Faithfulness is a discipline," she said with moral conviction. "For us it's essential, because it's a basic trust issue that lets each of us be ourselves."

"That was a very big change for you."

She smiled. "That's right. At the very beginning of our relationship I worried about his other love interests. The last guy I went out with was always leaving me for someone else, but then he'd come back after three weeks or so. I realized I did this too. I would get attracted to other people as a way of ending a relationship. I was immature and couldn't be alone. So we were real clear about the need for trust. If infidelity happened, it would end the relationship. But we're not afraid of it anymore," she said, shaking her head. "It won't happen."

Realistic about the dangers and temptations of this world, Beth relied on her trust in herself and her husband to face down the threats — and not on false piety or denial or naive hope. Kit and Beth felt strongly that each could be trusted in the face of danger and that they were responsible for their own behavior. Affairs don't just happen, as Beth saw clearly. "It's a choice. Infidelity is not something you fall into."

She smiled conspiratorially. "You know, it was hard for me to get rid of old habits. I used to go through his pockets, you know. To see if there were names of other women. And of course I found them, because he works with women. I would be jealous that he was going to lunch with so and so, and he would say, 'Of course I'm going to lunch with her. We work together and we're friends.' My suspicions made him furious. But it was real important to us both not to restrict each other's lives, because that's a prison and that's where the freedom of our relationship comes in. I have very close male friends, and he has close women friends."

"Have you ever been tempted to be unfaithful?"

"Sure I get tempted. It's natural. I don't think life is without its attractions. But I don't worry about them because I'm not going to carry them anywhere. I make sure I never get into a situation that will get too close. If it does, I cut it off. It's easy to do."

"I take it you haven't been sexually harassed or caught in a situation you couldn't control?"

"No, I've been lucky. It's not been an issue in my professional life."

Beth is actively making sure her marriage is safe. The moment she thinks of straying, she says to the man and to herself, I'm not available, don't get any ideas. And she takes steps to block both her impulse and his. Her degree of candor might baffle her grandmother.

"There's no doubt in either of our minds. There really isn't — ever. I mean I know we'll go through another forty years of ups and downs, but it would be absolutely inconceivable to me to think that we won't make it to the end of our lives. And I think that he feels that way too. And that gives you this incredible sense of safety and comfort, knowing that you just don't have to ask those wrenching questions over again. I don't know if he'd say that, but I know that's at the core of our sense of security — in an insecure world."

# 15 &

# The Sixth Task

*Exploring Sexual Love and Intimacy*

<br>

THE SIXTH TASK OF MARRIAGE is to create a loving sexual relationship and to guard it well so that it will endure. A good sex life, however the couple defines that, is at the heart of a good marriage. This is the domain where intimacy is renewed and the excitement that first drew the couple together is kept alive. The bedroom is a privileged place for lighthearted play, laughter, adventure, passion, pleasure, where a couple can achieve freedom from childhood taboos. There is no better antidote to the pressures of living than a loving sex life.

Like Beth, Kit spoke candidly about his sexual experiences before and during marriage. "I felt reborn sexually with Beth. It was like night and day compared with my other experiences. I like women a lot, and when I was in my twenties I had a lot of sexual encounters. I also lived with one woman for two years before Beth and I got together. The truth is that I had trouble in that relationship. The woman I was living with wanted an open sexual relationship, and I just couldn't handle that. I suffered with premature ejaculation. I was really feeling badly about myself as a man; I was afraid that no one would want me. With Beth I feel mature and comfortable. And it continues to be absolutely satisfying. Sex during pregnancy was the most wonderful experience in the world."

Beth said, "I knew when I married him that sex would be less intense. It wasn't a matter of technique; it's that the security of marriage makes sex less arousing. But also, the best sex I've ever had has been with Kit."

Kit and Beth, like others in the study, were able to work out earlier sexual anxieties within the marriage. Nevertheless, they had to make trade-offs. Although Kit was very pleased with their sex life, he had to overcome a tendency to have a roving eye and become a faithful husband. Beth had to give up the sexual excitement and wild fantasies she had enjoyed with other men. Sex was tamer for her and less frequent than she wanted, but no longer felt tortured. They had found a solution that worked for both.

People mistakenly assume that because couples nowadays enter marriage with sexual experience, building a sexual relationship requires no special attention; given two healthy people, it just happens. But in truth, the new sexual freedom means that people today have much higher expectations. They expect more from themselves and from their partners. Those who have had problems in earlier relationships, as several people in the study confessed they had, expect to resolve them within the marriage. Thus, although building the sexual relationship is one of the most pleasurable tasks of marriage, it certainly is not the easiest. It requires delicacy, sensitivity, and patience. It takes time and a willingness and ability to accommodate to the other person's needs.

The early days and months of a relationship are usually a time of intense sexual excitement, when the man and woman engage in a great deal of play and exploration. Mostly they ask and answer the wordless questions, "Does this please you? Does this feel good? What is permissible? What are the boundaries? How can I make you happy? Let me show you what makes me happy." They learn to read each other's sexual messages and invitations, when to push past reluctance and when to refrain, when to seduce, and who seduces whom. They learn as much about themselves as about their partner as their erotic world expands. But this complex sexual dance doesn't happen without trial and error. Everyone runs into problems before finding breakthroughs. Everyone needs to explore.

Each partner comes to the marriage with a history that has shaped his or her sexual appetites, fantasies, inhibitions, and anxieties. These cannot be anticipated during the more public courtship of falling in love and getting to know each other in conversation and shared activities. Each person's sexual needs are as individual as a thumbprint, a composite shaped by many influences, including the events of childhood and adolescence as well as more recent adult experiences. There may be a wide discrepancy between the two partners in sexual experience. In the past, men usually had more sexual knowledge and therefore were expected to take the lead in the sexual courtship. But that is no longer the case; as we saw in Beth's story, the woman may be the more experienced partner.

Building a sex life that continues to satisfy requires subtlety and imagination. This realm is entirely the creation of the man and the woman together; it relies exclusively on their resources. If it is rich in feeling and excitement, if it is experimental, it is their creation. If it reinforces old fears or is mechanical and lacking in tenderness or passion, that, too, is their creation. Whether it lasts throughout the marriage or ends earlier depends on what the couple bring to this private world and what they are able to create together.

Teresa and Peter, both in their early thirties, took me to the heart of their sexual courtship. Although their desires and experiences appeared discrepant at the start, this couple created a passionate sexual relationship that became the core of their romantic marriage. Like all of the couples in the study who married in the eighties, both had had considerable sexual experience. Peter had been married before, and his divorce had left him reeling.

"I never realized anything could be so painful," he said. "My divorce left me with serious sexual difficulties. It was like all of my misery spilled into my sexual performance. Teresa and I have a wonderful, exciting sex life, but it began with a fiasco. The first time we made love, I came the moment I touched her. She was good and understanding. Thank God she liked sex. She was the first woman I ever met who really liked sex a lot. On our third date we were having dinner at a restaurant. She reached over, grabbed my hand, and pulled me outside, where we embraced and kissed passionately. It was like she began to set me free. She has a nice dirty mind that feels wonderful. We have both had a lot of desire for each other over the ten years of our marriage. We are accomplished lovers."

Teresa said, "When I first met my husband, sex was okay, but I was used to better. I'm from an Italian family. Italian girls are brought up to be seductive little things. I'd been in touch with my own sexuality since I was fifteen. Having had good sex, I wanted the same with Peter. Being the aggressor allowed me to take a leading role in the sexual action.

"We both understood that it was not only sex but our whole relationship that was involved. It wasn't easy. I wanted to get my needs met. I wasn't just willing to get him off. We talked a lot about physical contact. I tried very hard to help him, to loosen him up. I would cry, and he would say, I don't know unless you tell me. My view was, if you really wanted to give it to me, I wouldn't have to ask for it. His idea was, you have to ask me, because I don't know. Finally I realized that he was right. If I asked, I got it. He was consistent, so I believed him. Finally it all began to balance. I didn't have to ask, because he started to understand and to sense, and we just both wanted to give it. I began to trust him. It balanced just fine." She laughed. "Sometimes he can be a wild and crazy man."

Teresa and Peter took time and made imaginative efforts to build their sex life, from which they derived great pleasure and pride. In their very successful courtship, the woman led the way, and the man happily followed and eventually caught up with her. Obviously, not every couple undertakes this task with their dedication and skill.

A harmonious sex life adds powerful new strands to the relationship and affects all other domains of the marriage. As a couple finds sexual pleasure together, their perceptions of and fantasies about each other expand. Their self-images are profoundly changed by their shared erotic experiences, the memories they have created, and their new physical ties. A good sexual relationship strengthens self-confidence, affirming a man's pride in his manhood and a woman's pride in her womanhood. The ability to give and receive sexual pleasure is a major dimension of adulthood. Achieving it together is not only a source of individual pride but an affirmation of the couple's unity and commitment. As Peter declared, "I'm confirmed in this marriage. I feel confident about myself as a man and about myself as a sexual partner." Teresa said, "I've always tried to hold him as close as I can. It makes me feel a sense of power that I can give him such pleasure."

Many men and women emphasized the close tie between their sex life and their emotional bond. One woman in her forties said, "Sex is very important to me because of the intimacy, the validation of each other. It's a rejuvenating force for us because it transcends other things. It's a way of making our emotional connection and recalling our love for each other." A man, also in his forties, said, "Our sex life is very good, but it's not only sex that's important. We are very affectionate. Many times a day we touch each other. There is a mutual desire for the constant contact. She'll just walk by, and I'll reach out to touch her. It's become part of the bargain of our marriage. We always see each other as sexual."

Sexual intercourse combined with love demands trust. It's a risky business to come so close to another person emotionally and physically. Both partners must feel safe, and this takes time. People are never more vulnerable than when bodies and personae are interpenetrated, when boundaries disappear and the excitement is high. Indeed, the essence and much of the excitement of sex lies in taking the risk of giving up physical and emotional boundaries. For some people, sex without love is easier; for others, love by itself is easier. The combination can feel very scary.

It is important to recognize how fragile people are in sexual matters, how easily put off or discouraged. Sexual courtship involves allowing oneself and one's partner to overcome shyness, inhibitions, the fear of letting go, of regression, of losing control — a thousand and one fears rooted in the sexual taboos of growing up and the anxieties of a close sexual relationship.

Love and sex are inevitably accompanied by anxieties and ambivalence. The anxieties stem from the earliest mother-child attachment, the first model for all later relationships. The mother who provides love, nurturance, and protection also punishes and deprives. The mother who nurses and holds you is the mother who weans you and sends you out into the world. The mother who is the center of life is the mother who displaces you with the next child. You depend on her totally, but she will not always be there when you want her.

Thus from the very beginning of life, love and anxiety are joined. Every love relationship and every sexual relationship has a push-pull quality. There is no love without hate, because love involves intense need and dependency. There is no love without envy, because loving someone involves wanting to be like that person or to be that person. The challenge in every marriage is to balance the mixture of love and hate so that love is predominant, and to maintain that balance throughout life.

A colleague of mine in Brazil eloquently described this issue as a postscript to our conversations about marriage. He wrote, "Maria and I have loved each other for four decades. We have worked on our love for each other every single day of those years by keeping a close rein on hate and its courtiers, envy, jealousy, and fear."

When primal fear and hostility are overcome by love, the sexual experience can be the most powerful of a couple's lives. As Matt told me, "Sometimes when I make love to her, I disappear." This would terrify many men who are less able to trust the woman they love. But in a fully realized, loving sexual relationship, such a feeling can be a source of enormous happiness and gratitude, not only for the ecstasy of the fusion, but for the joy of finding absolute safety, love, and satisfaction after taking such a great risk.

Combining sex with love was a real change for those in the study who came to marriage with many prior experiences of casual sex; some had become active as early as fifteen. But having made the transition to a good sex life within marriage, they found it surprisingly easy to close the door on the past. All of these young people stated that they had been entirely faithful, not only since the marriage but since making a commitment to each other.

For instance, the youngest couple in the study, Nancy and Joe, met in their freshman year at college, moved in together two years later, and married at twenty-one. Both now held university appointments. When I interviewed Nancy, in the tenth year of their marriage, she was almost ready to deliver their third child. She described not only the events but the feelings she and Joe had had when they first knew each other.

"Both of us spent our first two years at college with really weird people, lots and lots of one-night stands. All this time Joe and I were really very good friends and spent a lot of time together. We used to sit under a special tree and talk. We helped each other with all of the problems of being far away from our home communities and our families. But sex and friendship were strictly separate, and crossing that border was out. Those were the rules.

"One night we both went barhopping, and when we came back we went to bed. But he didn't want to have sex. I climbed on top of him, but he said no. It was the first time in my life that a man rejected me. 'No sex?' I said. 'I don't get it. What's the matter with me?' I was really hurt."

Joe told the same story, but from a different perspective. "There we were in bed, and she's on top of me. But the intensity of my feelings scared me. I wasn't ready. I knew that this was going to be important, and my fear was connected to this knowing. I wasn't brave enough to say so at that time. It was the first time in my life that I couldn't perform. I thought the world was coming to an end, that I was cursed for life.

"I was impotent for several weeks, and finally we pursued each other and we made it together. Sex with her was stronger, it was more intense, it was plainly better. But the thing is, the sex was less intense than my feelings. It wasn't the sex, it was my feelings that scared me. My feelings were so intense. Only gradually did the sex come to match my feelings."

When they moved in together, Nancy said, "We had sex two or three times every day, and we both graduated with honors." But now, at age thirty, she said, "Sex is not as important. Sometimes I don't think it's as important as the fact that we have a commitment to each other. And if for some reason we could never have sex again, I don't think that would ruin our relationship. Of course I feel that sex is the time we have together, when we don't have the kids. It's our time, it's fun time. In that sense it's very important. But it's not why we married. We married because we loved each other. There's only one man in the world I ever loved besides my husband. Otherwise I didn't love them. I had fun with them, but I surely didn't love them or think that I did."

It is evident that for these young people casual sex was a form of play. But combined with love and true, caring friendship, sex was serious. The rules seemed to change almost overnight. Suddenly sex was tied to permanence, to tenderness, to giving the other person's needs equal weight, which made all the difference between fun and seriousness. In a loving sexual relationship the feelings are as powerful as the instinctual drives. As Joe related, his feelings were even stronger; he was terrified by the sudden confrontation with adult love and the beginnings of commitment. When sex is no longer a game in which the rules are easy come, easy go, people become frightened. This new game is for keeps. If things go awry, there is no new person waiting in the wings.

It is commonly believed that sexual activity is at its height during the early years of marriage. But that was not always true for the couples in the study. Nor did sexual activity necessarily decline over the years. In many marriages high activity in the early years was followed by a decline when the children were young and then a strong rise after the children left home, continuing into the retirement years.

In some of the marriages there were pronounced differences in desire between the man and the woman. In one quarter of them the woman wanted more sex than her husband, as was true for Beth. In another quarter the man, as in Keith's case, wanted more sex. The remaining half were evenly matched in desire. The level of sexual activity, even when it was lower than one of the partners wanted, was rarely a source of intense conflict, though the early years of Tina and Marty's marriage could be seen as an exception.

The level of sexual desire also varied over time, so couples found it necessary to fine-tune their sex life to accommodate changing needs. The birth of a child inevitably thrusts marriage into a new, harried phase that interferes with lovemaking. These couples did report that their sex life was strained and sometimes put on hold for months after the first child was born and for much longer if two children came close together.

At menopause and in the years afterward, some women experienced a sharp rise in sexual interest and passion, whereas others found their interest waning. Discrepancy in the level of desire between men and women was most likely to be a factor at midlife. One menopausal woman said, "I find myself wishing that we had more of a sex life. I'm hoping that in the next phase of our relationship we will be more creative with sex and passion." Her husband said, "We have sex about once a week. I know she would like to have more, but after twenty-six years of marriage, I don't feel the same passion."

All of the older couples, however, continued to enjoy sex. Those in their sixties said that they regularly had sex once a week. Partners were candid with each other about changes in sexual desires and feelings. Some found that although sex was less frequent in later years, the excitement was more intense. One woman in her fifties said, "We have sex less often as we have gotten older, but my orgasms have gotten stronger and quicker and more intense over the years."

A few of the couples at midlife and later read sex manuals for suggestions on adding variety to their sex life; others tried videos. Most found that allowing plenty of time and choosing a romantic setting was increasingly important. Men especially reported that their earlier sexual vigor returned when they were rested and away from home. Despite their sometimes rueful recognition of diminished desire — "I used to be a hotter number," said one woman — they tried their best to avoid disappointing each other.

The intensity of sex varied also with the type of marriage. In romantic marriages sex was more frequent and more passionate than in the other types, and the couples were more likely to find time and beautiful places where they could enjoy each other. In companionate and traditional marriages sex was often less central to the relationship. As one man said, "Friendship, not passion, is primary in our marriage."

In many second marriages sex was at the center of the relationship. Often remarried couples had come together after a long period of sexual deprivation and were eager to have a fuller sex life to make up for the hurts of the past. Those in rescue marriages varied a great deal in their sexual activity. Several women, like Helen, preferred cuddling and being held by their husbands to intercourse. But others very much enjoyed sex when they felt comfortable and trusting in the relationship.

A couple's sex life is the most vulnerable part of the marriage. Unlike casual sex, which can be fitted into the time available, sex within marriage depends on a measure of inner tranquillity as well as on privacy and freedom from interruption. Without the safeguards of some peace and privacy, a couple may be unable to turn to each other lovingly. When sex is regularly postponed because other demands intrude with greater urgency, it can become perfunctory and unfulfilling, weakening the marriage.

Married people come to bed with many needs, not just the gratification of the sex drive, important as this surely is. Sex provides a unique opportunity to create an island of pleasure, which we all need. One woman said, "It's really critical that we make intimate time for each other. Otherwise we'd drift apart. One of the differences between us is that I don't like to have sex without intimate conversation, and he makes connections with me through sex. I need intimacy as a prelude to anything physical. To him, intimacy is physical. What I love is his willingness to keep our differences in mind."

People are vulnerable to hurt and rejection, even within a well-established marriage. "You have to be careful when you say no to a man," said one woman. "They're fragile. There are times when one of us is too tired, but we're very careful about that. I'll say, 'Look, I love you, I find you desirable, but I'll make love to you tomorrow.' And he'll do the same for me. We make sure that the other knows it isn't that we don't want them."

For all of these differences, the quality of the sexual relationship in these happy marriages was light-years away from the troubled sex lives of those who divorce. The greatest contrast between happily married and divorcing couples may well be in the domain of sex. By the time people file for divorce, sexual deprivation of many years' standing is shockingly common. In some cases the sexual relationship was never established, and in others, sex was mechanical, merely a vent for one partner's physical needs. In the happy marriages, sex was never a one-way street and was never deliberately withheld to punish or express anger. It never required violence as an overture. Sex was not a battlefield or merely an avenue for reconciliation.

Sex is remarkably sensitive to what's happening in all areas of individual and family life. Illness, especially surgery, as well as depression, worry, fatigue, and stress at work can affect a man and woman's intimate life. When a baby cries or a child has a nightmare or a teenager is out late with the car, the couple's private time together may be postponed or disrupted. And when sex declines or disappears for a sustained period, sexual frustrations may mount, at the very time when the marriage is least able to ward off the dangers.

Work may interfere with a couple's sex life, especially early in their careers, when they are putting in long hours. Mothers caring for young children are often exhausted and feeling decidedly uninterested in sex by the end of the day. It is not unusual for even young and vigorous men and women to fall exhausted into bed at night, wondering if they'll ever find time for each other again.

Couples in the study found that their sexual relationship was richer when life was less stressful. Men and women alike looked forward to vacations as times when they could be together and enjoy some freedom. Many people spoke with great yearning of their long-standing wish for extended leisure and privacy so they could spend time in bed together. In the ordinary course of life, couples found that the excitement and frequency of sex depended much more than they had expected on being able to shut out routine pressures and fatigue.

It is very important for all couples to find ways to protect their privacy, to cherish their sexual relationship, and to guard it fiercely. A richly rewarding and stable sex life is not just a fringe benefit, it is the central task of marriage. In a good marriage, sex and love are inseparable. Sex serves a very serious function in maintaining both the quality and the stability of the relationship, replenishing emotional reserves and strengthening the marital bond.

# 16

# The Unforgiving Workplace

TWO YEARS LATER, on my follow-up visit, Beth and Kit greeted me warmly. The house was still strewn with toys, books, children's clothes, and unfinished art projects, even though it was evening and the kids were in bed.

Beth said teasingly, "Well, we're still married! Nothing about the basics has changed."

Kit smiled in agreement.

"We feel luckier than ever," she said soberly, "especially when we see some of the problems other people around us are having."

"What do you mean?" I asked.

"Well, the recession is hurting a lot of our friends," said Kit. "We have more security than other people, but I can tell you it's affected us."

"How so?"

He was uncharacteristically hesitant. He sounded pained, maybe even a little depressed. "I'd really like to change jobs, but I can't take that chance. I have enough seniority that I probably won't be fired, but the budget has been cut to the bone, and there's more and more pressure at work. I do all my own secretarial work. Just typing reference letters for students is a minor nightmare. I bring a lot of work home these days. I don't have any choice but to stick with it. I'm really trapped. We need the health insurance and the money." He shrugged. "And there aren't any other jobs around. Most of the community colleges have laid off dozens of people. I guess I should feel lucky to have a job."

Beth jumped into the conversation, her voice more cheerful. "He's not telling you everything. He's working on a novel."

Kit looked at his wife and smiled. "Yes, that's one project that's bringing me a lot of pleasure. But I have a long way to go on it."

I asked Beth about her work.

Her smile faded. "Sometimes I feel caught in a vise. My practice is okay, but that's partly because I offer a sliding fee scale, and so many of my patients are in financial trouble. But I have to see more patients to meet my expenses. There's a lot of pressure at the hospice, and the upshot is that I've had to take more patients there too and work till eight o'clock three nights a week. This means I never get enough time with the children, and it drives me crazy!" Beth looked despairingly at her husband. "Plus Kit and I hardly ever see each other. We can't even have dinner together half the time. We sometimes forget what the other looks like." She looked down at her hands, as if ashamed of this sorry state.

"We're facing a new crisis right now," she said, looking up at Kit. "We decided after a lot of discussion that we want to put Martha in private school, but I know we can't afford it without skimping on everything in our lives. We're really agonizing. I've always believed in and supported the public schools, but they're getting dangerous in our neighborhood. We're struggling with the decision. It's one of the hardest things we've ever confronted. If Martha goes to private school, Kit will have to get a second job."

Social scientists have thought of work and family as separate spheres with a common boundary or interface. I suppose this notion may have been accurate when most women stayed home and men dutifully went to work. But in today's world the image of coexisting separate spheres utterly fails to capture the interaction between work and family. As Kit and Beth's story shows, the two spheres not only connect, they collide and penetrate each other with razor-sharp projectiles.

Time is a chronic problem in many families today. It is no secret that work intrudes on family life. Longer hours at the office mean fewer hours with the kids. To compensate, many parents subscribe to the concept of "quality time" — short periods of especially loving or devoted interaction with their children that supposedly distills the essence of good parenting. But children do not buy into the concept of quality time; they are foolish enough to clamor for "time time" — bedtime, playtime, story time, soccer time, just-being-together time, and not-watching-the-clock time. They don't go for nouvelle-cuisine parenting no matter how prettily presented, for they have figured out that the helpings are too small and only leave them hungry for more.

But there is another problem in our society that has not been addressed. Just as work intrudes on the family, it also penetrates the relationship between husband and wife. When two people don't have enough time to spend with their children, they usually have even less time for each other. They postpone intimacy, sex, just being together, and having fun. Obviously, time together is an important measure of a marriage; "quality time" does not work any better for a couple than it does for children. Sex that only satisfies physical drives does not serve its central purpose of emotionally restoring the relationship and nurturing intimacy. And as many women made clear, sex without time for intimacy and an overture of pillow talk left them bored, frustrated, and angry.

Business travel, which seems to be an increasing part of American life, also intrudes on a couple's life together. I think we have under-estimated the frustrations engendered by travel and its ramifications for a marriage. One man, a district sales manager, spoke of the impact of traveling on his marriage and especially on their sexual relationship: "We enjoy having sex. But when I'm in the middle of my seasons, which is half the year and I'm out on the road flying from one town to another, I come home just drained. And it takes me a few days to resume a normal life. And that's had a lot to do with the frequency of sex in our marriage. I think I may have disappointed her in this regard. She would have loved it more frequently."

An architect said, "I'm in our New York office for two months at a time several times a year. I am very lonely, and I don't like it. But my wife finds it even more difficult to deal with. She is very sensitive to being alone, and although she's wonderful with the children, she finds handling them by herself very taxing. When I get home, she's a wreck and I'm depleted."

As the couples in these companionate marriages attested, it's often impossible to satisfy the demands of two jobs, the needs of the chil-dren, and the couple's own needs. Sometimes children lose out, some-times the couple loses, and sometimes careers and the workplace are given a back seat. The pie is too small to meet everyone's needs.

Kit and Beth provided a poignant example of how a family is affected when parents put in extra hours on the job. Kit started teaching an extra course at night school to put some savings in the bank, which meant he was getting home after Sam's bedtime four nights a week. Not long afterward they called and asked my advice because Sam was despondent. He was uncommunicative at home and had started sucking his thumb at school and withdrawing from activities with the other children. More recently he had refused to go to school, which really alarmed them. What should they do?

I suggested that Kit sit down with Sam and show him a calendar with the ten-week academic quarter marked out. He should tell Sam that Daddy would be working very hard for those weeks, because the family needed money to send Martha to school and to buy Sam a bicycle for his next birthday, as promised. But after that he and Sam would go back to their routine. Kit would then be at home to put him to bed, read stories, and sing to him, as he always had.

Kit followed this advice, and when he talked to Sam he acknowledged his own sadness as well as Sam's. He asked if his son could wait out this period. Sam was enormously pleased and flattered to be taken into his father's confidence and relieved to know that his dad would be available again. Within days the symptoms dropped away. Sam announced brightly to several of his classmates that he and his daddy were going to be friends again very soon. He no longer interpreted Kit's work as a rejection of himself.

What long-term effect will companionate marriages have on children? We know very little at this juncture. Many of these children are much closer to their fathers than are children raised in other kinds of marriages. Kit, who was distant from his own father, said he was very happy with his role. But as Sam's distress showed, he had to live up to his children's greater needs and expectations. Many mothers, like Beth, believe they are offering a different and vastly improved role model to their daughters, the vision of a man and woman working as a team, sharing love, values, and a deep commitment to each other, to the family, and to their work.

What do the children lose under this arrangement? If the parents are under strain from workplace demands, they have less flexibility in responding to the children's needs. Full-time jobs cannot bend to the changing developmental needs of the individual child. Having a father more available is worth a great deal, but having a mother less available can be a grave loss to a child. If both parents are frenetic, life is no picnic for anyone. Many parents complain that they are running in place from dawn to dusk. They worry that the children are coming home to an empty house or to a changing cast of sitters and varying child-care arrangements. Because of the demands imposed by dual careers, children are expected to be independent at younger and younger ages. Some are able to achieve this and to thrive. But others need more individual attention and care, either when they are very young or at adolescence.

The parents in these happy companionate marriages were the first to admit that the new order often led to a tug of war between the needs of parents and those of children. One father said, "My wife is very busy in her career. She has no time for anything else, and I'm stretched to the limit. I'm doing most of the child care. We are together less, but it strengthens us. We both have such a passion for what we do. We both pay homage to what the other person is drawn to do. But I'm afraid the children are shortchanged. I worry all the time that our children are shortchanged."

One of many pressures in companionate marriage is the conflicting pull of two careers on the relationship. Unlike many of their peers, Kit and Beth did not have serious career conflicts. They were both in reasonably stable, middle-income jobs that did not threaten periodic geographic moves in the interests of promotion. But other couples, like my daughter and her husband, face serious career conflicts, which demand major adjustments in a marriage.

Husbands and wives who are both academics often find that getting two good tenure-track jobs in the same city is a pipe dream. One couple in the study adopted a drastic solution. The man gave up his academic career for another profession so that his wife could pursue her career. Obviously not every couple can or wants to do this.

Another couple faced the prospect of a commuter marriage in states five hundred miles apart. She had been offered the job of a lifetime, and he could not leave the business he had built from scratch. They would be together only on weekends. Both were dreading this move, worried about how it would affect their relationship and the children. They planned to stay in touch several times a day via electronic mail on their personal computers.

When both partners have highly competitive, demanding jobs, serious problems can arise, leading to emotional and sexual estrangement. One person may have to give way completely to the other, with the result that the ideal of equality breaks down for a time, and the changed relationship may have new tensions.

Even when couples have egalitarian ideals, a wife's successful career can pose a major threat if the husband's career does not match hers in status and income. Among the couples I studied, the only serious infidelity occurred in the context of a husband's anger at and jealousy of his wife's career. The husband, a labor mediator, spoke honestly to me about it. "Her interest in her work, combined with the fact that I was feeling bored and unhappy with mine, finally got us to a high-noon shootout. I had the sense that this goddamned job of hers was of primary importance and I was of secondary importance. That's the kind of thing that can make you wake up in the morning and think about it and go to bed and think about it. It drives you insane."

The husband experimented with several one-night stands. "It was more often the hunt," he said, "not the actual deed. I would go to a strange city on a matter of work, see friends, schmooze, meet women, and take them to bed. Sometimes I put my clothes on and went back to my hotel without even making love to them. I was embarrassed and felt that I was leading them on and being selfish in leaving, but I basically was not interested in them. You see," he said earnestly, "my wanting to fool around was really about my wanting her to pay more attention to me."

He continued, "After several months of my screwing around, she found out. It was a huge blowup. And then one day a light bulb went off in my head. I can sit here calmly and tell you, but at that moment it was exhilarating. I raced around to find her. I'll never forget. It was a realization of how much I needed her. I told her this standing on the street, and she thought I was crazy. I remember feeling good and happy and hugging her and going back to work. I guess I really discovered she was part of me and that I might be losing that. I was overwhelmed and realized that I needed her desperately. I still don't like her job. I don't hate it — I even get some pleasure from it. She works in an interesting, neat place, but I wish it would go away. When she has to travel on business I moan and groan. I know I'm being selfish, but her trips are painful."

This man was saying eloquently that he loved his wife, he didn't dispute her right to have a job, but he nevertheless resented the fact that her career took priority over his needs, especially when she traveled. He found it very difficult that her job was more interesting to her than his job was to him. But because he loved her, he would try to accept her commitment to her career as an ongoing strain in the marriage.

I asked the wife how she and her husband had worked out the conflict. "I wasn't going to leave my job," she said. "I don't think that would solve the problem, because it continues to be a good job for me. He resents my working, but on the other hand I think he wants me to work. We became more aware of each other's needs and how to deal with them. He's a much more temperamental person than I am. I'm more easygoing. If we had both been temperamental, it would not have worked out. We would have flown off in different directions. I spent a lot of time trying to make things work, but I was not going to give in and leave my job. I was more aware of his needs, and I was more sensitive. I tried to be more a part of his life.

"But I was also aware that as we drew apart, something was missing. Our blowup made us closer. It surprised him to realize he needed me so much, so for him it was a big change." She paused and added ominously and with great honesty, "I think you can go through something like this once but not twice."

These are some of the irreconcilable conflicts in a companionate marriage. Although the issues won't go away, people can address them by identifying with each other and building compensatory pleasures into the marriage. They can be frank in discussing how jealous one feels about the perks of the other's job or how lonely one feels when the other is traveling all the time. Most of all, they have to pay close attention to each other's needs and frustrations. Of all of the types of marriage, the companionate form requires constant vigilance.

One woman told me that her husband, a scientist, had gone on some overseas trips that were very important for him but stressful for her. "We just had a long talk about it," she said, "and I asked him to cut back. It's helpful, I know, for his job, and it's a wonderful perk. But going to China and Japan is an option, and I can't go with him because my job won't permit me to leave for two weeks. And somebody has to take care of the children. The expenses are high, and the lab will pay only for him.

"What's more, before he goes, there's a lot of hectic stuff as he gets his scientific papers ready for presentation, and when he comes home his desk is full of work and he has to put in long hours just to catch up. So it's not only the trip, it's the before and after. I've told him I'm jealous. I'd like to be in a job that involves the international community. I feel trapped in feeling that I can't be part of that. And he then said he could forgo the trips. He said he understands how I feel and it was better that I had told him."

She didn't whimper, "Poor little me, stuck at home with a job and the kiddies." She said openly, "I'm jealous. This isn't fair." And he said, "It's better that you told me," and he cut back on the trips. The episode captures the way issues of equality are dealt with in these marriages. She was not afraid to speak up and make demands on the relationship because she expected that he would listen — and indeed he did.

As I examined these companionate couples, I grew worried about the implications for the future of modern marriage. I worried also about how poorly we prepare our children for the complexities of adult life. It is all very well to have "take your daughter or son to work day" — and surely we *should* prepare our children to take their rightful places at work. But what about their rightful places as partners in marriage and as parents? We do our children no favors if we withhold from them an understanding of the difficulties as well as the rewards of combining work, marriage, and family. Doubtless growing up in a companionate marriage enables a child to observe the complex maneuvering that is required. But she may see only the difficulties; the rewards may be invisible. Moreover, the child may be more aware of her own reactions than of the subtle nuances of the adult experience.

In examining the effect of the workplace on companionate marriages, I've become increasingly uneasy about the way in which our competitive culture thinks about marriage and how little it does to protect working couples. The prevailing value system is a recipe for misery. If the boss calls, the working husband or wife is expected to jump to attention and put the family in second place. If the baby cries, the husband or wife must be the devoted parent — putting the marriage in last place. Buffeted by a never-ending stream of such demands, a couple finds their frustrations and deprivations mounting. They never have enough time to spend on themselves, on the marriage, on mutual nurturance. If a marriage is given priority only rarely, it is in danger.

Sadly, the workplace is a major source of stress for modern marriage, and the two institutions may well be on a collision course. Despite the many advances made by women in recent decades, the world of work is still dominated by the view that an employee's first loyalty must be to the job. If circumstances call for working late hours or on the weekend, too bad for the family; the company can't worry about it. This arrangement may work in traditional marriages, where one spouse works full-time and the other stays home to raise the children. But this is not the choice of millions of men and women today who have opted for two careers and companionate marriage. They have chosen to live by values that are in direct conflict with those of modern corporate America.

It is not within the scope of this book to explore how to cope with this clash of cultures. Policymakers are suggesting many solutions, such as extended family leave, quality child care, and flextime. But most of these suggestions are designed to protect children — not the marriage — by making parents more available during the preschool years. While employers may argue that it is not their responsibility to protect marriage, the expectation that a worker will be available sixty or more hours a week is a key part of the wider social problem.

For people like Beth and Kit, who come together with a high moral commitment, the companionate marriage can be powerful enough to withstand the forces tearing at it from the outside. But for couples who are less committed to idealism, who are less self-confident and less imaginative, this form of marriage can be frighteningly fragile.

On the other hand I feel strongly that women and men should be free to pursue their interests and develop their talents fully in the workplace. The pleasures of a satisfying career and the self-esteem that results from making an important contribution to the community should not exclude the joys of motherhood or the satisfactions of a good marriage. Working parents are here to stay. The question is, are we wise enough to help couples protect their marriages so that work and family can operate in harmony?

What emerges very clearly is that companionate marriage needs to be stronger and closer at its core to withstand the powerful external forces that can tear a couple apart. Companionate marriage requires heroic effort and extraordinary energy, the ability to take a lot of pressure without falling apart and the capacity to maintain inner balance and a sense of purpose. Mostly it requires a firm commitment to the marriage. Building togetherness based on real intimacy is the critical task in companionate marriage, and as the couples in this study show, it can be done.

# 17 ⅋

# The Seventh Task

*Sharing Laughter and Keeping Interests Alive*

Lthough raising a family and making a living are serious pursuits, marriage has an equally serious purpose in providing an arena for play, humor, and lively interests. Just as a sexual relationship can become stale and lose its spontaneity and passion, so too can a marriage become frozen into a dull repetition of daily routines. The nemesis of a good marriage is monotony unrelieved by imagination.

Not long after I began this study, my husband and I had dinner with Joan Erikson, the wife of psychoanalyst Erik Erikson and a scholar in her own right. The Eriksons had been happily married for sixty years, and I wanted to ask Joan for advice. This is a couple that radiated mutual love and respect whenever they were in each other's company. Their many friends admired and sometimes envied their marriage.

After describing my research, I asked Joan what she thought was the most important ingredient for a happy marriage. This ninety-year-old woman sat tall and straight, dressed fashionably in regal purple. "Well that's easy," she said without hesitation. "A sense of humor. Without humor, what have you got? Humor is what keeps everything in balance!"

Over and over again, the couples in these happy marriages said that shared laughter was one of the most important bonds between them. Many used the word "funny" to describe a spouse. But by humor and "funny" these couples meant something deeper than the latest jokes making the rounds. They were referring to an intimate way of relating to each other, a low-key, spontaneous bantering that kept them connected.

"She's smart, nice, and funny." "He's a delight to me, and he sees things with a different eye. What drew me to him in the first place was his humor. He's really funny and makes me laugh, after thirty years of marriage." "She has spontaneity and a special kind of whimsy." "He adds spice to my life." "She makes me laugh. She has a great sense of humor."

Even a woman who had divorced her husband after many years of unhappiness confessed, "What kept me with him for all those years was his incredible sense of humor. He's a very funny man, and I loved his puns." She added, still in awe, "He could pun in three languages."

The task of using humor and laughter to replenish the relationship lasts a lifetime. This is not something reserved for vacations and anniversaries; it is part of everyday life. A healthy, plesurable tension between husband and wife provides a zing that keeps the marriage alive and exciting.

When I arrived at James McGrady's house, he had just woken up. He apologized for oversleeping. As we sat in the kitchen waiting for the coffee to finish dripping, his wife walked in.

"I see you didn't remember your appointment this morning," she said in mild reproach.

"And you didn't remind me," he said, smiling. "After all, you are responsible for everything I do." He looked at her and then at me. "That's why men marry women."

"Being in this study has gone straight to his head," she said, turning to me in mock exasperation. "Now he fancies himself an expert on marriage!"

Later, when his teenage son came into the kitchen, he continued in the same playful vein. "Son, you will have to leave us alone. This lady is doing a study of delinquent children."

As I began to think about the role of humor in marriage, I reflected on how my husband and I interact. In our careers and interests we are serious people, yet as I recorded our informal conversations over several days, I found that we engaged in a lot of light bantering. When he comes home from work each day, he is likely to tell me about some paradox, something out of his usual routine, something that piqued his curiosity or annoyed him or, very often, something he thought was very funny. His wish is to amuse me. And we tease each other, sometimes flirtatiously. This kind of interaction has been a lively and important part of our daily life together for more than forty-five years. It is the dead opposite of taking someone for granted.

In many of the couples I talked to, lightness, fun, and playful teasing were a treasured aspect of the relationship. Bantering brightens the day, hinting at a private world with a secret language and a shared sense of fun. Sometimes word play has sexual, erotic overtones, but more often a couple's banter pokes fun at the ups and downs of everyday life, including everyday marriage. Laughter is worth cultivating.

I have come to believe that teasing, flirtation, and laughter, which always carry a hint of insecurity — not so much as to create anxiety but enough to banish tedium — are an important part of a satisfying relationship. A good marriage is not a business partnership, although it surely includes some of the same elements. Nor is a good marriage a form of friendship, although husbands and wives need each other as close friends. Nor is it just a support system for times of adversity. The distinctiveness of a good and happy marriage lies in its electricity, in its power to light up the participants and enhance the excitement and pleasure of their lives.

Humor, of course, has serious uses. Few strategies are more useful in defusing anger or tension or restoring a wounded ego. And there is no better tool for putting the little annoyances of life in their place. As every married person knows, petty irritations often cause disproportionate hurt and anger. How could you have lost twenty dollars? Where did you hide the car keys? Why didn't you return the library books when they were due? Or, in a more serious vein, how could you have insulted me in front of my coworkers, my children, the neighbors? Dealing with these situations with humor can cushion the inevitable frustrations of daily life and restore a true perspective. Laughter counteracts frustration by providing immediate pleasure, restoring the connectedness that is threatened by exasperation and self-righteous anger.

This is what Joan Erikson meant when she said that a sense of humor is needed to maintain balance in a marriage. Tactful, nonjudgmental, gentle humor can indeed keep a marriage on track.

But humor is only one aspect of the task. The other is keeping interest high. Many happily married people say that boredom is their greatest enemy. A marriage that has gone stale, in which the partners pass each other like ships in the night, hardly seems worth the effort. How did the couples in the study avoid boredom?

They genuinely found each other interesting. A radiologist said of his wife, who worked in city planning, "I much prefer listening to her tell about her world over mine. I sit looking at slides, and she is involved actively with people and whole neighborhoods. I find it fascinating and follow it daily. I know all the people she works with as if I had met them."

"We're both strong-willed," said one man. "If we only had one car, we would wrestle each other to the ground about who should drive. But we've never been bored with each other. There's never been a dull moment around here. I promised her an interesting life, and I've delivered on the promise."

These couples enjoyed the time they spent together; they did not live silently side by side. In the joint interviews I was impressed by the way they listened to each other's responses. If they felt that their partner was going to say something predictable, they did not betray it. On the contrary, I often sensed that they expected to hear new and interesting views.

"It's the day-to-day of the marriage that is happy," said a woman who ran a printing business. "I look forward to having breakfast with him. We have a lot to say to each other. Sometimes I need to make lists to make sure that I get to all the things I want to talk about. It makes me happy to spend time with him. I enjoy him. We laugh a lot and draw the kids into it."

These couples had the imagination to recognize that marriage consists not only of externals — where we live, what we have, whether or not we can refrain from fighting — but of the important extra dimensions of imagination and symbolism. They imbued their daily activities with meaning beyond the immediate present. Thus the children were enjoyed as individuals and also as the fulfillment of a shared vision. Home provided both real and symbolic pleasures. They appreciated the present satisfactions of their marriage and understood that it represented the fulfillment of a lifelong wish for a loving companion in adult life.

The men and women in these happy marriages were remarkably open to the idea of ongoing change. They anticipated change in themselves, in their children, in their relationships, in their marriage, and in the world around them. They were flexible and readily adopted new ideas. Knowing that they would not remain forever young and in good health, they kept their eye on what lay ahead, preparing for major milestones in advance. Their belief in change allowed them to seek out separate interests and to alter their course at critical points by beginning a new career or going back to school at midlife, for example.

One reason these couples were open to change, I believe, is that they wanted to create marriages different from those of their parents' generation. They were courageously reaching out for new models, as we saw in Kit and Beth's companionate marriage and in Keith and Helen's rescue marriage. Their adventurousness added enormously to the liveliness of their relationship and to a quickening at its core. All the couples in the study seemed well adapted to today's rapidly shifting social milieu.

Being part of this study meant an investment of many hours of precious time. But these couples were intrigued by the idea and decided to be a part of it. In follow-up interviews I found that many couples had continued to talk about the issues we discussed and had come away with new ideas for improving their relationship. Several made important changes in their lives. One man, who had abandoned his religion when he reached adulthood, decided to seek out a church where he could renew his spiritual ties. He attributed this turnaround to his conversations with me, in which he had recalled the religious experiences of his childhood. A woman decided to take a ten-thousand-mile journey to her mother's grave after discovering a deep sadness in the course of our discussions and realizing how much she had repressed her early history. She reported that this momentous visit had altered her life, especially her relationship with her children.

Finally, the people in these happy marriages were engaged in worlds outside the family. They pursued professional and personal activities individually and together. A good number enjoyed the out-of-doors, hiking and camping as a couple and as a family. Some were involved in politics, others in the arts. A few belonged to religious organizations. None led entirely isolated lives. In my experience, couples who divorce tend to lead more isolated lives and to have fewer friends and community contacts. In some cases one person remains engaged in the world while the other shuts down, and the marriage suffers. It takes two to carry on a conversation, and both must be open to ideas.

Couples in companionate marriages, where husband and wife straddle two worlds, may find it easiest to avoid boredom. Kit's and

Beth's lives are enhanced by their access to each other's professional world and by their shared political values.

In most cases the couples enjoyed some activities together and others separately. There was encouragement and sometimes pressure to share the same hobbies or interests, but they did not believe that marriage conferred the right to impose one's own taste or values on the other. One man said, "We've always honored each other's freedom to pursue the activities we each enjoy. Marriage is not a straitjacket." In several couples only one partner belonged to a church. Recreational travel was usually shared, but some couples vacationed separately on occasion. The women tended to have more friends and to spend time with them while their husbands stayed home.

Their mutual and separate interests contributed nicely to the ongoing conversation. A man in his late thirties put it well: "We enjoy talking to each other. Sometimes we sit on the bed and talk together for hours. It might be about family or friends or gossip. Or we might talk about a movie we've seen. And we talk a lot about politics. The war in the Middle East really troubled us."

He leaned forward. "We have a lot of interests and we love to talk about them. She's getting a Ph.D. in psychology, and I find that very stimulating. I'm in marketing for a big corporation, and I'm a little jealous about the books she gets to bring home and read. But there are aspects of my job that I like to tell her about, like solving problems. Other interests we do not share. She's crazy about opera, which we can't afford, but she goes because it's important to her, while I baby-sit. I'm crazy about baseball, which is certainly not her thing. We both love music. Every now and then we do something we really can't afford, just for the adventure of it."

Often activities within the marriage itself can provide the nourishment. One man described his great contentment at coming home nightly and spending the evening with his wife in the kitchen, helping her cook and enjoying the serenity and warmth of the relationship.

A woman described a courtship so pleasantly uneventful that her friends thought she was crazy. "I would come up to his place after driving fifty miles. We would have sex and then we would spend quiet evenings together. We both like to read mysteries. I would lie on one couch and he on another, and we would open a bottle of wine and spend a quiet weekend. We still love that."

Typically a marriage goes through cycles of quickening and slowing down. But the quickening of interest and excitement is always partly under the control of the partners. They know each other well and understand better than anyone else what excites and what diminishes the other's interest. Tending this aspect of the relationship is a very important and seldom acknowledged task of marriage.

# PART FIVE

# Traditional Marriage

# 18

# Nicholas Easterbrook

WHEN I WAS GROWING UP, my friends and I, no matter how talented we were or where our interests lay, all knew that the real goal of college — the real core curriculum — was to find the right man to marry. This powerful, unspoken agenda influenced men and, especially, women in all walks of life. Although some swam against the tide, they didn't pretend it wasn't there. We knew that in choosing a man we were choosing a life. There would be no easy second chance if we failed to pick wisely, so we gave it everything we had. Naturally we expected to fall in love, but there was no harm in linking love to other agendas.

The kind of marriage we all expected to have was a traditional one, in which husband and wife have different roles and responsibilities, separate spheres of operation. Although the spheres overlap, they constitute distinct psychological and social realms. In the idealized form of the older model of traditional marriage, the man's primary job and self-definition is to provide for the economic well-being, protection, and stability of his family. The woman's job and selfdefinition is to care for her husband and children and to create a comfortable home that nourishes everyone, particularly her husband, who comes home each evening drained by the demands of his job. The home that the woman creates and the man supports is the haven where the children are raised. Motherhood is regarded as a full-time job when the children are young. Furthermore, home is where standards are maintained; well-ordered, ethical behavior is expected, and moral principles are a guiding force — in sharp contrast to the often cutthroat, unpredictable world outside. Making and protecting the home is the primary shared commitment of every traditional marriage.

Today's men and women have many more choices in the intimate relationships they create, as the section on companionate marriage attests. However, I found that traditional marriage was alive and well among young adults and in second marriages. Although its place in society has been transformed by the social and economic changes and by the sexual politics of the last two decades, traditional marriage offers many advantages, and people have not rejected it out of hand. But those who choose it may find themselves bucking a powerful tide of opinion, which states that women who stay at home in traditional roles are trying to turn back the clock. When a woman forgoes the economic security of a career, the argument goes, she puts herself and her children in jeopardy; if the marriage fails, she probably will not be able to reenter the work force at a high enough level to support herself and the children. Moreover, by not participating in the marketplace, women in modern traditional marriages seem to threaten the social equality and economic opportunities that so many of their sisters and mothers fought hard to achieve.

Nevertheless, for many men and women in my generation and also for younger couples, traditional marriage has brought deep satisfaction. A significant number of the couples in this study chose traditional marriages. That group included all of those who married during the 1950s and early 1960s and 25 percent of those who married in the 1970s and early 1980s.

Traditional marriage has changed in recent decades; the most important innovation is the division of adult life, especially for women, into several chapters. Couples who choose this form of marriage today still regard the raising of children as their first priority. They firmly believe that a full-time or nearly full-time mother is important to children's healthy development and that the loss of a second income is worth the trade-off. The women in this study who chose traditional marriages in the 1970s and 1980s deferred their careers to be at home when the children were growing up. But many kept a hand in by doing some part-time work while their children were small. When the children were older, the mothers planned to go back to work. In the new traditional family, motherhood is regarded as one chapter; marriage is no longer a codex in which each character plays a fixed role from wedding to fiftieth anniversary.

The older couples in the study, those who married in the 1950s and early 1960s, were also affected by societal change. Although the women began their married lives expecting to stay at home throughout the marriage, most were later influenced by the women's movement and changing mores. Many of them entered the work force at midlife, after their children were grown.

Many men are drawn to the traditional form of marriage. Often they have never considered any other possibility; this is simply what marriage is. Some, who are on fast-track careers in business or science, want the wholehearted support of a wife who raises the children and creates a comfortable home. Others are less driven by the need to succeed in the workplace, but they prefer the quality of life in a traditional marriage, convinced that it has immense advantages for husband and wife and especially for the children.

What do these men expect to receive, and what do they expect to give in return? The traditional man marries for love and to have a family. He wants his wife to be content. He assumes that she enjoys raising children and brings a special sensitivity to this task. Sexual passion is welcome but not central. His wife may not be a perfect housekeeper or parent or lover, but he expects her to do her best in all these realms. He does not want her to serve him like a prince or adore him like a lord; what she gives, and what he wants, is her care and tenderness, her respect and admiration for his efforts as husband, father, and breadwinner.

In return, the man in a traditional marriage provides all or most of the family's economic support, especially when the children are young. He regards breadwinning as his enduring responsibility, whatever the fluctuations and stresses of the job market. He expects that his work will take priority in terms of where the family lives and in many of the daily decisions that affect parents and children. He takes care of his wife and children during emergencies, sickness, and other times of need. He may not have a lot of time to help raise the children, but he does plan to be a major presence in their lives. Being a father is an important part of his manhood.

These are the values that draw men into traditional marriages. Being human, they do not always succeed at living up to their goals. For those who do succeed, the rewards are high.

In later chapters I discuss the issues that confront younger couples in traditional marriage. Here I have chosen an older couple with whom to explore the nature and inner core of traditional marriage. Not only is this form more common among older couples, but it presents specific challenges at later stages in life.

Thus I was drawn to Maureen Easterbrook, who was one of the first people to volunteer for this study. A traditional homemaker, she is also a grower of extraordinary orchids and other exotic plants. Although I did not know Maureen well, I had long admired her warmth and gentle manner, and I was very pleased when she called me.

As it turned out, I first interviewed her husband, Nicholas, age fifty-five, the founder and chief executive officer of a large biotechnology company in the Bay Area. He was well known in the community as a successful businessman whose company did important scientific research. When I stepped into the lobby of his corporate building, I was struck by the display of Chinese art, a collection of extraordinary breadth and beauty. From a Han Dynasty figurine to a Mao-era tapestry, the evidence of a discerning eye was everywhere. I wondered whether Nicholas or Maureen was responsible for the decor.

Nicholas graciously ushered me into his private office. A huge window faced San Francisco Bay, where a flotilla of boats with full spinnakers sailed before a gentle wind. My eye was immediately caught by the ancient Chinese scrolls on the walls. Nicholas, noting my interest, explained them to me in detail. He also complimented his wife for playing a critical role in developing his artistic sensibility.

Having a successful career is no guarantee that a person is a successful spouse, and I was curious to find out how Nicholas had been able to combine an obviously high-pressure job with a good marriage. But before I could ask my first question, he began to interview me instead. Where did I go to school? With whom did I train? Where did I learn to work with children? What was the purpose of this study? Why was I interested in his marriage? His questions were discriminating and intelligent, but I was aware that I was being carefully scrutinized.

It was only after I had passed this test that he agreed to participate in the study and allowed me to take the lead. He had succeeded in placing both of us in our traditional roles — he, the man, in gracious command and I, the woman, in willing acquiescence. It was for both of us a familiar dance; I was amused by it but not put off. I read his attitude not as arrogance but as his perception of our respective roles. Even though Nicholas was used to being in command, we did establish a good rapport as equals. Propelled at first by intellectual curiosity, he became emotionally engaged in our discussion and confided in me.

In response to my opening question, "What is good about this marriage?" Nicholas began, "We comfort each other. We have shared and continue to share a great many interests. I have a tremendous amount of respect for Maureen as a wife and as a mother. She's a very charming woman." He looked at the silver-framed photo of his wife and four daughters perched on the corner of his immaculate desk. "I very much appreciate the fact that she's independent and that her life does not fully depend on mine. She's a kind, caring, generous person. She's more generous than I am. She is given to charity and to good works in the abstract, which I am not. That part of her balances the more pragmatic, the more practical, the more realistic me." He smiled. "I enjoy being with her. I enjoy being with my family."

Sara and Matt, in their earliest comments, had spoken of passion and sex; Helen and Keith had emphasized saving each other from the abyss and from solitude; Beth and Kit had focused on partnership and sharing. Nicholas, on the other hand, spoke of comforting. I asked him if comforting was central to his marriage.

"Yes. We take care of each other. I need all the things that she does. Home is her place. It's entirely Maureen's making. She has created a safe place, safe from all the bullshit out there. She is safe, and our home is a great comfort."

Nicholas then told me about his grueling work schedule, with long business trips and late nights at the office. I said it sounded bruising and exhausting, and he responded, "Yes. But when I come home, I never, never bring my work with me. It's important that you understand that my marriage has always been separate from my work. I've kept it that way."

"How do you manage to leave all your work at the office? That's not easy."

"I discipline myself. I direct myself. I park my work at the front door." He began to reflect on the past. "When the children were young, I loved them but spent little time with them. It's a pity, because I always wanted a family, and it was sad for me that when they were small I was away so much of the time, getting my career under way. My wife was the buffer, and she took the responsibility for raising them. I'm not the kind of man who does things in the house. I figure my responsibility is supporting the household, and I do that, and I've always done that well. Money has never been an issue for us. But I try to protect my life with the family. I work long hours, but home is home. And I try whenever possible to be home for the weekends."

"How late do you get home?" I asked.

"At eight-thirty or nine. She often waits for me, and we have a late dinner together. Since I started this company, I've been on the road more and more, and often I don't get back into town until after midnight."

Nicholas was describing some assumptions underlying traditional marriage, namely that in the world of work the man acts in accord with its rules and his status there; the world of home is created by the couple but run by the woman. A home that works well for the breadwinner is one where the intense needs and anxieties generated at work can be let go. He spoke of his great relief in feeling safe at home, in the safe space created by his wife. Like the giant Anteus in Greek mythology, who regained his strength each time he touched Mother Earth, Nicholas drew sustenance from his home and his family. Home presumably offset the danger he experienced "out there." Of course, a home can serve as refuge only when the boundaries between the two worlds are carefully maintained. Nicholas understood that and had learned to leave his work concerns at the office.

"Has work been this hard throughout your married life?"

"Unfortunately, yes," he said. "I wish I had known early on what I know now. I had a strange model of family life in my parents. Both of my parents worked. My father was a nuclear physicist at Los Alamos and was completely incapable of separating work from home. There was for him no world separate from his work. He spent most of his time in his lab, trying to come up with ingenious equations that would put him on a par with Niels Bohr or Richard Feynman." Nicholas sighed. "I think you could say that I've rejected a lot of what I was brought up with. I wanted out of that kind of life. I tried not to work seven days a week and to protect my home. I like being on a different track. It was a conscious decision to be different."

He gazed at the sailboats out in the bay. "Of course, it didn't start out this way. When I was a student at Caltech and later an assistant professor at Stanford, we had very little money. The first year we were married, we lived on thirteen hundred dollars a year. But then I began to move up. And eventually I struck out on my own outside of academia. We've never been spendthrifts. Actually, by the standards of what's out there, we are pretty frugal, but now we travel first class and enjoy fine wines, and we love our home. But we started off with very little and climbed the ladder. Everything we have, we built together. No one gave us a dime."

"Was your father proud?"

"My father," said Nicholas, with anger close to the surface but well contained, "has been dead for five years. But he made goddamned sure that I would be on the fast track in a scientific career. You see, my father was an unrelenting tyrant. He was never very successful. But he thought he was brilliant." His tone was derisive. "Let me tell you about the kind of man my father was. When I was seventeen, I was a finalist in the Westinghouse science competition. I remember getting the phone call that I was a winner. I ran into Dad's lab with part of my experiment under my arm to tell him and show him what I had done. I laid out the chemical reagents on the table and began to demonstrate the steps in my experiment when he said, 'Okay, hotshot.' Then he swept out his arm, broke three of the vials, and said, 'Go ahead. You're such a hotshot. Let's see you fix it.'"

I was stunned by the father's cruelty to this sensitive, gifted youngster and by the hostile competitiveness in the relationship. "Was that kind of taunting typical?"

"Yes, typical. My father couldn't stand that anybody else would do anything important. He did it all. But he made sure that I would spend my life trying to get to the top. My mother every now and then stood up to him, but she always lost. My mother was a kind and gentle woman who worked full-time in the lab and came home exhausted to take care of everything at home. We never did anything together as a family. My parents' whole marriage was played out where they worked. My father was an attractive man, a bright man, but he drove us without mercy."

Nicholas looked uneasy, but he was obviously a man of courage and did not hold back about his troubling personal history. "You have to understand that my father has been the main adversary of my life. But the only issues I've ever cried about have to do with my father. I cried with my father's illness. I cried with my father's death. My whole life has been organized to deal with my father. But it was my mother who taught me right and wrong."

Nicholas ascribed his own fierce competitiveness to his relationship with his father — a hated, loved, and admired figure who represented the central conflict of the son's life. His mother, although powerless in his upbringing, taught him how to be moral. I thought that his description of his wife as comforting, kind, and gentle may well have drawn on his image of his mother, whom he described similarly. Work was the central passion of Nicholas's life — in the fast lane, where his father drove him. The devils he competed with, fought, and conquered all lived in the workplace. He returned home every night like a warrior from the battlefield to have his wounds salved and bound for the next day's battle.

He continued, "I don't know whether you know anything about science, but it's not the ivory tower it's made out to be. It's cutthroat and competitive. People steal ideas and take credit for work they didn't do. I had to be as good as the men I worked with, the profs at Caltech, who are among the brightest in the world, and it would have been easy for me to fail. But I was driven to succeed. I discovered early on that I had a talent for molecular biology and that I could fight my way in the world. I became a really good bench scientist and developed some early cloning techniques that are still used in labs all over the world."

"But," he said, in a changed tone, "I think you might say that with my spending so much of my time and commitment in the lab, there were years that were difficult and lonely for my wife. I have to admit that I wasn't there for her and that because I was away so much our life suffered, including our sex life. I had to put my work first, my marriage and family second. I really had no choice. When I trained in science, all my colleagues worked in the lab seven days a week, often past midnight. We were expected to give everything to our research. The top people in the lab had families but you'd never know it from how much time they spent at work.

"And it was no different when I went into business. To build something like this" — he swept his arm toward the room — "you have to fight and fight and fight. You can't have a successful career and build a biotech company by working nine to five, or even eight to eight."

Nicholas's story was familiar to me. My husband and two of my children are in academia; I've watched them and their friends and colleagues struggle with the conflict between work and family. In many professions, including academic medicine, law, and science, an ambitious person is expected to put work first. If you slip backward for six months, you may never be able to catch up. In these fields the competition is constant, and those who make it to the top make enormous sacrifices.

"Let me tell you about an episode in my life that will help you understand our marriage," Nicholas said. "When I was in my late thirties, I woke up one morning very early. My heart was racing. I was in a cold sweat and felt as if I couldn't breathe. I woke Maureen, and she got the doctor immediately. They hospitalized me, suspecting a heart attack, but the tests showed no heart involvement. They called it an acute anxiety attack. It felt, of course, like a blow from on high. It came at a particular time in my life. My father had wanted me to stay in an academic career, but I had decided, over his strong objections, to venture out on my own and start this company. The panic never returned, but I took it as a message. I went into therapy and learned pretty damned fast that the break with my dad was at the bottom of my panic. Although I was almost forty, he still held me in thrall. It was like his fist was in my gut.

"I'm sure that during that time Maureen felt very frightened and alone. I was very careful to explain to her that my attack was entirely unconnected to my relationship with her."

"And she believed you?"

"She has always believed me. During that entire frightening time, she was wonderful. She was calm, sympathetic, reassuring, but never intrusive and certainly never hysterical. Whatever she suffered — and I'm sure she did, we both did — she protected me. She gave me the support and the space that I needed. She acted as if she never doubted that I would work it out, as I had worked things out before when they got tough. And I did, and went on to carry out my original plan."

The way Nicholas and Maureen handled his severe panic attack, a serious symptom that certainly could have derailed his career, if not his entire life, illuminates the central dynamics of the marriage. In the remarkable minuet of their relationship, they contained the threat. He got a diagnosis and immediately sought competent therapy. Acting with calm compassion, she took him to the hospital, then brought him back and left him in control, which is what he needed in order to recover. She carefully refrained from adding to his burdens by not giving in to her own distress, which must have been very great.

Judged by the psychological fashions of today, when people expect a quick fix by expressing their feelings and demanding access to each other's inner life, Nicholas and Maureen handled the crisis in a very different, reserved way, maintaining the boundaries between them. They treated each other as civilized adults who would meet emergencies, solve problems, and seek appropriate expert counsel when needed, but would not allow themselves to regress or to lean too heavily on the other. Maureen's ability to steer clear of his struggle with his inner demons was a sophisticated achievement. She maintained stability, continuity, and order in the life of the family.

An important aspect of their marriage was Nicholas's concern for and protection of Maureen. He expected her to support him emotionally, but at the height of his crisis he thought to protect her and to limit her distress. As Maureen later told me, in the marriage he was a more tender, humane, and moral person than he was at work. Even during a difficult time he was considerate of his wife. It's fair to say that without a good marriage, he would be a much more hard-edged man and more driven by demons.

I asked Nicholas, "How did you choose Maureen?" I generally asked people how they met their spouse, but with Nicholas the word "choose" seemed apt.

He laughed. "I was lucky. I was in grad school at Caltech, and she was entering her sophomore year at USC. We met at a party in Pasadena."

"What was it about her that attracted you?"

"She was pretty. She was intelligent. She was gentle and generous with her friends and family. She wasn't easy to get — she had a lot of admirers. That was pretty important to me, as you can probably figure out by now." He added, "She was interested in a world of beauty I knew nothing about — art, flowers, and nature. My world was so dark . . ." He looked around the room with its beautiful art and furnishings. "I loved her hands and the way she touched things. She has a way of soothing."

I asked him to tell me about the early years of their marriage.

"We got married young because that's what you did in those days. She was twenty and I was twenty-three. We got an apartment in Sierra Madre, and I went to school. Everybody was young. Everybody had nothing. There was a large group around us, a mutual community of interests. It was a wonderful equilibrium. It was intellectual and exciting. I look back on it with nostalgia. And then, shortly after that, the children started. The babies took all of Maureen's time, and our paths became increasingly divided into home and career.

"Also I started to travel soon after the babies were born. This was hard on both of us. But whenever things got really out of balance, she'd tell me. She wouldn't have to yell or anything. That wasn't her style. She'd just tell me, and I would realize it was my problem. It was always my problem. It was never her problem. And I tried. I found out she felt reassured if I phoned from wherever I was. And I phoned every night."

Later in the interview I asked Nicholas what place sex had in the relationship.

"It started off disappointing," he said. "I would have liked a freer, less inhibited, better physical relationship. Something more experimental. I guess my wife was very much influenced in her upbringing by her mother, who was a religious Christian woman. Maureen has always been inhibited, and sex was hard for her to enjoy in the very beginning. But it's gotten better. She's come to enjoy it more. We had more sex when the children were young and less when they were adolescents. And it's better now when we go traveling and there's more time. We have sex about two times a week, except for a year when we had some problems. It was a serious problem that occurred when our youngest daughter became a teenager. Thank God the episode is completely over. I think she should tell you about it."

Nicholas talked at some length about his daughters, whom he got to know better when they were older. His relationship with them as adolescents and young adults was gratifying for him. He spoke of his oldest daughter's interest in science and his hope that she might follow in his footsteps. She had done some interesting work in biochemistry, and he hoped that she would make a real contribution. Another daughter had a good head for business, and he shook his head ruefully, saying that she would soon outstrip him. He described the concern he and Maureen had shared about one daughter, who had been in an earthquake when she was in Mexico; she had been badly traumatized by seeing several dead children who had been trapped in a fallen building. She had undergone treatment, but it had taken her several years to recover. "She's our sensitive one," he said. "And she pays the price that goes with it."

He also talked about how Maureen loved being a mother and how close she and the girls had been when they were growing up. He admitted wistfully that he wished he had been closer to them at that time. "This is one of the penalties of my career, but as adults, I see them a lot more." He remembered coming home from work late and going in to kiss them good night, often when they had already fallen asleep. "But there was great joy in seeing them peaceful and protected. At least I was able to give them all that I never had as a child."

He added, tellingly, "I would have liked a son, but it's probably lucky we didn't have one. I'm not sure I could have been a good father to a son. Or maybe I would have bent over the other way. It's easier for me to love my daughters, to encourage them but not to drive them."

# 19 ❧

# Maureen Easterbrook

H AVING MET NICHOLAS, I wondered what the marriage would look like from Maureen's perspective. What satisfactions would she describe, and how would they mesh with what her husband had told me?

Maureen greeted me at the front door of her spacious home, set back from the road. Like Nicholas's office, the entryway and living room were decorated with exquisite Asian antiques. The decor was not only beautiful, it set a tone of tranquil orderliness, like the floating world of Japanese art. The colors and textures combined to create a serenity Nicholas must have appreciated when he came home from the biotech battlefront.

As Maureen served me a cup of good coffee in a quiet, plant-filled patio, I had the sense of having entered a safe haven. But it was not overly formal. Maureen was dressed in jeans, a canvas shirt, and a gardening hat. She'd been working in the garden and had a touch of sunburn on her nose. I looked at her closely. She was not a beautiful woman, but her clear blue eyes, cropped brown hair, and tall frame were pleasing. She spoke softly.

When I asked her what was happy about her marriage, she plunged right in. "We enjoy each other's company. That continues to add to the marriage. He is generous, kind, and caring, as a husband and as a father. We have four wonderful daughters who give us a lot of joy."

She laughed, as if recalling some incident. "He has a great sense of humor. He always sees the funny side of things. We laugh together, and that's important in a marriage and in life." She paused and added, "He's an excitable man, and we sometimes argue. We come from different backgrounds. He's direct. He calls a spade a spade. He's very critical. Politically, he's sure he's right. He's opinionated about a lot of things, about people, whom he approves of and whom he disapproves of, including my own family. We disagree about my generosity, my philanthropy, my giving money for the rain forest, which he considers a waste. But he certainly wouldn't stop me.

"I think it's important that you understand that I was the middle child and I don't like to fight. I'm used to being a buffer, and I'm used to being buffered. I learned early on to state my piece and to stop. I don't like to argue and I don't."

"Does that help the marriage?" I asked.

"It surely does, because he has had to learn to listen to me. If we disagree, I state what I want. Mostly he comes around, but not always. But we don't go on and on. It's a civilized home."

Somewhat incredulously I said, "Always?"

Maureen smiled, realizing that I was pushing her. "Well, in the mornings I'm at my worst. I don't do very well. I tend to talk too much. I tend to nag. I tend to really act like my mother. So I found that I was telling him to do this and do that, and the way we solved it is we never have breakfast together. He makes his own breakfast. I stay in another part of the house. I get up early and go for a walk. I love to walk early. I like the fog and dew before it burns off. He plays tennis or works in comfort in another part of the house. I stay away when I'm bossy and difficult, and that solves it fine."

This struck me as an ingenious solution. Essentially, instead of changing her behavior or changing his response, which another couple might try to do, she just stayed away from her husband in the morning. And the serenity of the marriage was protected. It was a solution by avoidance, by the setting up of boundaries, which I sensed were at the core of the marriage. Maintaining the calm of the household seemed to be a top priority for both Nicholas and Maureen. This strategy also reflected their preference for keeping a dignified distance. On days when they were both at home, their relationship did not begin until midmorning.

She added, "My husband is not a patient man, and he is often under great pressure at work. I'm aware of this when we disagree, and I make a decision as to whether an issue is worth a struggle."

"You consider his needs?"

"Of course," she said. "That's what marriage is about. We consider each other, and we have tried to teach that to our children." She smiled mischievously. "Anyway, he's better at fighting than I am, but time is on my side. Mostly I get what I want. I've learned how to handle him."

"What's the secret?"

"It's the approach. I don't bark or give orders. I speak softly, but I know how to keep things going and to bide my time. He has many wonderful qualities, and he doesn't dwell on things. He's a human being who can be headstrong and stubborn, but underneath he's vulnerable, and he needs me."

I asked her how she met Nicholas.

"Well, I was very lucky. I was a sophomore at USC, and he was at Caltech. I had a lot of boyfriends, but he was especially good-looking and competent. He was very bright. He was always interesting and talked incessantly."

"About what?"

"He talked about his plans for the future. In fact, for the first six months we dated, I thought he was an orphan because he never talked about his family. All he talked about was work, what he was doing and what he planned to do."

I was interested that she stressed his competence, his good looks, his drive. She did not mention love or a sense of destiny, of being swept away, as Sara had. She did say, "We share the same values. He was ambitious. He wanted a career and family, and I did too. Plus I wanted an exciting man with potential." She added softly, "Of all the men I ever met, he was the one who attracted me, and that's still the way he is. Also, he was the opposite of what my mother had in mind for me. She liked button-down, proper types who said yes ma'am and no ma'am to her in just the right tone. He's never done that."

"I married him my senior year," she continued. "I left college to get married, which was not unusual in those days. It was 1959. Nicholas had a stipend for grad school, and we lived on very little money. It's hard to believe we did it on so little, but I don't remember feeling deprived. We had a lot of fun."

"How was it leaving home?" I asked. At twenty, girls are still in the process of separating from their parents, even if they live in a college dormitory.

"It was traumatic to break away from my parents. I was very attached to my mother's apron strings. In those early years of the marriage Nicholas did a lot of traveling to Third World countries as part of a research team that collected and studied viruses. I had no experience of living by myself. I was quite shaken by it. Shortly after we married, my father died very suddenly, and that made me even more dependent on Nicholas. And then," she said, throwing up her hands to emphasize the point, "after he finished grad school, we moved to a new community where I didn't know anybody. This made me more dependent on my husband. I missed my mother and father. Since we knew so few people, Nicholas was my only friend and my strength."

Maureen was entirely unprepared for this major life change. Until her marriage she had led a protected life in a stable, middle-class family. She was barely an adult when she married Nicholas, and almost immediately she found herself alone among strangers. It's understandable that she relied on him for almost all her needs in those early years. Because she was so lonely and frightened, he was her security and strength.

"It took me a while," she said, "to move out on my own. In the early years of my marriage, and I'll never forget this, the central question was, how will I survive when he travels? Sometimes he was gone for a month at a time. Finally I asked him to call home more, and he became very good at this. The two of us have worked on this throughout our marriage."

Maureen's request for telephone calls from distant places seemed very modest; she did not ask him to stay home, nor did she say she would stay with her family when he was away. She coped courageously with her situation.

"Our first child was born less than two years after we got married, and the second came along right after that. And then two more. And with the children, there was no way I could figure out how to get out and meet people. But I didn't need it. I loved being a mother. I loved taking care of my children. My loneliness disappeared after my first baby was born." She laughed. "I realize that's not what I was supposed to feel. I was supposed to be sorry for myself. Housebound and stir-crazy. But the truth is, I felt wonderful. It was a rich time for me. To put it in modern lingo, I found it enormously liberating."

What does a woman gain by choosing a traditional marriage? What does she lose? I can find answers in my own life. Although I did not go directly from my parents' home to marriage and had been launched in my career for several years, like Maureen I felt that the time when I was a young mother was the happiest in my life. Unlike many women today, I did have part-time help, which made a big difference. We also lived within walking distance of schools in a safe neighborhood.

In those years my husband worked all day and went back to the office three or four nights a week for training seminars. It never occurred to either of us that he would help with the housework or with the children. He saw them at suppertime and played with them on weekends. When the children were born, our marriage changed abruptly from a close, romantic partnership to one in which I took care of the children and he worked long and hard to support us. His frequent absences inspired our children to invent a game called "Daddy goes to seminar." My husband and I tried to arrange our schedules to have time alone together, but it was never easy. That phase of our lives was a different marriage from that of our first five years, before we had children. And it had different satisfactions.

For me, being a mother held priority, perhaps because I had never had the experience of being a child in a stable household. I loved the responsibility, and I loved bringing up my children according to my values. My husband loved being a father, but he was preoccupied with a competitive career. Although he and I were less close than before, I did not feel lonely or isolated. The children were always there for me. I became part of a society of young mothers and young children, which I enjoyed. The close friendships forged at that time have withstood the years and the vast distances that now separate us.

Of course, this division of roles was expected in my day, but what about young women today, who are expected to throw themselves into careers? My younger daughter deliberately chose a traditional marriage. From her earliest years she wanted to be a mother. At age three, she announced to the family solemnly, "Mommy takes care of me, and I take care of my animals," referring to the fifteen or so stuffed creatures that lay on her bed for years. "They need me in the dark." Although she was brilliant in math, and my husband and I had proud visions of her making her mark in a male-dominated field, she had other ideas. She took lots of advanced math courses because for her they were easy A's. But she was as unimpressed with the ideology of the women's movement as she was with our ambitions for her. She knew exactly what she wanted — to be a mother with two or three children. So she chose the field of clinical social work, which allows her to stay home while her two children are young and to reenter the job market when she's ready.

Most important, my daughter married a man who shared her values and for whom family is a top priority. He wanted an attractive, interesting wife who would establish a warm, loving ambience for him and his children. She is a very happy woman, though she admits to a twinge of sadness as she watches her college friends advance in their careers. "But," she says with a wry smile, "they watch me with more than a twinge of envy."

Many women are drawn to traditional marriage because of a deeply rooted wish to be a mother. As little girls they played with dolls, stuffed animals, and more dolls. Efforts to get them interested in trucks or even pink Legos went largely unheeded. Whether this is a function of nature or nurture hardly matters as long as women who want to stay home to raise children are allowed to do so without feeling like second-class citizens. Full-time careers, such as my older daughter's, are tremendously rewarding. But it is easier to pursue them without children or with only one child.

What women gain from a traditional marriage is the opportunity to raise their own children. The most frequent lament I hear from young mothers is not "When will she grow up?" but "She's growing so fast, I wish I could slow her down." These years are precious because caring for children is an enormous pleasure. Holding and comforting a child, playing together, putting the children to bed — all of these commonplace experiences have no counterpart in other domains of life. What's more, they will not wait. Women in traditional marriages do not want to delegate these tasks, not only because they worry that others might not do so well by their children but because they don't want to give away that precious time. The richness and variety of being a mother have gotten little attention in recent years. But young and old women know about it, and many want that experience.

Maureen mentioned the emotional support she had received from her children, which had kept her from being lonely. We're used to thinking of adults as supporting their children, and indeed they do. But a relationship with a child is a two-way street. It's certainly true that the never-ending work is exhausting. And the responsibility can be terrifying, considering the many dangers of modern society. There is no way to bring up a child without crises. But the payback in being loved and unreservedly admired, in warding off loneliness and being central and indispensable to your child's life is incalculable.

I asked Maureen, "Why did you marry so young?"

"Well, it's very simple," she said. "You didn't fool around unless you were a rebel, and I surely wasn't that. My mother gave her reluctant approval to our marriage. Actually, we gave her no choice. She insisted that I someday go back and finish college, and later on I did. You don't mess around with my mother."

Maureen searched my eyes. "You have to understand my mother to understand me. She's a very powerful woman, and that's good and bad. She adored my father and took wonderful care of him. He needed a lot of care, because although he was very good at what he did, he drank a lot and she covered for him and took care of him. Also, she's a very staunch Christian, very puritanical and strait-laced."

"What results of that do you see in you?"

"I've always had some residue of trouble with sexual passion. I enjoy sex and I find Nicholas exciting, but I was never passionate about it. It's probably affected our marriage and disappointed him."

She trailed off, and I waited for her to continue. "It's been good. I don't initiate sex and I never have, but I have warm feelings and make myself available. I never say I'm too tired. I never have a headache. He knows how to pleasure me. I've gotten much freer over the years. We've enjoyed sex together. I think love expresses itself in many ways, and sex is just one form of love. I'm loving in many ways aside from making sexual love. It's a festive night when we make love. On a normal night there is no romance. But I'd say we have sex two times a week."

In most traditional marriages sexual passion is not regarded as central, and when the children are young it may even be pushed to the periphery. Although sex was valued by all of the traditional couples, as Maureen and Nicholas made clear, it was not as frequent or as exciting as in some other marriages.

"How much is your life built around Nicholas's career?"

"A good deal, though not all of it. I do give it priority. When he needs me to entertain or go to meetings or spend time with the wives of visiting venture capitalists, I always do. But I don't pretend to know anything about his business, nor do I want to.

"I put a lot of time into what has become more than a hobby, which is breeding orchids. We were able to build a magnificent greenhouse, and this has enabled me to grow orchids and other exotic flowers that are hard for many people to attempt successfully. I travel, without Nicholas, to international exhibits several times a year, and I make annual trips to Brazil and Central America. It was there that I became interested in the rain forests because of what I saw firsthand. You might say that I didn't want to spend all my life at luncheons and fundraisers. I prefer making beautiful things grow. And if it's challenging, so much the better."

She turned the discussion back to her husband. "You have to understand that Nicholas works very hard. Coming home is very important for him emotionally. I try always to be upbeat. I make sure that I'm cheerful, and I never greet him at the door with an 'Oh, my God, guess what happened to me?' He puts very complicated deals together, deals that if they work will benefit all of us greatly. But they're high risk, and he has to be in a lot of places at the right time. He has to raise money for the company on Wall Street and work with international investors in Japan and Europe.

"We've more than met our expectations. But now that the girls are older, I have more options of coming and going, traveling with him or staying home and working in the greenhouse."

"Which do you prefer?"

"I'd rather be with my husband alone than with anyone else," said Maureen. "Recently we went to see a film and then met some friends afterward. But only when we were alone did we really get to talk about the movie and what we took from it. It was a much better conversation. We didn't sit silently in the car when we drove home. We never do. We had a terrific discussion. I find him a very interesting man." She paused, considering. "The best thing is, we've been able to maintain a sense of freshness in our marriage."

"What's the secret?"

"The main thing is to distinguish between big things and little things, learning not only to overlook little things but to forget little things, knowing what's important, knowing what's worth fighting for. For Nicholas, a very important thing is not being bored and having a chance to recharge his batteries."

"How does he recharge?"

"At home. He is a very warm and soft person. He adores his family and is very sensitive to his daughters. Yes, he's been very successful and has earned a lot of money. He takes strong stands on lots of things, and I abide by his wishes generally. That's the side that the world sees. He also understands about commitment. And he loves me."

"And you?"

She smiled. "I understand him. His moods, his disappointments, his deep sorrow, and his amazing successes. And I love him."

Maureen was clear about what she had gained and lost in her marriage. She enjoyed her protected, economically secure family life, and when the children grew up, she was free to develop her own interests. She felt needed, respected, and appreciated by Nicholas, whom she considered a fascinating life companion. His many enthusiasms and wide contacts enlivened her world. Secure in her self-image, she credited herself for raising four daughters, creating a beautiful home, pursuing a challenging hobby, and supporting the causes she believed in.

Maureen did not see herself as an adviser or business partner to her husband. Her job was to build a parallel life, not to enter into his work. In their marriage they followed what I have come to consider an unwritten protective code. He protected her from the ups and downs of his life and, as much as possible, from his mood fluctuations. Undoubtedly he felt anguished by the defeats he suffered occasionally, but he strove gallantly to leave his problems at work. It's no accident that at the height of his crisis, he assured her that his panic attacks had nothing to do with their relationship. She, of course, devoted her life to protecting him from himself by maintaining relative calm and stability at home. Mutual protection was at the heart of their marriage.

Maureen still thought of herself as a middle child, whose role was to carefully orchestrate her moods and wishes so that her husband would not be angry or disappointed with her. She described a lifelong dependency on her husband that was both financial and emotional. Although she commanded his respect and gratitude, her power and her role were not on a par with his: he led and she accommodated. She could have taken a degree at the university and pursued a career in botany or forest ecology, but she never considered doing so. She might have made an important discovery in horticulture or become an inspiring teacher. However, she chose not to do these things. She declared, "We have had an interesting life, and we are reaping the harvest. I don't know anyone with whom I would change places."

\* \* \*

What about younger traditional marriages? Will they turn out as well as Maureen and Nicholas's marriage?

Children are still central to the traditional marriage, but in many other respects the ground rules have shifted over the last two decades. Men's and women's roles are less rigidly defined. It is no longer assumed that the woman's job is to accommodate to the man's needs; both partners are considered equal in the power hierarchy and decision-making. Women today know the frustrations of working in an office, and men know how difficult it is to take care of young children. They recognize that both jobs are difficult and that each person needs nurturance and support.

When I met Alice and Nelson Harris, they were ten years into a traditional marriage after living together for five years. They had even bought a house together before getting married. Today they lived in that house on a quiet, tree-lined street in San Mateo, where they were raising three children, aged eight, five, and three. Nelson commuted to his job as a junior partner in an architectural firm in San Francisco. Alice, who was thirty-one when they married, had wanted to have a child as soon as possible. She had worked full-time as the office manager of a computer company until her ninth month of pregnancy. She did not work outside the home after that.

The wish to have a child played a major role in the Harrises' decision to marry. The realization hit Nelson like a thunderbolt on a sunny afternoon in a neighborhood park. "We'd been together quite a while," he said during our interview. "Alice was getting restive because she wanted children, but she wasn't pushing hard or anything. We had not discussed marriage up to that point. But one day" — tears welled in his eyes — "we were strolling in the park, and I saw this little boy walking along the trail. Suddenly I was overcome and just started to cry. I want one of those, I said to myself. I desperately wanted a child of my own. I could hardly stand it. It was like I suddenly realized that I was no longer a child. I was an adult and I needed to have children.

"I didn't say anything to Alice at the time, but as soon as we got home, I went upstairs and wrote her a poem proposing marriage. And we did it — a large, bang-up traditional wedding, including a bridal registry at Macy's, the whole bit."

Nelson grinned as he talked about the children. "The birth of our first child was one of the high points of my life," he said. "There was something about Jack's birth and the things that happened around it that was really a passage. I felt totally committed to my marriage and family, and I still feel that way. There's no ambivalence about it. I don't ever want to leave this relationship.

"Alice and I do have fights at times, and sometimes I want to punch her lights out. She's a temperamental lady, and she has no trouble letting me know how she feels. But behind all the anger or whatever, I know we'll make up and go on. The relationship between us is never threatened."

When I asked about their quarrels, he replied, "Well, she yells, I yell, she cries, whatever. Then we apologize and try to talk about what's going on. And then we kiss and make up and feel better for it."

Nelson reflected for a moment. "Alice and I have an equal relationship in our marriage. We both make the major decisions together, which is the only way it can be. Early on I tended to want to be in control, but after Jack was born I realized that that wouldn't work. It was a major transition for both of us. I don't need to be in control of everything, nor should I be."

He explained how they had partitioned their time. "We decided that we would combine being together and being apart," he said with an air of satisfaction. "We have three kinds of vacations — family vacations, vacations for just Alice and me, and time that we each take alone. She's currently away for three days, and I like that. I like being with the kids all by myself and doing the kid stuff without her telling me how to do it. I also like it when I go away alone, having time for myself without responsibilities."

Nelson discussed how he relied on Alice for encouragement. "I get into these neurotic numbers where I blame myself for everything. And she really helps me. Like I feel bad if I think that I did a bad job of getting the children's lunch, that they're going to get into trouble if I put the wrong thing in their lunch boxes. And she'll say, 'What's this? They can make their own goddamned lunches.' You have no idea how helpful that is to me. Recently we had some trouble at the office, and my secretary messed up. I was really worried. Alice said, 'It's going to be all right. Don't worry.'" He smiled. "I feel like I have a childlike trust in her. If she says it's going to be okay, it relieves my anxiety. What's more, it works out that way."

When I asked about sex, he said that Alice was very passionate and not inhibited, as he was. "I've never totally overcome all my inhibitions. She's helped me loosen up a lot sexually. When we first had sex, her passion blew me away. It was one of the major surprises in our relationship, and I loved it."

Nelson went on, "I'm less inhibited with her than I've been with any other human being. She helps me not be a workaholic, and I try very hard to keep that inclination under control."

A week later, when I asked Alice what was happy about the marriage, she first mentioned children, then described her friendship with Nelson. "We understand each other," she said. "It's been like this from the beginning. I seem to know what he's thinking, but it's not that I'm telepathic or anything like that. It's that we're soul mates. We can talk about anything. We agree on most things, we have similar reactions to people, we like to do the same things, and what's more, he won't allow me to sit on my feelings and mope. We'll have loud fights, but we resolve them. We can have fun and be silly together, but most of all, he's a wonderful father, which makes me love him even more. He takes care of me, and I'm supportive of him as well.

"I was a gawky kid, and I thought I'd never get a date. But now I sometimes think I've gotten everything I ever dreamed of, and I just marvel at it all. I love being a mother, and I loved being pregnant with all three kids. I didn't mind the morning sickness, and I even loved giving birth. It makes me feel sad that I won't have more babies, at least in all likelihood. That whole period was the most exciting time of my life."

Alice's happiness showed in her every move and facial expression. "I haven't worked since Jack was born, and I feel very good about it," she said. "I sometimes worry about my ability to earn a living, and I'll probably go back to school one of these days. But Nelson and I wanted me home full-time with the children. Sure, it would be nice to have more money, and with three children we often feel strapped. But there was never any question that I would quit my job when the children arrived.

"Nelson is a wonderful dad," she repeated. "He's loved every minute of it, including diapering the babies. Sometimes he loses patience, but he's really good with the kids. I wish that he'd play basketball or baseball with Jack and do those father-son kinds of sports, but Nelson's not into that. He helps the kids with their homework, with practicing music, and he even helps with the PTA.

"This is a child-centered home, though we try not to let the kids play us off against each other. We present a united front when they get out of hand. Parenting has strengthened our marriage, but it's also kept us apart. I wish we had more time to be together, just the two of us. I can't imagine how working mothers do it all, because I can never find enough time."

Asked about disappointments, she said, "He has one lovely fault that bothers me at times. He's too careful of me. If he's worried about something, he keeps it in and doesn't tell me, sometimes for months. I keep saying, 'Look, I know there's something wrong, tell me.' He protects me, and I tell him I don't need protecting."

Alice's other disappointment was that "sex is not a burning passion in the marriage. It's comfortable, but I have had better, more exciting sex. It's not as important to him as it is to me." She thought for a moment. "The biggest surprise of my marriage is how successful it's been. I haven't seen so many good marriages, and I wasn't sure someone would love me enough to really stay married to me. But he has loved me enough.

"There's nothing I would change about my marriage, and what I'd like for my daughters is that they maybe go farther with their careers before they get married, because I don't have enough to fall back on should something bad happen. I'm not sure how the women's movement has affected me," she confessed. "My husband doesn't mind helping me with the kids, he does the dishes regularly, and he makes me feel happy. He recognizes my needs and respects me as an equal. I don't know whether I'm a feminist or a humanist. I'm just for people. But what I want for my kids is that I hope they'll be good parents."

The young traditional marriages I studied had many features that were not present in earlier generations. For example, Nicholas took for granted that he would have children, whereas Nelson was bowled over by the sudden recognition that he wanted to be a father. Alice and Maureen both loved being mothers, but Alice saw herself as part of a parenting team, even though she was a full-time mother. Maureen operated as a parent pretty much on her own, with little help from Nicholas.

Unlike Maureen, Alice wanted Nelson to share his concerns at work and felt hurt when he kept her in the dark. Thus the emphasis on carefully separating family and work had no counterpart in the more recent traditional marriages. Younger couples were less interested in building walls than in cutting back on the encroachments of work on family life. Although Nelson admitted to being a workaholic, he welcomed his wife's help in curbing his tendencies to overwork; he was less ambitious than Nicholas.

The families handled conflict differently. While Nicholas and Maureen valued a calm home with little argument, Alice and Nelson fought openly and took it in their stride. He was surprised at her hot temper, but there's no reason to think that he would ask her to be quieter or that she would submit to such a request.

Finally, power was negotiated in different ways. In the Easterbrooks' marriage, Nicholas was the dominant partner. Alice and Nelson, like the partners in companionate marriage, shared equally in the power and decision-making. They were equals and soul mates.

The two marriages did have much in common in the emotional dependence that was at the core of the relationship. Maureen kept Nicholas on an even keel, and Alice kept Nelson from feeling guilty about every little thing that went wrong. Despite their maturity and competence at work, both men had an almost childlike belief that their wives would rescue them from inner problems and anxieties. And both were not ashamed to admit their dependence on their wives. For her part, Maureen expected Nicholas to protect her economically and socially as a quid pro quo of the marriage. Alice felt that Nelson overprotected her, but she referred to it as a "lovely fault." Finally, sexual passion was not at the core of either marriage or of any of the other traditional marriages.

Both husband and wife in the traditional marriage see the family as requiring commitment and, when necessary, sacrifice. Each person expects to give up something important for the good of the family. But the father does not necessarily spend a lot of time in play or conversation with his children, and he may not actively participate in their care. Nevertheless, he can remain powerfully connected to his children, and the love he feels for them can be a central part of his life. He is no less morally committed to his children than the father in a companionate marriage, who spends far more time with his children.

One man, who worked eighty hours a week throughout his children's lives, told me about a fire that destroyed their home. "I'm not sure whether I would have gone back into the burning house for my wife, whom I love with all my heart. But I know for absolute certain that I would have returned for my children and died with them." A father's love for his children and his moral commitment to them cannot be measured in units of caregiving.

My findings about fathers and children in traditional marriages run counter to the popular notion that if a man is interested in his children, he will share in the day-to-day work of raising them. But this view overlooks the fact that a father can have a strong connection with his children via identification with his wife, their mother. Her psychological role in this connectedness was described in various ways by the men in the study. Some called her "my surrogate." Others referred to "my extension" or "my partner." Whatever the term, the man felt that he shared in the daily lives of his children via his wife. He stood by her side in spirit and substance. This commitment to his children was central to his self-image and integrity. As in the familiar child's circle game — the farmer takes a wife, and the wife takes a child — the father, by holding his wife's hand, connected with the child. There are, of course, very many strands to the father-child relationship. But connectedness via the mother was singled out by the men in traditional marriages to whom I talked.

The father of a two-year-old and a five-year-old said, "We give priority to our children. That's the central idea of the marriage. I view myself as a father figure, as a provider, as someone whose responsibility is to provide adequately for the family." After explaining that he made sure to spend every weekend with his children, since he saw them very little during the week, he said, "You know, the only thing you really contribute to the world is your kids. We are placed here on earth to serve the needs of our children. They grow up soon enough. The important thing is to make a commitment to the children. They need a mother, and she is my surrogate when she's home. She takes care of them at school and at home, and we support each other. Our home is child-centered."

Asked what was happy about her marriage, the wife said, "We are a family with young children. It's the family unit. Actually my husband and I don't have as much time together as we would like. I enjoy having time to myself. But it's mainly that we're a family and that we have young children, and that's happy at this time in our lives."

Although the men in these modern traditional marriages had more contact with their children than Nicholas did, they reflected sadly on missing out on doing things with their young children. And although they were proud of their own contribution to their children's care, they spoke of their wives' closeness to the children with some envy. When men are the sole wage earners, they pay the price of reduced family time. Young men who work in professions that demand the long hours that Nicholas put in do not have a choice. Like young mothers who work full-time, they agonize over whether they are doing the right thing. And, as the women know so well, there is no satisfactory answer to their dilemma.

Like the other forms, traditional marriage fills some needs and expectations but not others. These marriages are no less vulnerable to the economy and shifts in the job market than any other type. For these relationships to function, the man has to provide economic stability. The wife has to feel she has the resources to create a safe, stable, and comforting home. If money is uncertain, it is impossible for a wife to create such an environment or to stay at home.

People who call for a return to old-fashioned values fail to realize that traditional marriage cannot work without financial stability based on one income. Moreover, the family needs to feel securely buffered against crises — particularly the economic threats of divorce, prolonged illness, unemployment, or the death of the breadwinner. Because the woman has given up her place on the economic ladder, she needs protection for herself and her children. When disaster strikes, she needs far more than a safety net at an economically marginal level. She also needs rewarding educational and work opportunities that are commensurate with her ability and ambition when she reenters the work force. Traditional marriage can flourish only in a society that rewards the breadwinner with a stable salary that can adequately support a family and protect parents and children against economic misfortune. The society must also provide generously for the reentry to the workplace of the parent who stayed home with the children.

# 20 &

# The Eighth Task

*Providing Emotional Nurturance*

OUR NEEDS FOR COMFORTING and encouragement are deep and lasting. A main task of every marriage from the early days of the relationship to its end is for each partner to nurture the other. The loneliness of life in cities, the long commutes, the absence of meaningful contact with people in so many jobs, the anonymity of suburban life, and the distances that separate close friends and family have all sharpened our emotional hungers. The faceless machines we spend so much time with in our offices have increased our sense of isolation. We feel tired, driven, and needy. More than ever before we need someone special who understands how we feel and responds with tenderness. Love begins with paying attention.

The eighth task of marriage, therefore, is to give comfort and encouragement in a relationship that is safe for dependency, failure, disappointment, mourning, illness, and aging — in short, for being a vulnerable human being.

Nicholas said, "Maureen has always understood my moods and known how to soothe me." Nelson said, "I feel like I have an almost childlike faith in her ability to help me feel better." Finding shelter, love, and reassurance in a treasured partner's arms is what marriage is about.

Replenishing each other's emotional reserves does not mean infantilizing each other — quite the reverse. Paradoxically, providing for a partner's dependency needs as these needs arise strengthens the capacity of both people to maintain their adulthood, for adulthood is built on occasional regressions. We all regress when we cry, when we admit helplessness and failure, when we feel discouraged and depressed. We turn to each other for a welcoming lap or a strong shoulder to lean on. If we never let down our guard, we become brittle, fragile, and boring. As adults we take two steps forward and one step back. If we do not, we risk depleting our reserves for the next step upward.

This kind of compassionate help begins with an accurate assessment of the cause of the other's suffering, followed by a genuine effort to relieve it or to head it off. Comfort within a good marriage rests on mutual understanding and genuine caring — not on generalities and platitudes. A marriage that does not provide nurturance and restorative comfort can die of emotional malnutrition. Why get up in the morning to face the daily responsibilities of adulthood and family life if the rewards seem so inadequate compared to the effort required? The need for sympathy and for restoration of battered self-esteem, which receives much less press than the search for sexual adventure, is a major component in infidelity.

"A man's home is his castle" once referred to a private space that was heavily protected from intruders by thick walls surrounded by a deep moat and fortified against trespass by law or arms. Nowadays we might say that a man and woman's marriage is *their* castle, a private space where they can withdraw from the stresses of the public world. In their private world, both can find replenishment for dealing with the demanding tasks and challenges outside.

It has been difficult for our society to acknowledge that satisfying men's and women's needs for nurturance should be a high priority. Women who do not work outside the home have long been assumed to be dependent on men and to need lifelong economic protection; but replenishment of their emotional reserves has not received much attention or sympathy. Under the rules of older traditional marriages, the wife was expected to give bountifully to her children and to her husband, while taking care of her own emotional needs. Men traditionally have viewed dependence on others as a negative reflection on their manhood. Women, however, know that their maternal role has always been an important aspect of marriage. As they age, both women and men become more dependent.

Some other societies have been less timid about recognizing these human needs. In Japan, which is an overtly hard-driving, competitive culture, there is a much greater acceptance of the continuing dependency needs of both men and women. The Japanese psychoanalyst Takeo Doi used the term *amae* to capture what he calls "the intense drive to gratify dependency wishes, to be responded to, taken care of, cherished." This drive, he argues, is a powerful force in adult man-woman relationships.

To clarify the importance of nurturance in marriage, it helps to look at the notion of the mother as providing emotional refueling for the child, who goes back and forth from independence with his peers to his mother's sheltering care. The toddler ventures away from her mother's safe lap to explore the exciting but hazardous world of the playground. She returns at intervals to have her tears dried and complaints kissed away, then returns to the serious business of conquering the world.

The same to-and-fro occurs in adult life. One or both partners venture out to face the perils of the workplace, then return to the safe, emotionally supportive relationship of marriage and home to gather nourishment and confidence to venture out again. If the satisfactions of the home are sufficient, a balance is maintained. If not, the man or woman feels depleted and unappreciated.

The relief that people seek at home is often evident as they enter the house. The businessman's first gesture is to undo his tie and top collar button and remove his jacket. The businesswoman kicks off her shoes. "Thank God I'm home" is the message. "Bar the door, I need a rest." And, perhaps most of all, "Take care of me." The need is to relax, take off the public clothing, and give up the smiles, the public geniality of the salesperson, whether he or she sells legal advice or neckties. The many masks required by public life are no longer needed, and we happily doff them along with our public uniforms as we enter the privacy of home. Even John Wayne needs to take his boots off. Even the dean of the law school needs to undo her bra.

Of course we can and do relax with a hot shower, a martini, or a favorite TV show or magazine. Many external remedies can offset bad feelings and restore a happier mood. There's plenty of room for self-parenting. Indeed, sometimes we just want to be left alone. But people want and need more than this from their marriage. Men and women alike need a person they trust who reassures them, saying, "You did the best you could," who alleviates their worry, saying confidently, "You couldn't help it, so why blame yourself?" and who sends them back to battle with the message "You can do it, really you can." Everyone needs a regular retelling of "The Little Engine That Could." How else can we keep going?

In this private arena, there is an urgent need to unload, to admit to anger at the boss, to reveal the failure to negotiate that contract, the loss of an expected opportunity, the anguish of deciding to let a worker go. We all need a sympathetic ear for our confession of an unfortunate loss of temper and the fear of the possible consequences. But our failures are not the only issues that we need to confide. We all long for an audience to celebrate our successes, someone to whom we can describe how truly superior we are to colleagues or competitors and crow about our successes, someone who will share in our pleasure at a victory scored or a competitor's defeat, without our having to dissemble. Sanctimoniousness and hypocrisy go by the board at this time.

Equally important is the scenario of the mother who spends her entire day taking care of a baby or young children, who is also depleted after driving them to school, to play with friends, to the pediatrician, to the market. The physical and emotional demands of raising children are exhausting; her feelings may alternate between resentment at the enormous effort involved and guilt about the resentment. Over the long haul, the satisfactions of raising children are very great. But on any given day many a young mother would consider climbing Mount Everest an easy alternative. At times she yearns to climb into someone's lap for a good cry — or even to run away.

Unless there is an acute crisis, what a couple talks about when they unwind is less important than that they are together and listening to each other. Most people do not expect to be rescued from whatever is bothering them. They do not expect their partner to change the world or kiss away their narcissistic hurts, and they don't really want to give away the children or quit their job. But they do want to be heard. And more than that, they want real understanding and sympathy, not an automatic "uh-huh." They expect that their partner will understand the part that hurts most or frightens or angers or frustrates most.

In many marriages, recognizing that the other person needs comforting is a surprising discovery. One young wife said, "I learned from long trial and error what kind of nurturing Tom needs from me. When I first met him, where we both worked, I saw a handsome, supremely confident executive who could skate circles around everyone else in the office. It took me years to realize that he needed any support at all. It just didn't occur to me. If he was moody or blue at home, I took it personally, assuming that I had said or done something to annoy him. I never guessed that he could be feeling *discouraged*."

Observing the other person is the first step in this task, and a very important one. Hearing what is not being said is even more important. People in good marriages read body language as well as words. Although this knack requires no special talent, it does demand attention and practice. We learn to read body language at our mother's knee, quickly mastering the signals of when she is on the warpath or just making an idle threat. We learn to tell if Dad is ready to blow his top or if he is still distractible, and we understand when the neighborhood bully means business. Sometimes we miscalculate the bully's intentions, but not for long, for we know our chances of reaching adulthood intact may be in serious jeopardy.

This lifetime experience of reading body language pays off in marriage, for it enables us to give our partner compassion and nurturance even when the need is unspoken. The popular emphasis on communication in marital therapy — just tell her how you feel — hardly captures the subtleties of these deeper modes of communicating. Marriage partners need to observe each other closely to make judgments that are reasonably correct. They need to distinguish between blowing off steam and being seriously disaffected, between tiredness and exhaustion, sadness and despair, urgent need for relief and moderate complaining, chronic depression and a temporary low. Sometimes silence speaks volumes.

Signals that are not read or are unheeded can lead to trouble. Most people tolerate a spouse's mistakes in this regard and don't expect ESP or brilliant deductions in every exchange. But they cannot deal with a partner's "blindness" or "deafness" to their feelings. A partner is not required to heal all wounds, but he or she is required to hear and take seriously a cry for help or relief, however awkwardly expressed.

Men and women need to understand each other, because the daily aggravations of life have an important influence on relationships. The greetings given and received at the end of a long day set the tone for the rest of the evening. It's important that partners resolve the issues between them within the compass of the day so that they can comfort each other when they go to bed, even if they are both exhausted. The need to maintain emotional connectedness is serious. This is not to say that a marriage will break with one missed cue or even many. What breaks marriages is the anguish of being emotionally abandoned by a partner who is oblivious to these needs. Eventually, feelings of emotional abandonment generate depression and then rage.

Partners can help each other in many ways. Some people need to talk; others prefer to be left alone. Some need to be held and comforted. Others need music or tennis or a nap. One young woman said, "In the evenings I need time to replenish or I'm lost. I don't want sex after a hectic day with a two-year-old. I sometimes don't want conversation. I want to curl up and shut out the world. I want to sit down with a book." Some people need to be listened to right away; others need to delay until they have begun to sort things out. Some need humor. One man said, "The stock market is so boring to me that each morning I can hardly return to work. But her lively chatter cheers me immensely. Her humor helps me maintain my sanity." Individuals have their own patterns of what makes them feel better. What would be insulting to one person is exactly what another needs. It is essential that both partners know what strategies will help the other bear the everyday stresses of life.

Just as important, both partners need to be able to tell when a crisis has reached flood stage and requires immediate action, as when one parent is overtaxed by an ill, distressed, or colicky child. In such situations the other parent can take over or find outside help to provide some needed respite. Acute situations also come up in connection with work or in relation to illness or death. People need to decide how much support a partner needs and to act accordingly. Recognizing the urgency of the situation can be harder than improvising a remedy. There is often an unfortunate, though understandable, impulse to downplay bad situations, and such a response may mean that a partner's cry for help goes unheeded.

A marriage that is capable of rising magnificently to an acute crisis cannot always handle the boredom, fatigue, tension, and unmet needs that are part of everyday life. But routine frustrations are always serious if the partners' needs are on a collision course. It is a drastic mistake to overlook these frustrations and assume that time will automatically take care of the problem. Although time may indeed provide a remedy, the so-called remedy may not heal the marriage. It is always better to acknowledge unmet needs than to deny them; at least they can be recognized and examined in the light.

The hardest part of many modern marriages is that both people feel overwhelmed and in need of comfort at day's end. An exhausted wife, too tired to even wash her face, confronts a man who is also totally done in. Each wants comfort from the other, and each feels too depleted to give it. Competition for the limited supply of emotional relief can lead to disaster. Emotional crises occur occasionally in all marriages with young children, as well as in companionate marriages where both partners have stressful jobs. When the marriage includes two careers and young children, the results can be explosive.

There is no magic trick to prevent the occurrence of such blowups or to remedy them when they happen. The only recourse is to call on our own common sense, good will, and sense of fairness to find ways to avoid future explosions. In one marriage in this study, the wife had spent years caring full-time for a handicapped child; her husband felt miserable and rejected because she had little emotional support left to give him. When they faced up to these feelings, they decided to place the child in residential care for a year. That allowed them to turn the marriage around.

Other solutions were less radical. Some couples, like Alice and Nelson, took mini-vacations together and separately. Alice, who had been reluctant to spend three days alone, was surprised at how much she enjoyed the opportunity to replenish herself; she regarded her husband's support for her time alone as a gift. Some couples took turns helping each other with burdensome tasks and found, to their surprise, that the tasks became less dreadful when shared. Some helped with pressing school assignments or work overload. Several partners in this study helped a stressed-out spouse write university papers in fields they knew little about. Others found ways to give each other space protected from invasion by children or telephone calls.

Maintaining and restoring each other's self-esteem is another important aspect of marriage. The task of continual encouragement goes hand in hand with replenishment of emotional reserves. Contrary to what many people believe, self-esteem is not established once and for all early in life. Although its foundations are laid down during childhood and adolescence, self-esteem fluctuates during adulthood. It reflects not only our own view of ourselves but how we feel we are regarded by the people who are important to us. Does he love me? Does she think of me as having integrity, as someone to be trusted? Does she think of me as a competent person in whom she can have confidence? Self-esteem is not a single idea; rather, it is like a tripod whose three legs are feeling loved, feeling virtuous, and feeling competent. If all three are strong, they support high self-esteem and self-confidence. If they are weak, the result is a poor self-image and a chronic expectation of failure.

Each part of the tripod of self-esteem is challenged every day of our lives. We give ourselves new grades with each important experience. If we do something well, we are proud of the achievement, pleased with ourselves as a parent, a cook, or a lawyer. If we perform poorly, we chastise ourselves for being so incompetent, for having lost the contract, for having come down too hard on an innocent child, for having burned the dinner and ruined the party, for having lost an important case. Then we are ashamed or guilty, angry at ourselves for being so klutzy and so unlovable. Our self-esteem sinks and we feel shaky, even depressed.

If an individual's self-esteem is firm because she has always been pleased with herself and felt loved and appreciated, she may need less reassurance from her partner. When she fails, she counts on having another chance to do better and bounces back with relative ease. But even people with generally high self-esteem have periods of profound doubt and disappointment. At such junctures we turn to others — a husband or wife, children, or good friends — to help restore our inner sense of self-worth.

In a good marriage we turn first to our partner. After all, he loves me and knows my merits. She reassures me that whatever makes me feel shaky, it is less important than I think, that it will soon be past history, and that she adores me. Together we review and thrash out what happened until we are able to close the door on that failure and move on. Helping one's partner maintain self-esteem and continue without getting discouraged and giving up is an important task of marriage.

But when our self-esteem has been shaken by the hurt of a close friend's rejection, or when we are afraid to take on a really uncertain venture because we fear failure, we need our partner even more to tell us that we are lovable and capable. A good marriage is critical in strengthening our resolve to try again. As one businesswoman said, "There's no one else in the whole world of whom I'm sure that whatever he says about me will always be good — who is always there, who will always take care of me, in the best sense of the word. I always know that my interests have priority with him. He is the one person in my whole life who is always saying to me — and Lord knows I've needed this many times — 'You can do it. You really can do it. Go ahead.' He's the one person in the whole world who is always in my corner."

We expect a husband or wife to stand by us and provide loving support and encouragement. We especially need this vote of confidence when things look bleak, but we need it as a reserve all the time. Our self-esteem needs to be shored up when we look in the mirror and realize that we look a little (or a lot) older or fatter. An achievement, whether it is cooking dinner or writing a sonata, needs to be acknowledged first by the person we married. Our need for emotional nurturance by our partner is inseparable from our need for encouragement.

In the good marriages I studied, each partner had a genuine respect for the other. They truly thought of each other as virtuous, competent people, as good fathers and sensitive mothers. Each hoped fervently that the other would succeed. They loved and respected their partners and were eager to provide encouragement. But they did not expect perfection or heroic performance. They surely expected occasional failure.

Finally, these people were not envious of what they gave to the other. They did not dole out kindness with the expectation of immediate reimbursement. They did not weigh their gifts or keep records. Supporting and encouraging the other was a given. They accepted this major task not only as fair but as necessary to make the marriage succeed. As an actor told me, referring to his work in a new play, "I suddenly got it about ensemble work. Ensemble is when you work as hard for the other guy's moment as you do for your own." That feeling is at the core of a good marriage.

# 21 🙟

# Adolescence

## A Wolf in Denim Clothing

EW PEOPLE REALIZE that an adolescent in the household is a wolf in denim clothing. By their very existence, teenagers are a powerful trigger for turmoil in marriage. Every family in this study that had adolescent children reported a high wave of anxiety when a child turned fourteen, and some felt it even earlier. One man said he was shocked when his eleven-year-old experimented with pink lipstick and blue eye shadow. "I suddenly realized what was coming down the road."

When a child enters adolescence, he or she suddenly seems ten feet tall, casting a dark shadow on all aspects of family life.

"We defied the odds! We're still married," one woman exulted at our follow-up interview. "What's new is that we have a teenage daughter. It's a shock. We knew it would be different. Our house is hot, passions run high."

"How old is your daughter?"

"Fourteen going on twenty-one."

"Has she gotten into trouble?"

"Lord, no," her mother replied. "It's enough that she's fourteen."

This anxiety is not necessarily in response to the teenager's overt behavior; just as often it comes from the parents' fear of imagined behaviors. What are all those boys doing hanging around in the den? Are they experimenting with drugs? What is she really doing at the party? What are they drinking and how much? Who is driving and how long has he had a driver's license? Fears extend to accident, death, pregnancy, and rape. There is a general fear of the rising aggression exhibited by teenagers, whose dynamic energy hints at challenge and sexuality. None of these are small concerns.

The adults in the study rarely responded to the challenge in a modulated way. One man, who had never raised a hand to his children, said, "My son questions me at every turn. He defies me all the time. I want to kill him. I want to knock his teeth out."

Many parents are more upset and anxious when their daughters reach adolescence than when their boys hit that stage. Perhaps this is because teenage girls' bodies change more obviously, and they tend to act more sexual within the family than boys. Whether it is because she crowds the rest of the family out of the bathroom, hogs the telephone, parades around in skimpy clothes, or attracts young swains to the door at all hours, a teenage girl occupies center stage. She is more challenging and provocative than a boy, who isn't as likely to flaunt his sexuality at home. Even when teenage girls remain demure and strait-laced, anxiety about their potential behavior rises to the surface.

What makes this anxiety intolerable to many adults is not only that their little girl or boy is really growing up and becoming sexually stimulating but that the changes bring to the fore their own memories and unconscious transferences from the past. Many people can't recall early childhood, but most remember adolescence, with all its dangers and thrills, vividly. The harrowing mix of memory and fantasy stirs parents up to the point that they don't entirely trust their own judgment. This only compounds their anxiety.

Parents also know what the young people do not: that behavior has lasting consequences. Fast cars kill and maim. A college education makes a difference. Sexually transmitted diseases cause sterility and death. The parent feels panicked by all the dangers faced by teens, who are blessed with an implacable sense of omnipotence and timelessness. Nothing the parent says will change these attitudes — we all remember ignoring our own parents' admonitions.

These anxieties easily dominate every aspect of family life, including the relationship between spouses. For the parent experiences this adolescent challenge as a demand. The teenage child, speaking for the next generation, is saying, "Move over, I'm on my way." In establishing his manhood, the boy pushes at his father, who sees the behavior as insolence and defiance. Overthrowing the king is risky, and this is where the boy is most vulnerable. He needs his parents to give him structures and rules, but he also needs a vote of confidence, a welcome into the camaraderie of men. This is a complex message for parents to hear and respond to.

The sexual challenge is equally complex. Looking at her daughter, a mother hears a replay of "Mirror, mirror on the wall," but only the daughter fully expects to be told that she has won the contest. She, not Mom, is the fairest of them all. Mother is seen as fading rapidly in beauty and sexuality.

A father intuits that his daughter expects him to protect her from living out the impulses and fantasies she directs at him. She wants her beloved father to find her charming, attractive, irresistible — and absolutely off-limits at all times. For her, this is a fine but all-important line. If she is developing at a normal pace she feels that she's the one who is turning elsewhere for love and intimacy. If she is developing more slowly or unevenly, she may feel unattractive and unlovable. She needs encouragement from her mother to help her build a confident self-image as someone who is attractive and feminine. She needs her mother's permission to move to young womanhood.

In families where there's been a divorce, the sexual issues are further complicated. A young stepmother may aggravate the generational competition. And a stepfather, who does not have the same long-term history with the girl as an infant and young child — which strengthens the incest taboo in the biological father — has a harder time dealing with the sexual excitement that the adolescent inevitably generates. One way that the young person helps to keep sexual impulses under control is with the convenient fantasy that the parents are asexual. But this psychological device may fail in recently remarried families.

An hour into our interview, Maureen sat up stiffly, smoothed her shirt sleeves, and looked me in the eye. "What I haven't told you is the worst episode of my life," she said in a confessional tone.

I leaned closer. "Tell me about it."

"It's such a bizarre story. I'm almost too embarrassed to discuss it." She pushed a stray hair back into place with her ring finger. "But then, it did affect the marriage, and I think it's important that you know."

She heaved a deep sigh and struggled to begin. Up until then she had been straightforward in describing her marriage. She had spoken easily about being a full-time mother and about having a husband whose work consumed him and whose frequent business trips left her feeling lonely. A dignified and intelligent woman, Maureen prided herself on having everything under control. But the story she told reveals how easy it is to lose control.

"When my daughter turned fourteen, she started to go out in a serious way with a boy who was sixteen. He was a big boy, into body building, and he had a beautiful body, sort of like an Adonis." She sighed again. "And I lost it for a whole year, Judy. I became an adolescent again. I had this gigantic rescue fantasy for this boy. His mother was alcoholic and had been abusive, and he in turn was abusive to my daughter. Nevertheless, I treated him like my son. I became preoccupied with him, as if he were my son, and my other daughters and my husband resented it mightily.

"This boy became the focus of my life. If he hurt my daughter, I was hurt. If he treated her badly, I felt bad. If he abused her, which he did, instead of telling her to reject him, I felt helpless — just as she was. I felt abused. I had gone crazy. I thought about him constantly. I dreamed about him. I could hardly eat. He became an obsession."

"How physical did the relationship get?"

"It was very erotic. He was a stud. It was an affair, but it was all in my head. I knew that my daughter was sexually active with him, and I could do nothing for her. I was immobilized as a mother." She talked in a rush, afraid that if she stopped, she wouldn't be able to continue. "Even though the boy drank too much, I took him with us to all kinds of places. I let him drive my car. I even let him take my car home with him and return it the next day. I was absolutely wild in what I did with this boy and for this boy. It was a vicarious relationship in which I was living out something via my daughter, and I couldn't stop myself."

"How do you explain this?"

"Have you ever had a teenage daughter?" she asked. "I think it does things to you. It's just that I was more vulnerable. Maybe if I'd had lovers I would have built up some antibodies. But I was just so vulnerable."

"How so?"

"I was a late bloomer. There must have been something missing from my adolescence. The truth is" — she flushed in embarrassment — "it was his beautiful body. It was sexual. It was lusting for adolescence and being the lusty adolescent I wasn't able to be. I had been kept under strict supervision by my mom." She paused for a second.

"Maybe it's part of approaching midlife and having adolescent kids. It was all of those things. It was a real obsession, with many, many threads. But it's over. Thank God it's over."

The changes of adolescence have a strong impact on the marriage and on each parent. The teenager, as we saw in Maureen's story, strengthens the parents' sexual impulses, especially desires that were never fully gratified and that now spring to new life. "I never had a real chance to play." "He's the only man I've ever known. I wonder what sex with somebody else would be like." "I wonder what sex with a young woman would be like, especially these new-style young women." "My daughter's girlfriend looks like a million dollars. Maybe, from the way she looks at me, I'm not over the hill." All of the issues of adolescence are revived in this internal chorus.

The extent to which a parent can control these impulses depends on how insistent they are and on the constraints holding his or her behavior and feelings in place. The ascendancy of love and friendship over anger and deprivation in the marriage, as well as moral conscience, the capacity for judgment and impulse control, and of course the external forces of family, church, community, and tradition are all critically important at this time. It is a complex balance, and the scenario plays out differently for each parent as the adolescent child rubs salt into old and new wounds.

One mother of a teenage boy said she and her husband had recently visited a site in the Sierras where the family used to go camping, and she experienced a tremendous sense of nostalgia, of time passing. It was fall, and the leaves were drifting to the ground. Although she talked to her husband about how things had changed since their boy had begun high school, he did not feel the same nostalgia. He had not been as deeply involved with his son in the early years but was now enjoying a greater sense of kinship based on manhood and the fact the boy was attending his alma mater.

The weekend was intended to be a romantic interlude. "I took a hike by myself, and it reminded me how much I like the quiet of being by myself," she said. "And then we took a hike together. And we got to this lovely place in the mountains. I sat down by the river and I started to cry. I was crying because I was so stressed out with work and family. And I was crying because my son was getting older and because life was moving on and because of the fall, the falling leaves.

My husband was very sweet about my tears and treated me with a special tenderness and consideration that I really appreciated."

For this woman the autumn leaves symbolized the fact that her son's adolescence has brought her into a new season in her life. She turned inward, mourning, thinking summer was coming to an end. She was crying over all of it together.

Whether such tears are dominated by a gentle wistfulness and the recognition that this is what life is all about, or by anger and a sense that life isn't fair, depends a lot on the satisfactions of the marriage in the past as well as at that time. If the marriage has been reasonably gratifying and it is able to bend to meet the new needs, the crying may be gentle. Having a loving partner is a great advantage. But if the person feels deprived, the tears can be driven by rage and by thoughts like "I didn't get what I deserve. I didn't get what I needed. And time is running out." Anger is an inevitable component of this mourning process, but if satisfactions from other sources are not available, the anger can be directed with great force at the partner or at oneself. All of us have seen adults driven by the need to recapture their adolescence and by the refusal to accept the march of time.

These feelings are often expressed directly as anger at and envy of the adolescent. When Nicholas's father said, "Okay, hotshot," and broke his experiment, he was trying to stop time, roll back the clock, recapture his own youth and a chance at the prize. Adolescents correctly perceive such words and behaviors as intense, sometimes mean-spirited rivalry.

Thus the teenager may force his parents to turn to each other with new needs reinforced by new hungers, especially sexual hungers stimulated by the adolescent's presence. Much rides on the response these couples offer each other. Unfortunately, many couples told me, just as their sexual desires were rising, they had less time and privacy to enjoy each other. Waiting up late for a teenage daughter to come home or having one's son walk into the bedroom to report on the evening's adventure put a crimp in the parents' sex lives. What these couples did not state was that anxious fantasies about the youngster's activities can also stimulate their own sexual impulses.

Partly through identification with the teenager and partly in preparation for his or her departure, every couple at this stage is forced to look at their marriage and themselves. What is good or bad about our relationship? Is there enough in it? Where are we going, separately and together? What lies ahead? There is change in the air. We examine unrealized ambitions, a promotion not received, a house not purchased, a career change that can no longer be postponed.

Questions of identity — who am I, and why did I choose this road? What if I had gone into another field? What would happen if I gave up the whole rat race, the eight-to-eight shift that enslaves me? Oh, to have another chance to be young, to start at the threshold of life and be able to make other choices. Not surprisingly, the narcissism of the adolescent is contagious, and we become preoccupied with our appearance. Am I too fat? Am I looking old? Am I wrinkled? Am I still attractive?

One woman said, "The whole balance of our marriage is changing. We feel a certain shyness with each other, and we are both unhappy with being a little overweight. Ted loves me as I am, but something has changed in our relationship. It is as if we are suddenly getting to know each other in a new regard. What's looming ahead is that the kids will go away, and we need to take stock and know who we are. A major factor in our lives has been the children and the family. We are not so good at re-creating ourselves, and we have to work on this. The later years will be a challenge. We will have to reconnect as a couple. It's hard for me to look ahead, even in fantasy."

In thinking about the power of adolescence to unhinge a marriage, I wondered what had gone on between Nicholas and Maureen during the period she was obsessed with her daughter's boyfriend. I asked, "Were you and Nicholas having trouble that year?"

"Well," Maureen said reflectively, "he was away a lot at that time. He was here and abroad. But," she added emphatically, backing off from finding flaws in the marriage, "he always traveled. No, it was not the marriage. It was all me and my lost adolescence. And it was about me and my daughter. The truth is, she was growing up and getting ready to leave me — if not with this boy, then with another." She took a deep breath. "Fortunately, it all came to a head when we went on a family vacation — me, the girls, and the boy. My husband joined us after the first week, and immediately the you-know-what hit the fan. Vacations are important to Nicholas, and one of the things he likes is having time and leisure for lovemaking. So I was kind of expecting this to happen, and I was probably more sexually eager because of my fantasies about the boy. Instead, Nicholas turned a cold shoulder on me. He showed no sexual interest, and I was taken aback. And then he exploded." Maureen trembled at the memory and began to pick nervously at her fingernails.

"And?"

"And at that point I got scared," she said. "It was the first time in my life I got that scared, because it finally crossed my mind that there might be a point of no return, that he would leave me. I realized that I had to save my marriage. It was hanging in the balance and was seriously threatened by my crazy obsession. This woke me up. I hadn't betrayed him. It's very important that you understand this. But it was an internal betrayal."

"You mean nothing physical actually transpired between you and the boy."

"That's right. Nothing. It was all in my head. It was like the adolescence I never had fully, and I was living it again through my daughter."

"What happened after Nicholas exploded?"

"It came to an abrupt end. I threw the boy out. I yelled at him like I've never yelled at anyone in my life and said 'Get lost and don't you ever dare come back.'" Maureen smiled. "And then I set the proper constraints on my daughter, who was planning to follow him. My husband and I got together and reined her in. She was crying hysterically, I was crying, but Nicholas and I were working together. We sent my daughter on a trip and separated her forcibly from this crazy relationship.

"In her freshman year at college she wrote a paper in school about a master-servant relationship, using *Jane Eyre* as a point of reference. She's twenty-two now. So, after a one-year episode of losing it, I'm free. I became free when I threw him out. And I've recovered."

Maureen was especially vulnerable to her daughter's adolescence and caught up in a mixture of identification and envy in part because the world had changed since she was young. Like so many of her friends, Maureen had been "a good little girl," whereas her daughter inhabited a more open, exciting, adventurous world. Also Maureen had married at twenty, before she had lived independently. She went from being a protected daughter to being a protected wife in a traditional marriage. Her role as homemaker further distanced her from the world of men.

Her sex life with her husband remained somewhat inhibited, but what had seemed satisfactory for many years was suddenly challenged by the open sexuality of this young Adonis and her daughter. She longed to take her daughter's place with him. How conscious or unconscious her wish was at the time, I do not know, but she clearly understood the erotic nature of her attachment to him when she told me the story.

Maureen was doubly and triply vulnerable because she had reached midlife and was more aware of mortality and death. The death of her own mother and of Nicholas's father contributed to her sense that she would soon be displaced by her young and pretty daughter. Her fantasies about "the young stud" muted her fear of mortality and pushed to the periphery her preoccupation with feeling older and less attractive.

What held her back was her self-awareness, her good sense, her conscience, her genuine love for her daughter, and her love for and loyalty to her husband and to the marriage. But it was Nicholas's brief rejection of her that made her aware of the consequences of her behavior and forced her to bring the situation to an abrupt end.

Maureen wondered whether every woman experienced similar fantasies of reliving her adolescence. Yes, all adults do have the wish, consciously or unconsciously, to be the adolescent they are fighting with, to displace the youngster who is trying to displace them. We love our children, but at the same time we envy them. We want them to grow up, but we know that it's us they are replacing. Our pride in their achievements as young adults mutes our anger and envy, allowing us to step back and let the next generation grow. But it does not banish our wish to be young again, to be standing in their shoes. How could it?

A child's adolescence is also a time of mourning. We grieve because the youngster will soon move out of the home, and we recognize that the teenager's emotional detachment is the first step in that process. We lose our special relationship with the child and the feeling of being essential to his life. We lose the role of wise parent who knows and can do so much.

All of these feelings affected Maureen, who had been close to her daughter. I asked, "Has your daughter forgiven you?"

"I hope so. I think we're good friends again. But it took a lot of doing. I'm sure it will never happen again."

"For her or for you?"

"For her," said Maureen. "The young men she goes out with now are very different. And I think she'll find someone who will take care of her. I want her to have what she needs."

I was interested that she wanted a young man who would take care of her daughter, much as Nicholas has taken care of her. She continued, "I don't want to excuse my behavior, but my hunch is that it's not so unusual for women my age to long for young lovers. I'm sure it's always been true of men."

"How did this episode change your marriage?"

"I don't know," she said. "At one point I would have said it had changed a lot. I felt, until that episode, that I was the most important person in Nicholas's life, and that hung in the balance during the episode. I may be deluding myself, but I feel we're back again. He has no one but me. I provide the emotional support that he needs. We have a deep love for each other. He would never leave me. This is a forever thing. And I have become more sensitive to that. Maybe this was an early midlife crisis. I don't want to be middle-aged. I don't want to be old. Who does?" Maureen's voice was wistful. "I think I was young again with that rescue fantasy."

She seemed lost in fantasy for a moment. "My daughter's very much like the way I was. She's a young woman of great passion in her soul. But it's no longer 'we,' she and I. She and I have separated. We were very close, but this way it's better for her and probably for me, if I can ever believe that. But the main thing with my husband is that I don't pretend that it's both of us. I take full blame. I nearly lost it.

"I also have become more tolerant. I had a friend I was very intolerant of, because something happened with her children and she didn't react in a way I thought was appropriate. I went to her, and I said, 'I owe you an apology, because I judged you and I shouldn't have judged you. And I've learned that nobody can judge anybody else. You know,' she said, shivering a bit, "it chills my soul to talk about this." She smiled, pleased that she had had the courage to tell me this story.

At the end of the interview, in a gesture that was out of keeping with her careful reserve but that reflected the changes she'd experienced, Maureen rose and put her arms around me, and I hugged her back. She knew and I knew that what she had told me was a rarely mentioned but omnipresent part of a long-term traditional marriage — namely, the wish to break out.

I drove away genuinely stirred by her story, thinking how powerful in all of us is the wish to be young again, to take our children's place, and to fly away from marriage, parenting, moral constraints, and adult responsibility.

# 22

# Infidelity in Fantasy and Reality

SEXUAL FANTASIES provide a steady hum in all our lives. They are present in the boardroom and the grocery store, in subways and buses. Sometimes these fantasies rise to a crescendo when temptation calls or anger flares. But most of the time, particularly in happy marriages, they are held in check or are incorporated into the couple's sex life as a stimulus for excitement. Although Maureen was especially frank in talking about the teenage Adonis who so attracted her, I heard many erotic fantasies from the men and women in these happy marriages.

Some people believe that fantasies of infidelity are a symptom of an unhappy marriage. That can be true, but I saw no evidence that it is usually the case. Sexual fantasies are a normal part of adulthood, and the desire to have an affair is part of the human condition, especially in today's sexually exciting milieu. At one time or another, everyone imagines having sex with a stranger, covets the lusty neighbor down the street, or daydreams about going to bed with Sharon Stone or Tom Cruise. The only thing new about sexual fantasies is that now women are more open about discussing them. It's just not true that men want sex and women want love — both sexes want sex and aren't afraid to admit it.

Many women fantasize about sex with the forbidden stranger, the demon lover, the notorious outlaw with long hair to his waist or, as in *The Bridges of Madison County,* the nomadic Robert Kincaid who appears and then, after a few splendid nights of adultery, disappears. They dream of wild, passionate lovemaking that breaks out of the mundane restraints of everyday life, of sex suffused with danger. These current fantasies remind me of a folk song that probably goes back to medieval England and is still popular on college campuses. It tells the story of a lady who leaves her castle to run off with the raggle-taggle gypsies. When her lord comes looking for her, riding high and low through the woods, he finds her standing in the open field and beseeches her to return. She replies, "I would rather one kiss from the gypsy's lips than all your land and money-o." And she remains with the gypsy — anticipating wild sexual pleasure "on the cold open field."

From early adolescence on, men have fantasies about sex with a passionate, beautiful, exciting woman, often one who will do his bidding and fulfill all his sexual appetites. She may be a harlot or Marilyn Monroe or the *Playboy* centerfold. Or she may be Lolita, the virginal, natural young girl with untapped passions. She's everything that he wants her to be.

Fantasies about people from our past are common among both men and women. We all remember our high school and college days, when burning physical passion and sexuality were paramount. People fantasize about the adolescent sweetheart who married someone else or the lover who remains, at least in memory, larger than life. Memory and fantasy are fused. Men and women often go to school reunions with these fantasies inflamed by the illusion that one really can recapture adolescent pleasures and banish the woes and limitations of midlife.

Even a great marriage leaves some part of each partner unsatisfied. In the best marriages both people feel that their most important needs are met, but those that are not met become part of the individual fantasy life. I marry a stable man and find that my fantasies about wild sex continue to excite me. I may embroider them as time goes by. I marry a woman who is brilliant but not tender, so my fantasy is of a tender woman who will caress me and take care of me.

In companionate marriages the relationship is egalitarian, and wives are somewhat less nurturant. Several of the men in such marriages talked wistfully about their fantasy of a delicate, attentive lover, which reminded me of the geisha fantasy — the erotic mother and concubine who takes care of all your needs, who feeds you, strokes you, musses your hair, and makes love to you. The fantasy of a sexual, nurturing woman who does your bidding and devotes herself to you caters to the yearning for omnipotence. A man in his fifties said, "It's funny. I'm very supportive of women's lib. I like to think of my wife as a professional who goes for the top. But it would be so nice if she could achieve all those goals of women's lib and match it with feminine wiles." The fantasy suggests that sex with a seductress who tempts and teases can be more exciting than sex with a partner who regards herself as an equal.

In a good marriage the partners accept that they can't have everything, that some wishes will always remain unmet. But the line between fantasy and behavior can be thin. Moreover, some fantasies can be as threatening as real infidelity; Maureen felt conscience-stricken and suffered as much guilt over her fantasy relationship as if she had actually been unfaithful.

To begin a discussion of infidelity among these happily married couples, I used two open-ended questions — one indirect, "What would break this marriage?" and one direct, "How faithful have you been?"

Nearly everyone in the study, from the passionate, romantic lovers to the most sexually reserved couples, had sexual fantasies and had thought about infidelity. They had also discussed infidelity with their partners. In today's culture of divorce, it is an omnipresent issue. In every type of marriage, the question of faithfulness is confronted and resolved many times.

All acknowledged the excitement of risky sex and recognized that it is readily available, given the number of single and divorced men and women. Anyone who wants to stray will find a ready partner. Our whole society is in transition, and profound shifts in attitudes about sex and infidelity are part of this change. We all live with constant sexual temptation in a culture that equates happiness with a willingness to live in the moment. The fear of AIDS may limit casual encounters, but it does not stand in the way of relationships between long-term colleagues and friends.

Sex is ubiquitous in the workplace. Every successful male executive that I talked to admitted being sexually interested in women he worked with, and some of them were sexually attracted to him. Nicholas said, "Ladies call me. Women do that nowadays. It's new. They have all kinds of agendas. The inducements are high, but essentially I let it be." Several men confided that colleagues were in love with them. Similarly, working women said they had to give explicit signals that they were not available. Friendship and collegial activities can shade imperceptibly into sexual interest and liaisons unless one person clearly draws the line.

One woman told me about planning to attend a conference out of town with a married colleague and friend of many years. He approached her directly. "You're so attractive to me, I'm not sure I'll be able to keep my hands away. Perhaps I should warn you." She countered, "Perhaps I should warn you that one of my great failings is that I'm in love with my husband." She arranged to stay in a different, less convenient hotel during the meeting. The women in the study complained less about sexual harassment than about their sense that they constantly had to define the boundaries in their relationships with male colleagues and friends.

Many of these men and women said they would be tolerant of a partner's casual infidelity brought on by loneliness when traveling alone on business. One man said, when I asked him what would break his marriage, "Well, infidelity wouldn't help, but I don't know that it would break it. We've been together a long time. Anyway, I think it matters what kind of infidelity. A quickie on a business trip, that's one thing. Sleeping with someone's best friend, that's another. After all, sex is readily available in this society."

A one-night stand would not break the marriage, these couples told me. "There would be hell to pay, but it wouldn't break the marriage," a woman said. "I'm not going to throw my marriage away over one incident. But it would matter if he stopped caring." A serious love affair would be unpardonable, they all agreed. If the core of marriage, emotional love, was threatened, the marriage would be over. "If my husband came home and said he was in love with a colleague, that would be intolerable." "If my wife had a lover and said she loved him more than me . . ." This is the new moral Maginot Line. But casual infidelity? According to these couples, it was not an unforgivable sin.

So much for what they said. On the rare occasions when one spouse discovered the other's infidelity, however, there was great suffering. It was *always* a serious crisis. One woman cried for two years after discovering that her husband had spent one night with another woman. Eventually she was able to forgive him, and the marriage recovered. Despite their claims of open-mindedness and acceptance of infidelity, people who were cheated on were shocked and miserable, even if it was only a one-night stand. Their unhappiness surprised them.

No matter what people say or how sophisticated they sound, no one takes infidelity lightly. A tolerant attitude — a casual affair is no big deal — lasts only until your partner cheats on you. Discovery of betrayal is as painful as it's ever been, "modern attitudes" notwithstanding. No one in the study realized how upset they'd be, and one-night stands led to pain that far outweighed the sinner's pleasure. Such revelations didn't break the marriage, but they left people in misery for far longer than anyone thought possible.

Most of the transgressions I was told about had not been discovered and had little or no impact on the marriage. Spouses were absolutely convinced that their husbands or wives had never cheated on them. Since I had promised each person full confidentiality, I knew when they were wrong.

Sixteen percent of the women and 20 percent of the men in these long-term happy marriages had had one-night stands or brief affairs. There is no study of infidelity in California or among educated middle-class Americans with which to compare these figures. But a 1994 national study based on 3,432 men and women aged eighteen to fifty reported that 15 percent of married women and 25 percent of married men admitted to having had sex with someone other than their spouse. There have been several surveys in recent years yielding different results. An unsolved question, of course, is how much credence to put in the data. Also, the large-scale studies do not provide details of the sexual encounters, as my interviews with these men and women did. As a result we do not know how heavily invested the participants were emotionally, whether the infidelity represented a one-night stand or a love affair, whether it was confessed or discovered, and whether it led to estrangement or breakup.

One woman traveling among archeological ruins in a distant land accepted the invitation of a fellow traveler to spend the night in his bed.

"How was it?" I asked.

"Wonderful," she said.

"How guilty did you feel?"

"Not at all." She laughed.

"How was your marriage at the time?"

"It was fine. But the moon was full, and my husband was five thousand miles away."

One woman, who felt depleted by her husband's breakdown and depression, told a different story. "I gave myself the present of a brief affair with a younger man," she said. "It was great but of course temporary."

Brief infidelities occurred in all types of marriages — romantic, rescue, companionate, traditional — but I did not learn of any infidelity among the couples who married in the early 1980s. It's impossible to say whether these marriages were made of stronger stuff or whether more years of marriage would increase the probability of cheating.

I found no evidence among these couples that intense sexual fantasies or infidelity was related to a person's sexual experience before marriage. Some women who had become sexually active at fifteen and had had many lovers had no affairs after marriage. And some who had been virgins at marriage were curious about relationships with other men but did not necessarily rush out to enlarge their experience at midlife. As one woman with three young children told me wistfully, "What I long for is a passionate fling that would last exactly one week."

The temptation to have an affair can strike at any age. Laura, at seventy, was one of the oldest women in the study. Lively and attractive, with green eyes, white hair pulled into a bun, and a slim figure, she had been married for forty years. On the day I met her, she was wearing jeans, a cotton sweater, and light makeup. When I asked what would break her very good marriage, she told me the following story.

"Before I got married, I had a love affair that lasted almost two years. It was passionate. I've never been sure why I didn't marry him, and I took the initiative in leaving. I hadn't seen him in over forty years. During all this time I knew where he was, and he wrote to me once or twice. I wrote back, just to say hello. At one point he indicated that he wanted very much to see me, but I didn't follow through on this. My husband had seen his name on a letter that arrived at home, and he had been very angry and quite jealous. So I didn't respond to the letter.

"Then I found myself one fine day in the city where my former lover was residing, and I decided to call him. I was leaving the city that evening, and I called him in the morning and said I'd have some free time that afternoon, and if he was free I'd like to get together. He hesitated and said he might be busy, then he decided suddenly that he could meet me. So we did."

I listened spellbound.

"I wasn't quite sure how I would greet him, but it seemed sort of silly, when you've been in bed with somebody, to greet them with a handshake. When I saw him, I recognized him immediately. He looked very well. He was tall and good-looking when I knew him, and he is tall and good-looking at seventy-five. He has maintained his figure, which I've always liked in men, and I found it very easy to go over to him and to put my arms around him and hug him. He was pleased and pleasantly surprised, and it was, as we sat down together to have tea, as if no time at all had elapsed.

"He told me that he had married and had several children, all now grown up. It had taken him two or three years of real anguish to get over me, and he had succeeded actually in repressing me and our history almost totally. He had solved it in that way. His wife knew about me, but his wife was a very beautiful woman. He showed me pictures of her and his adult children. He'd attained an eminent position in his field and obviously had at least externally a good life. He wanted to know in detail about my life and marriage, and I told him. He was very disappointed that I didn't have pictures of my children.

"It soon became clear that as we were talking, we were each falling into who we used to be. It was as if history had vanished. We were recalling memories of our time together. He said he'd been trying a few days before to remember the song I used to sing. Actually, I hadn't thought of it since I last saw him, and to my surprise I found I could sing it with a clear voice and I remembered all the verses.

"It was clear that we were talking out of a context of the relationship that had been. He was watching every one of my movements. And I was very aware of his presence physically. We were a man and a woman across the table from each other, a man and a woman who were profoundly attracted to each other, and there was no gainsaying that.

"I left to take a taxi to the airport. He did not offer to drive me. As we left, he embraced me. I turned my cheek when he kissed me, and he kissed me on the cheek, and then we almost kissed. I left in the taxi, and he stood as if frozen on the sidewalk, waving me off. I waved and left.

"The most interesting thing happened after that. I was like somebody on fire. I couldn't get him out of my body. I couldn't get the longing for him out of my arms, out of any part of me. I was on fire with a sexual desire for him, and there was no way that it seemed quenchable. I went home and seduced my husband and that didn't help. The song I had sung ran through my head day and night. I was preoccupied with fantasies of his calling, of meeting him. What I would say, what he would say. What's more, there was no doubt in my mind that he was experiencing the same.

"It's interesting that what restrained me from calling him was an image of my oldest grandchild. Perhaps our parents restrain us when we're young and our grandchildren restrain us when we're old. This intense fire, this intense excitement, the sense of being overwhelmed by every love song I'd ever heard, by every snatch of love poetry that I remembered, was an amazing experience that went on with all the other activities I was doing. It seemed not to interfere with my activities but was a sort of permanent excitement and preoccupation, a passionate preoccupation alongside of whatever else I was doing.

"Had he called, I don't know what I would have done. During the first two weeks, my fantasy reply to his call was 'What took you so long?' As the weeks went by, my fantasy response changed to 'I'm glad you didn't call, because I would have met you anywhere.'

"I tell you this because I think we have an entirely wrong view of adults in the aging process. I don't think there's anything atypical about me. I don't think it's in keeping, however, with the view of men and women in their seventies. On the other hand, maybe this is something that is coming down the road, an awareness of passion and sexual excitement as occurring naturally for many people, or maybe for just some people, late in life.

"Incidentally, none of this was associated with not loving my husband. There wasn't the slightest sense that I was in love with this man. There was the clear sense that I passionately wanted him. But I also was able to put together in this episode, from some clues that he gave me when he spoke, the reasons why I had left him in the first place. And this also, instead of giving me closure about the experience, opened up the flood of memory and sexual passion."

I was reminded of Gloria Steinem's proclamation on her fiftieth birthday: "This is what fifty looks like." Laura's story was what seventy looked like for her. Passion and sexuality are not lost with aging, despite what the younger generation may want to believe about their parents and grandparents.

Like Maureen and Laura, most of the men and women in these happy marriages did not act on their sexual fantasies. The fact is, a good marriage depends on giving up certain things, and these couples were highly conscious of that. To protect your marriage, you hold your fantasies in check and honor your commitment. That may mean you have to settle for a tamer sex life.

Keeping fantasies in a safe container is one of the primary requirements of marriage in any culture, but especially in a divorce culture, where there are so few external controls — Big Brother or the mullahs are not watching. In these marriages, fidelity was not based on a list of do's and don'ts or on religious principles but on recognition that behavior has consequences. What restrains people from infidelity is not the lack of fantasy or desire but a strong moral commitment to the marriage.

People also felt that if they ventured into an affair, their spouse could venture as well, and they considered that unacceptable. No one claimed to have never been tempted, but many admitted to sexual fantasies they did not act on because they did not want to hurt the other person. A man in his fifties said, "You never stop looking at women. Only when you're blind or dead. As for action, there's none. For moral reasons and because I love my wife." A woman in her late thirties said, about a developing flirtation she cut short, "We stopped because I'm not good at guile."

What mattered most, the couples said, was the emotional meaning of behavior. Real infidelity is a betrayal of the heart. But a sense of morality, loyalty to the marriage, love, and protectiveness toward the other person can keep infidelity at bay.

# PART SIX

# Renegotiating Marriage

# 23 &

# Confronting Change

BECAUSE PEOPLE AND LIFE circumstances change over time, marriage is always a work in progress. Like the human heart, it can only function dynamically; stasis means death. The challenge for every married couple is to stay connected, not just in terms of legal marriage but in terms of friendship and attraction in spite of the inevitable kaleidoscope of change. Marriage is always a gamble because it poses a tricky question: will two people living together for many years change in ways that are mutually congenial? The answer, of course, is as varied as the human population. Some marriages change so little over time that the couple seem much as they were during courtship. Other people and marriages change so radically that they bear no resemblance to how they started out.

Many couples seem to think that just as they can't slow down the human aging process, they can't do anything to alter the aging process of marriage. They let the relationship take its "natural course" by happenstance until it threatens to break down, and by then it may be too late.

It does not have to be this way. Sure, marriage *is* a gamble, but it's possible to stack the deck in your favor. It's feasible to win, not by leaving everything to chance, but by attending to the changes that occur as we age and the marriage ages. Along with the everyday changes, which accumulate slowly, there are predictable times of major transition, comparable to the developmental milestones of growing up, when changes in the individuals and in the family structure destabilize earlier patterns. The couple is forced to revamp their relationship to bring it back into balance. Unfortunately, these periods tend to be so unstable that the marriage may be in jeopardy.

I've already talked at length about one of these predictable milestones, the transition from being a couple to being parents, when the marriage undergoes a profound metamorphosis. Similarly at midlife many people have strong fantasies about being young again as they watch their adolescent children strut their sexuality and aggression. This is a time of important psychological and physiological changes in men and women, and couples again need to redefine their relationship. When the children leave home, the marriage undergoes another metamorphosis as it reverts to being just two people. This too is a time for renegotiating the marriage tasks.

Retirement is another period of redefinition, as people experience the changes associated with aging and think more about illness and death. In retirement men and women spend more time together than at any other time during their lives. With work no longer providing the basis for self-definition and a link to the outside world, this stage opens new opportunities for enhancing the marriage as well as new hazards. Although only a few of the happily married couples in the study were in retirement marriages, the similarities among them were striking, especially in terms of how couples dealt with the marriage tasks.

A different kind of transition is the second marriage, which has its own unique characteristics and challenges. A remarriage that includes dependent children from one or both first marriages demands special understanding and thoughtful planning. Some of the issues that arise have no counterpart in first marriages, and those who remarry are often ill prepared for the new conditions that await them. Although the psychological tasks of marriage are the same, the context in which they are dealt with is very different.

Every couple needs to review how they have resolved the tasks of their marriage on a regular basis rather than waiting until disappointment, restlessness, or anger brings the situation to a flash point. Many people seem to focus on external questions. Should I take the new job? Should we send Jimmy to private school? Can we afford to buy a bigger house? But it's equally important to explore the inner issues: the new job is great, but is the emotional cost too high? Or, I've been feeling lonely, stir-crazy, bored, restless, exhausted, and fragmented; what can we change in our lives to deal with these feelings? Or, our social life has grown meaningless to me. How can we revise it? Or, what I want more than anything in the world is the space, time, and money to write or paint or travel; what can we do to make it happen?

If a marriage has become shaky, the very process of negotiating the tasks again can help the couple reconnect. Finding ways to revitalize the marriage should be a central theme for every couple. Indeed, one of the great virtues of modern marriage is that it allows for much greater flexibility than in the past, when conformity prevailed.

In these final chapters I discuss how couples in the study dealt with the developmental changes of midlife and retirement and with second marriages. I hope that their experience and wisdom will help others facing similar life transitions.

People used to view adulthood as a plateau. You reached it, coasted along for a number of years, then got old. But in recent decades many researchers have explored the psychological and social changes that occur in the adult years, especially during midlife, which is variously defined but generally considered to be between the ages of thirty-five and fifty-five.

Midlife is sometimes seen as the noon of life, the period of highest achievement before aging brings declines in mental and physical prowess. People at midlife realize that time no longer stretches ahead forever. Somber thoughts are often triggered by the illness and death of older parents, by the aggressive behavior of teenage children, by the empty nest, and by changes in one's own body. Midlife is also a time to take stock of one's accomplishments and disappointments. Some people, like Nicholas, can say, "I met and conquered the giants on their own turf." Many others say, "I am a disappointment to myself and to my family." Or "I am underappreciated and underused." And there is the inevitable and important question: "Have I found love and sexual satisfaction?"

While the midlife issues of individuals have been examined extensively in recent years, less attention has been paid to marriage at this critical juncture. But all of these concerns have their counterparts in marriage. At midlife, couples are at a crossroads of change, just as individuals are.

Unfortunately, a time that is ripe for change does not necessarily bring change, and marriages can grow or become stale at this time. Some couples merely live side by side, united only by their common history and shared interest in the children. Others expand their horizons and develop a new, more intimate relationship. Some despair about their future together and decide to divorce.

The challenge understood intuitively by many of the couples in this study was the need to reshape their marriage at midlife to meet their changing needs and new circumstances. As the children left home and coparenting no longer bound them in familiar routines, they set about establishing new bases for togetherness. As individuals they found new paths to satisfy the need for independence, and they encouraged each other to undertake new ventures. Together they addressed discrepancies in their sexual interests.

At midlife the original task of marriage, separating from the families of origin and establishing new connections, must be solved anew. Now, however, the task is to separate from and make new connections with young adult children. Both aspects of the task — separating and reconnecting — are important, and neither is easy. At this stage the issue is to let go of the marriage that was defined by children and to create in its place a new one in which the partners are once again focused on each other.

Although the transformation from family back to couple may have been anticipated and discussed in hundreds of conversations, when it occurs it does so with dramatic suddenness. Sometimes a couple is hardly aware of how much their self-identity and their perception of each other has been modified by the years in which the children were growing up. But whether or not the couple is aware of the differences, a marriage that has finished with active child rearing is by its nature a different entity. The midlife couple's identity as parents fades, and new identities emerge.

As with the separation from our original families, the separation from our children is both a painful process and a welcome prospect. We mourn the loss of our children's daily presence, and we mourn for the family as a child-centered unit. Fortunately this process occurs over a period of time, sometimes over many years, depending on the number and spacing of the children. Parents often need several years to make the psychological transition that is required. For the young person, leaving home is a major milestone, and the transition to young adulthood is both welcomed and feared in varying degrees. The parents play foil to these powerful feelings while struggling with their own emotions.

At the same time, parents look forward to the freedom that the children's departure will bring. As one man said, "I've been looking forward to this empty nest. Our daughter wants to stay home an extra year, but we've convinced her to go to the university now." He was clearly impatient to spend time alone with his wife and had made many plans for what they would do together. Parents' anxiety about facing each another across a dinner table that no longer includes the energy and chatter of adolescents is offset by pleasure at the opportunity to engage in new activities together and separately. Most parents approach this new phase with a mixture of pleasure and dread. ·

Men and women in all of these families grieved when their children left home. Some men shed silent tears as their sons or daughters departed for college, even when the school was less than twenty miles away. In one child-centered traditional family, my interviews took place just as their son was leaving for college. Both parents were preoccupied with his departure and the changes that it would bring. While I was interviewing the husband, the young man returned from registering at the university. His father asked him if he had registered, if he had chosen courses, if he had done a number of other things he was supposed to do. The son, who towered over his father, kept saying, "Yes, Dad. Yes, Dad. Yes, Dad," clearly making an effort not to be irritated by his father's protective manner.

When we were alone again, the father turned to me and said, "I don't want him to grow up. I don't want him to go away from us. Berkeley is far enough. I don't want him to go any further. But he's ready. He's really ready to go. He's a man, and he's gone across the threshold."

Asked what was good about his marriage, this man replied, "The best thing about our marriage is our children. They are the focus of what we do, the way we are. Most of our other family live very far away, so we're kind of isolated. And I think just naturally we cling, we both cling, because we're so far away. We both thoroughly enjoy our kids. We love doing things with them. And now our children are at the point where they're leaving us. The world becomes bigger for them. We're still focused on them, and we're still doing for them, but it's a different kind of doing. They're becoming adults. I think we've gotten more clingy now because they're leaving, and my wife and I are focusing more on each other. I think that's good. There's some kind of a transition going on."

I asked him what he thought his life would be like now. "Well," he said, "it was great before we had kids. Meeting at five, going out for dinner. It will be great again. But I'm going to walk around the house, and it will be too quiet. My wife will miss them, and we'll probably spend more time talking about them. But we're not so stupid as not to realize that that's the way life is, and that doesn't mean we're not going to go out and have fun and be two people. We are."

His wife echoed her husband's inner struggle with the pain and the hope of the looming separation. "This has been a major emotional stand for us all. It's been awful because I think, in his need to separate, our son has made life difficult. Otherwise there would be no easy way to walk away. When we were ready to drive him over, it took him an extra hour to get out of the house. He's called many times, always with a purpose, but about things he could have figured out anyway. But he's a very strong, independent boy. He's not a mama's boy or a papa's boy in any form. We're just very close. Ninety-nine percent of the time we had dinner together. It was family time, and we sat and heard about each other's day. We'll miss that time."

The task of separation often takes a long time, especially in close traditional families. Two years later this family was still struggling with the transition. "He comes back once a month," the mother told me, "and we go to the theater together. But I think he needs to be away from us. I think it's important for him to do so, in order for him to feel his own strength. For both of us, though, this is a big loss." She added poignantly, "We need to focus on ourselves more." At the end of our talk she said sadly, "The family goes away when the kids go away."

There's no question that the children's departure looms larger for traditional families than for others because they are more child-centered and the mother has spent more time at home. These couples feel a greater sense of loss, and they face a greater need to reorganize the family. And, as is clear from the divorces that occur at this point in life, couples often find that in the hustle and bustle of child rearing they have grown apart, to the point that the children are all they really have in common. Sometimes the gap cannot be closed.

However these families dealt with the transition, they were aware that a major chapter in their lives was ending and another one was opening.

The task of establishing togetherness and autonomy must also be undertaken anew at this time. Couples who have defined themselves largely as parents need to rethink who they are as individuals and what their togetherness consists of. Autonomy has a new meaning, especially for women. Those who have regarded taking care of children as their major job face an exciting and frightening set of questions: who shall I be now, and what shall I do with the rest of my life? Women who have not been at home full-time face major changes as well. Should they now make a greater investment in their career or spend more time in other activities?

All couples must confront once again the questions they faced as newlyweds: how much emotional investment do we make in us as a couple? How much time will we spend in activities with other people or in individual pursuits? The issues are all on the table again. These decisions will determine the nature of the relationship over the next decades. This transition is especially important because of our lengthening life span. The average life expectancy for a woman is now seventy-nine, and for a man, seventy-two. Many people live healthy, contented lives well into their eighties. And the quality of the marriage has a significant effect on physical and mental health during later years.

Negotiating the midlife tasks is by no means easy, even in a good marriage, because despite the bonds that hold the couple together, the potential for being angry at or unhappy with one's mate also increases at this time. It's easy to find fault with a spouse or to lay the blame for one's own boredom or disappointment on him or her — "He is responsible for what went wrong." "If it weren't for her I'd be happy." If the children are having difficulties, a partner makes a convenient scapegoat. If work is unfulfilling, if one is feeling bypassed or fearing the onset of old age, it is also easy to lay the blame on one's partner, to take out frustrations on the one family member still left at home.

No one is immune from the urge to turn back the clock. And holding on to the earlier idealization of a partner becomes more difficult in midlife because people know that they have aged visibly and will continue to do so. Our anxieties about aging are readily projected: "I am feeling vigorous, but my wife looks old. The wrinkles on her neck disgust me." Or "I'm in the mood for passion, but he is bald and struggling with impotence." A couple's sex life may seem stale because it is so familiar.

On the other hand, men and women in all types of marriages

expressed a new restlessness and a desire for adventure at this juncture. Their new physical and emotional energies helped them undertake new ventures. Several men and women turned toward spiritual pursuits and religion; several rejoined the churches or synagogues in which they had been raised, even though they had not attended during their adult years.

Many women, especially, were successful in opening new chapters in their lives. In the midlife marriages I observed, all of the women were working, including those who had not worked while they were raising children. They were also doing more things on their own. One woman went on a fifty-mile hike with women friends to celebrate her fiftieth birthday; another took off on a rugged trip to Outer Mongolia. Another went on a pilgrimage to a Tibetan shrine. Some went back to school and took up new careers. One woman discovered that she had exceptional artistic ability and began to show her work in Bay Area galleries. Others decided to go to school full-time, not necessarily with a professional goal but simply to learn. All of these women were seeking a new emphasis for their lives, an endeavor that would engage and challenge them as much as raising children had and that would complement their husband's commitment to a career.

Men's lives change less at midlife, for they still go off to work each morning, as they always have; they do not have to reinvent themselves, as many women do, when the children leave home. Nevertheless, the men in the study, too, took stock at this stage. Several, like Nicholas, decided to start their own companies. Some decided to change direction in their careers; others withdrew much of their interest from work to concentrate on projects such as writing a novel or getting involved in community or political activities. The changes were very individual, but in each case there was a sense of having new energy and a restlessness that prompted the search.

There is considerable variation in the degree of external change people introduce at this point. Many are content with their careers, and others have little or no room to maneuver. Still others seek a radical change. Some midlife changes are barely perceptible from the outside, but they may represent important, subtle shifts in self-identity and in the perception of one's partner.

By contrast, some people became so intensely involved in their careers that they spent less time with their partners than before. At our follow-up interviews, some couples reported their growing concern that they were out almost every night and were spending much less time with each other. In companionate marriages like Kit and Beth's, where each partner's life is already quite separate, a shift toward less togetherness can pose a serious problem; without togetherness a marriage is surely impoverished and may collapse.

In most of the happy marriages, the individual changes lent a quickening to the marriage itself. There was a change in mood and a rising excitement in the couple's interaction, which helped overcome the notion that life from then on would be all downhill. Men and women encouraged each other in their new roles and ventures. One man said, "If I had three wishes in the world, one would be for her to get recognition for her art. She is so talented, and she's still afraid to show her work."

On the negative side, however, some men reacted with a mixture of pleasure and displeasure to their wives' new interests. Some felt demoted in the relationship and less cared for. One man growled, "She's going for a Ph.D. in public health. Whenever she goes back to school, life is hell." Some husbands envied their wives' sudden freedom to "play" at art or music or pottery. They felt that the marriage had been based on a fair division of labor: she raised the children while he worked at the office. The notion that she could now take classes just for fun drove some men wild. And even when the wives were working seriously at their activities, if they did not have paid jobs their husbands were resentful. At the same time these men were proud of their wives' newfound independence and success. They held themselves up as being a new kind of man, secure enough to accept equality in the relationship.

Despite increasing autonomy and independence, friendship becomes more important in the midlife marriage. After thrashing out the tensions caused by these changes, couples in the study tended to look at what they had in common. They talked about shared interests, their support for each other in and out of the home, and the time they spent together. Asked what was happy about her midlife marriage, one woman said, "It's easy; there are no hassles. We're good friends." A man said, "It's comfortable, we're good friends. Our roles are flexible." Others said, "Love is there, but it's not primary. Friendship is primary" and "We are each other's best friend, lover, and supporter."

This greater friendship and closeness gradually fills the gap left by the end of active parenting and becomes, in many instances, the basis for a new and different kind of intimacy. It is not about the past or about care of the children but is focused on shared concerns in the present as well as the issues ahead, including retirement and aging.

Men and women in the study spoke about having new feelings and about rediscovering each other. "We love each other differently now," said a woman. "The edges are softer, we're both more willing to give and take." Another woman said, "I look and feel different. I'm fifty; I'm settling in, and I've grown up, I've changed. I'm not looking for diversion anymore." A man said, "There has been a deepening of our feelings for each other. Until now, just keeping the family afloat and balanced was an absorbing task. Now we feel more together than ever before."

A woman said, "We're aging, and we can both see the ravages of time. I know that he loves me as I am. There's increased fondness and caring, and also shyness. It's like a new sexual and nonsexual relationship."

Many couples spoke about changes in sexuality, which required renegotiation of this important task. One woman said, "When you work from seven-thirty in the morning till eight at night, you don't have the energy you used to have. He would like sex more often. It's important to me, but my needs have changed." Others reported heightened excitement and desire. Men experienced less fluctuation in their sexuality at this time. By and large their level of desire was stable or began gradually to diminish. A few men reported episodes of impotence, which frightened them badly. One man said, "I thought my life was over."

To fill the gap of the children's departure, couples reached out more to friends and families, making an effort to reestablish connections with their siblings — with the clan, if you will. Some organized family reunions. Many people were tending to the needs of the extended family, not only aging and dying parents but siblings who were having problems. Men and women alike spoke of making vigorous efforts to stay in touch, by telephone or visits, with current friends and to renew ties with friends from bygone days who had drifted away. People who had never been to class reunions went back for the first time. Sometimes the children's friends became regular visitors and were welcomed as emissaries from the younger generation. People felt a greater need to join social groups organized around religious institutions or political work, which several of the families took very seriously.

At midlife people in a happy marriage are likely to be best friends who are on separate tracks; they understand the importance of holding on to each other but are actively reaching out as well to friends and family.

The factors that lead couples in happy marriages to rework the core tasks of their relationship at midlife lead other couples to seek divorce. I have seen many seemingly stable marriages come apart when the children reach mid-adolescence or when the youngest child leaves home. Marriages that were good enough when the children were being raised may not be able to weather the treacherous passage of midlife. Men and women may find their lives wanting in love, sexual gratification, and respect from their partner.

These feelings of deprivation, combined with the sometimes frantic sense that time is running out, lead to what I have called the "last-chance divorce." Sometimes an adult who leaves a marriage in midlife is trying to live out a fantasy of recapturing lost youth. Men wear unbuttoned shirts and gold chains. Women dress like their teenage daughters. Dissatisfied husbands and wives let their eyes roam over the sexual market, often looking for a younger partner. Some people are driven by the desperate feeling that if they do not act now to find love and sexual gratification, their life will have been wasted.

I recall one poignant case that showed clearly how that feeling of desperation can combine with the children's adolescence to precipitate a divorce. As in many other divorces at midlife, this was a marriage in which there had been no overt conflict; it had functioned reasonably well until that critical time.

Nancy Johnson, a forty-three-year-old mother of three teenagers, was hijacked, along with fifty-nine other passengers, on a flight to Miami. As the hijacker marched up and down the aisle, brandishing his Uzi and threatening people with instant death, she said to herself, "If I get out of this alive, I'm going to divorce my husband. I have to have something that makes my life worthwhile before I die."

Nancy, at eighteen, in an effort to escape the incestuous and increasingly difficult demands of her alcoholic father, had married a man she had known only briefly. The family lived modestly on her husband's salary as a bookkeeper while she raised the children. Nancy loved being a mother and was known throughout her San Jose neighborhood as a model parent. She was active in her church, the Girl Scouts, and the PTA. Her husband was very fond of her and appreciated her skills as a mother and homemaker, but she thought of him primarily as another child in the family. For her it was a loveless marriage.

After the terrifying ordeal of being hijacked, she made good on her promise to herself. She left her husband and three children and almost immediately became involved with a man she had long admired from afar. The feelings were mutual. He left his wife and children for her, and they married as soon as they were able.

When I saw Nancy five years later, she did not regret leaving her first marriage. She was passionately in love with her new husband, and despite some financial and health difficulties, the marriage was good. Even so, leaving her children was a continuing source of great sadness. Although the children had tried to understand, they were no longer close to her. Her ex-husband continued to feel angry, betrayed, and abandoned, although he, too, had remarried. Reviewing her decision, she said, "I didn't want to die without ever having lived."

All of the last-chance divorces I have seen were decided on by one person over the opposition of the other. Outcomes vary. Sometimes both people improve their lives, and sometimes both regret the loss of the marriage. More often, only one feels it was the right decision. Some of these divorces might have been avoided if the couple had understood the need to redefine their marriage at midlife.

Given the hoopla in recent years about the inevitability of midlife crisis and the havoc it plays with marriage, I was eager to learn how men and women in happy marriages coped with this phenomenon. Men and women who divorce at this time in their lives often say that the midlife crisis explains their partner's unexpected affair with a younger person. Or they speak about their own crisis, mentioning depression, restlessness, and dissatisfaction with their lives; they want to redefine their goals and priorities — and often they want to find a new spouse.

But among the happily married couples, I found no serious midlife crises, nothing that fit the definition of major psychological changes that propel an individual to make radical, unexpected decisions. No one threatened separation or divorce at this time. Maureen's erotic fantasy about her daughter's boyfriend had the makings of a full-blown midlife crisis, but it was short-circuited by her commitment to her husband and family and by her husband's threatened rejection. It was indeed a serious crisis, but the marriage contained its impact.

One forty-two-year-old man became moderately depressed shortly after his business burned down. Two years later he had not fully recovered and was continuing in psychotherapy, still casting about for a new focus in his work. His relationship with his wife was certainly affected, and their sex life had suffered because of his depression, but neither husband nor wife mentioned wanting to separate. In fact, he had become more involved in activities with his children and in responsibility as a parent.

No one has studied midlife issues in good marriages, but it is reasonable to assume that the quality of the relationship influences the individual's response to personal crisis. The support of a good marriage can mute people's pervasive dissatisfactions with themselves and their achievements at this life stage.

Typically, the people in happy marriages expected to help each other with crises. They were able to anticipate the children's departure and to discuss how they would deal with it. They knew it would be painful, but they also saw the advantages of life without the children and they thought about finding ways to fill the gaps. They were able to help each other deal with conflicting feelings and to encourage each other to embark on new ventures. They welcomed the idea of change in themselves and in the marriage. At the same time they were realistic in their expectations and not given to acting out impossible fantasies. As one man said, "We're more realistic than most people and less susceptible to middle-aged craziness. It's not giving free rein to fantasy, as one of our friends would like to imagine — that his responsibilities to his children don't exist."

My sense is that by introducing change into their lives by reshaping the marriage tasks, these couples blocked crises that might have disrupted their relationship. By finding new ways to strengthen the marriage, they infused it with new life. Instead of each person going outside of the relationship to seek new stimuli, they were able to refashion the marriage to fit their changed needs.

Midlife changes may be easier to appreciate in retrospect than when they occur. The restlessness that leads to change can be distressing, and the paths people take are rarely clear at the outset. Even when blessed with the fine antennae that these couples had, no one can fully anticipate the impact of this transition or the emotional resilience that it requires. Although these couples did rise to the occasion, they were sometimes surprised by the strains it put on their equanimity. All of these couples, however, were keenly aware of the exciting opportunities they could create in the decades that lay ahead. Some reported that their marriage was better than ever. Some looked back with nostalgia at their child-rearing years. No one said midlife was a piece of cake.

# 24 ⁊

# Ellis and Janet Boulden

## *A Second Marriage*

OVER THE PAST TWENTY-FIVE YEARS, my colleagues and I have worked closely with many hundreds of people in second marriages, many of whom had children from prior marriages. By the time we saw them, most of these couples were in serious trouble and had already decided to divorce a second time. For many, stepparenting was much more difficult than they had ever imagined. The hoped-for happiness in the second marriage had not come to pass.

I was eager, therefore, to see how happily remarried couples in the study had addressed issues that so many others have found overwhelming. A third of the couples in the study were in second marriages, and most had children from the first marriages. Most of the second marriages had begun in the 1970s and 1980s, when divorce rates were rising.

Actually, I know of no better argument for divorce than the happy second marriages that I saw in this study. And I know of no better argument against impulsively rushing into marriage at an early age than the painful stories these men and women told of their disastrous first marriages. All of them had married young the first time around; no one had been over twenty-two. The partners they chose were mostly marginal, troubled people. They married impulsively, often with hardly any courtship. "Marry me, it's my birthday," said one young woman to her date, who complied, and regretted it almost immediately.

Some of the young people were living away from home for the first time — at school or in a job, sometimes in a strange city — and married because they were unbearably lonely. Some, running away from wretched or violent homes, sought refuge with the first person who acted kindly toward them. Others married after a brief affair that resulted in pregnancy. One man said, "I didn't dare confront my father after she got pregnant. The marriage had nothing to do with her."

For all of these people, divorce was a gift, even a blessing. But it was a wrenching experience, which they described as the lowest point in their lives, even more painful than the bad marriage itself. And once the marriage was over, everyone had to face again the loneliness or guilt that had driven them to marry impulsively in the first place. Eventually the marriage and divorce melded together in their minds, and for many years afterward they experienced flashbacks in dreams and waking life.

The second time around, these men and women chose more carefully. Older and wiser, they were better observers of themselves and others. Though they yearned for love, they understood the meaning of commitment. But they also felt frightened of repeating their mistakes and failing once again.

To explore second marriage, I chose a family with two sets of children from the earlier marriages, primarily because "blending" children into a new family is so very difficult. Second marriages fail earlier and even more frequently than first marriages, and the most important factor in these failures is children.

Second marriages can belong to any of the four types; I chose a romantic one to demonstrate that a marriage which begins later in life can achieve the sexual passion and intensity that eluded the two people in their unhappy first marriages. The example presents a hopeful view of the potential of a good remarriage to undo earlier suffering.

I was introduced to Ellis and Janet Boulden through a colleague at the University of California in Berkeley. Ellis had taught a course with my friend, who spoke highly of their marriage. So I called Ellis, and after consulting his wife, he said they would be happy to cooperate.

The Bouldens have been married for sixteen years and have raised four children together. They married when she was thirty-four and he was thirty-seven; at the time each had a boy and a girl under the age of eleven. Janet's children lived with them and rarely saw their biological father. Ellis's children lived nearby with their mother, who remained bitterly angry at Ellis, even though she was the one who had sought the divorce. His children stayed with him and Janet every other weekend.

Ellis is a handsome man with a full head of brownish blond hair and the athletic physique of a distance runner. He greeted me in the hall of their turn-of-the-century San Francisco house and showed me into the parlor, which was dark and cool, with mahogany wainscoting and Victorian decor. Ellis is a medical writer for a city newspaper, and he peppered me with a journalist's questions. He asked about my work on divorce and its long-term effects on the family. His concern and the direct questions alerted me to possible problems in the Bouldens' marriage. I made a mental note to explore the issue of blending children in a new marriage later, but first I needed to know more about Ellis and Janet.

I began with my usual question, "What's good about this marriage?"

"We were both walked out on," Ellis said bluntly. "What's happy about this marriage is that we both wanted each other. Both of us came wanting particular things, things we felt were missing from our previous marriages."

From the outset Ellis used his first marriage as a reference point. And later, in my interview with Janet, she too began with comments about her first marriage and the fact that both she and Ellis had had previous failures.

"I was blind-sided," Ellis continued. "I had what I thought was a good marriage. When my wife left me, I felt castrated on the spot."

"I take it the divorce was unexpected?"

"Yes. I still feel regret and pain that the marriage ended, though I don't have feelings for my first wife. I don't want to rekindle that relationship or anything, but I regret the loss of the marriage. I'm even cautious about assuming my marriage to Janet is happy, because I felt my first marriage was happy."

He winced. "This is Janet's house from her first marriage, but if she decides to walk out, I'm staying." He laughed. "I'm settled, and I plan to stay in this house. It's not going to be me who leaves."

Although Ellis said he had fully detached from his first wife and didn't miss her, he was still haunted by her rejection of him. And although he joked about Janet walking out on him, there was a serious undertone to his laughter.

I asked him, "Do you think you knew better what you were looking for the second time around?"

He nodded. "What I needed in my marriage, and what I got with Janet, is someone who communicates, who tells me when she is hurting, tells me when she is upset instead of keeping it to herself. She doesn't expect me to be a mind reader. Janet is really up-front. She tells me everything, even when I don't want to hear it. Sometimes its painful. Sometimes it feels like too much, but it's what I wanted. I confess, sometimes I'd like to have a nice compliant wife who wouldn't say these things to me. But really, I'm glad about how she is."

"Tell me about Janet," I said.

Ellis smiled, and his mood changed. As he told the story, I had the sense that these images were burnished into his mind, that he loved telling the story to assure himself that it was true and to recapture his early excitement and pleasure.

"I remember when she joined a group that I was in," he said. "It's called Parents Without Partners. I remember what she looked like, her accent, her figure, her hair. She's stunningly beautiful. Plus she looked, you know, polished and urbane. I wanted to see her again after the group, so I sort of barged over to her house to help with a project she had mentioned she needed help on. So that was the first time I came to this house. I just dropped over unexpectedly.

"Our first date happened shortly after that. We went to the beach and stayed nine hours. We were both so hungry and vulnerable. We couldn't get enough of each other. We spent the whole day talking. It was a marvelous romantic day, and we ended up in bed with great sensual pleasure. We bowled each other over. Both of us were shocked. I guess you could say that we experienced the incredible rapture of being together."

"How soon did you two think about marriage?"

"Well, I was still stuck trying to figure out my relationship with my ex-wife, still hoping that it would work out. I was delighted by the passion with Janet, but I didn't intend to pursue the relationship because I still hoped to make up the first marriage. We broke up several times, mostly over the difference in our commitment to each other."

The transition between first and second marriage is inevitably rocky. No one I talked to in the study jumped quickly into marriage a second time. They were worried about trusting their own judgment, which had led them astray the first time. Several entered psychotherapy to explore why they had chosen so poorly and how they could do better. Many, like Ellis, rocked back and forth between the two relationships. Ellis's passionate attachment to Janet vied with his loyalty to his first wife and the children, even though his wife had left him.

He continued, "The thing is, I'm not geared up for casual sex. It seemed wrong to be leading Janet on with this great sex if in fact I wasn't thinking we were going anywhere in the relationship. So that was my only discomfort." He smiled. "The chemistry was phenomenal. Janet would be surprised if I didn't mention sex."

"Tell me about it," I said, pleased with his directness.

"For us, sex is number one. We both had some desperate needs for sex coming out of our first marriages. We were both deprived — Janet even more than myself, I think. But sex was absolutely one of the most important connections we made when we first met, and it continues to be an essential affirmation in our marriage. It's a very critical part of this marriage. Janet hadn't had sex in five or six years when we met and was desperate to include that in a healthy way in her life."

Ellis said that he and Janet had dated on and off for almost two years until "finally I realized that my wife had no interest in restoring the marriage. I told her, file or I will. Janet and I were ready to move on." He sounded positively cheerful. "Once we decided to get married, we moved right along. We put together our own wedding here at the house. We wrote our own service. We had my traditions and her traditions. We had a terrific time."

The change in Ellis as he described his marriage to Janet was striking. He was glowing and animated. "From the beginning, as a couple, we have had an emotional connection that's deep and strong and true and fulfilling. She is so special, energetic, a no-nonsense woman. I romanticize things. She's direct, honest, and has an incredible courage in facing things. But the basis of our relationship is that we are a couple, committed to making our marriage work. We've been together sixteen years. The truth is, I've been desperately in love for sixteen years."

His phrase, "desperately in love," may have been a reflection of the intense feelings that his first marriage had not allowed him to experience. To Ellis, Janet was a tower of strength, not at all like the immature young woman he had chosen the first time, when he was barely out of his teens. He and Janet were united by powerful sexual passion, by his deep respect for her as a woman of integrity and courage, and by their shared commitment to make the marriage work. The second marriage was not a substitute for the first but a far more important emotional connection.

Although people approach remarriage afraid of being hurt again, their capacity to love and be loved is not diminished if they make the right choice. Once they feel safe and know they can trust the other person, the new marriage can be deeply fulfilling — and they value the experience more for almost having missed it.

"You know," Ellis mused, "I never expected to get divorced. Divorce is unheard-of in my family. I come from a stable, conventional background. My father was a country doctor, and his ancestors fought in the Revolution and the Civil War. My dad was a gentle, lovely man. He was important in the community, but I really broke with him when I dropped out of medical school and again, of course, with my divorce."

"He was disappointed in you?"

"Very disappointed. I'm not sure he ever forgave me. In many ways my mother was the stronger figure, especially in day-to-day discipline. I fought with her more. When I was a teenager we really had some go-rounds. She was very strong, very traditional."

"Are you talking values?"

"Yes. In terms of the basic values in our family," he says, "the most important was to be a good person. To give something back to life. To create and be part of a big, happy family. To be responsible for yourself. Not just be a taker but to give something. We shared a commitment to serve, and everyone in the family was expected to do good, to do service. I could tell you everything my father ever did, what he said, looked like, wore, his mannerisms. But that wouldn't describe him. He had a healing way in his relationships." Ellis's eyes filled with tears and he choked on these words.

"You loved your father very much."

"Yes, but I would like to have done more of the things that other kids did. I would have liked more access to my father."

"You were lonely."

His eyes filled with tears. "Yes, I was lonely. That's one of the major themes of my childhood."

I thought about the disappointments he'd endured — loneliness within a stable family, a failed first marriage, not becoming the successful doctor his father had wanted him to be. He compared himself to his father and held himself to his family's high expectations, so I understood why he could not close the door on the sadness of not creating a happy family with his first wife. And coming from a strong moral and religious tradition in which divorce was not acceptable, he feared that he would be punished — that his new wife would leave him, just as the first one had. By his own standards he had failed. But I also saw him as a moral, good man capable of compassion, love, and commitment. He tried his best and took relationships very seriously.

"What happened to your plans to become a doctor?"

"I decided to go into medicine when I was a teenager. My dad was always stressing community service, and I liked the idea of being a doctor, of helping people in that way. So I planned to open a family practice in a small town. I met and married my first wife during my third year of college. We knew each other three months. We were really still teenagers. At the time it seemed just right. But then," Ellis said, dropping his voice, "I ran into some unforeseen challenges and failures. I really couldn't make it in medicine. The competition was too tough, and I dropped out of medical school midway through the second year. I got pretty depressed."

He pressed his eyes and rubbed his neck. "I remember driving along the highway, overwhelmed by my sense of failure and not knowing where to turn. I tried a lot of different jobs. We moved to California in 1970, found a place to live, and culture shock hit. It cost more to live out here than back east, and we were constantly broke. This was hard on my wife. She was used to a particular role, to a particular sense of importance. I think she was married to the image of a doctor and it was difficult for her to be a plain old person's wife."

Ellis was rarely home, there was no money, and he wasn't getting ahead financially. His wife was becoming depressed and feeling emotionally abandoned.

"I didn't know what was going on with her," he said. "And I didn't give her enough attention. I never had an inkling that we had a problem in the marriage. I never realized she was in trouble at all."

Conventional wisdom holds that if one person in a marriage is having problems, the other must know it, and the children must know it as well. But that's not true. In a good marriage the partners are tuned in to each other's feelings, but in one that is troubled, husband

and wife are often out of touch and leading isolated lives. I believed Ellis when he said he was not aware of his marital problems or his wife's suffering. He clearly continued to blame himself for the failed marriage.

He sighed. "As she became more and more depressed, she saw all her problems as being associated with the marriage, and she essentially detached. Finally she asked me for a divorce. But it was only at the very end I had a clue there was anything wrong. She had worked up a case that I was the real problem in her life."

"How did you feel?"

"I almost thought I wouldn't survive. In fact I thought a few times about jumping off the Golden Gate Bridge. I was left without a sense of order or connectedness, without a history essentially. It was as though she took away my life. It took me a long time to believe that it was true. I was devastated, as if my place in the world had been jerked away. I couldn't look my children in the eye. I felt like a failure. The despair was real and deep and lasting. A true despondency set in, and I had no clue as to how to pull myself back together. Finally I got into writing. Most of all, I met Janet."

The first task of marriage is to separate from the strong ties of childhood and to develop adult relationships with the families of origin. The first task of a second marriage is also to separate, but from different ties, namely the emotional attachments of the first marriage. Separating from a broken marriage takes much longer than people realize. Men and women remain attached in painful ways not only to the former wife or husband but to the house, the friends, and the extended family of that marriage. The full task of separating is accomplished as wounds heal, as trust with the new spouse is established, and as the second marriage begins to take its proper place. Both partners help themselves and the other turn away from past suffering and disappointments and look to new satisfactions. "Don't think about it anymore, we have each other," each says, silently or directly. Although the past never fades entirely, it is finally relegated to the wings, where it belongs.

The first step in separating from the earlier marriage involves mourning the loss of what that marriage represented emotionally and symbolically. Even if it ended miserably, there were bright dreams and hopes at its beginning, which must be lamented before being consigned to the past. Many first marriages contain some good along with the bad, so divorced people need to shed some tears before moving into a new relationship. Mourning is more painful when one person wanted the marriage to continue and the other wanted out. The husband or wife who has been rejected faces intense grief, but the one who wanted out must also separate from the dashed hopes and from the fear that he or she carries the seeds of destruction. And both of the divorced partners must loosen, if not give up entirely, their anger at each other, which can so easily dominate their lives. Closing the book on the first marriage requires heroic effort; in many cases it never closes.

I said to Ellis, "Tell me about the early years of your marriage to Janet."

"Well, it didn't just happen. This is a marriage which has been actively tended. We take care of each other. We rejuvenate. From the very beginning, we've gone away together for long weekends. We learned a long time ago, when we first married, that if we were always in the parent role, always at home taking care of the kids, we didn't get enough time together. I'd go on long drives that had to do with my business, and she would come along with me. Mostly we would talk about the kids or about us, but just being off together was an adventure — that was really important to both of us."

"And how about now?"

He said, "We continue to work on it. We both love to talk and walk, so five times a week we take long walks together, and I mean *long* walks. We have our stretch and exercise, but more important, it's an opportunity to be together, to communicate. We never do this TV-dinner number. We set aside a lot of time for us. And what we have finally created, and it takes time, is a sense that what we have is solid, and that's an important part of our happiness."

A week later I sat in the same parlor with Janet, who was wearing a dark green jogging suit. Just turned fifty, she was a petite woman with long black hair, blue eyes, and a fair complexion — a real Irish beauty. She worked as a copy editor at the newspaper Ellis wrote for. As I looked at this lovely, animated woman, it was easy to understand why Ellis adored her. She had a direct, refreshing manner.

At first Janet was a little anxious and said that she could take only two hours for the interview. I assured her that we would finish on time. As it turned out, we talked for nearly four hours. She really warmed to the subject of her marriage, as well as marriage in general. Like Ellis, she was deeply interested in the topic of children in second marriages.

In response to my opening question, Janet said, "Ellis had everything I was looking for. First I wanted kindness and gentleness. Then I wanted someone who was smart. And then I wanted someone who was willing to work hard on the marriage, willing to be in the marriage as a process. And for Ellis and me, it's worked out beautifully. We share activities. We have the same perspective on life and on politics. We're really close friends, and sex is great.

"My previous marriage was dreadful," she said in a low voice. "My husband was violent and abusive, very much like my father. As you know, Ellis was also married before, but he was in a marriage where he thought everything was fine. Then his wife left him. So you see, both of us were dumped." Janet smiled impishly. "One of the things that pleases Ellis about me is that I'm a loudmouth. I'm right out there with what I think and feel about things. He knows I'd never walk out on him without saying a word. I would just never do it. And I knew from the start that he was a kind, gentle person, that he would never hurt me. He's a good man. We came into this marriage wanting those things, and we both got what we wanted."

As Janet described her wretched first marriage, I realized she was telling me that I would have to study the present marriage in the context of their earlier experiences. She emphasized the contrast when she said, "I'm a loudmouth," unlike Ellis's first wife, who kept silent about the problems. In a second marriage the couple should have a good idea where the mines are, so they can take steps to avoid explosions. The Bouldens kept in mind the lessons they had learned from their first marriages.

"What were some of the challenges?" I asked.

Janet answered quickly. "The most serious problems were with the children, figuring out how to be a blended family with four kids below the age of eleven. Two lived with us, and two visited every other weekend. To be perfectly honest, sometimes I couldn't take it. I was ready to walk out. But that's a whole other chapter. The biggest problem for Ellis and me was finding the time and the space for privacy, for our life together."

"You solved that?"

"Yes, but it was hard to do. You see, we both realized that we needed to become a solid couple, but what I hadn't understood is how much I needed from Ellis. I had been deprived for so long, and what I needed was absolutely first in my mind. I needed someone to take care of me, to nurture me. I don't think either he or I understood that fully. After all, I was not a young woman, and I had been married before, for eleven years. But by the time I met Ellis, I desperately needed someone to care for me. And he needed me in return. We needed to take time, and we did. We'd go away alone on weekends to share adventures, to renew our relationship, simply to love each other. What pulled us through — and there were some incredibly rough spots — was creating that time alone as a couple and protecting it."

The hungers left over from a first marriage can shake the foundation of a second marriage in myriad ways. The couple begins the new marriage with accumulated needs, and each one wants to be taken care of, soothed, comforted, and held. At the same time, however, people in second marriages have more realistic expectations. They understand that each person has to accommodate to the other to make the marriage go. But because they have suffered so much, they need each other more, and their wish for immediate gratification is stronger.

Janet continued talking about the many years of humiliation and finally abandonment in her first marriage. "It was dreadful. My husband hit me a lot. I never loved him. I was only twenty when I met him, and it was disastrous from the start. He abused me, and he was a terrible parent. He divorced me because he was having an affair with somebody else. When the marriage finally broke up, we hadn't had sex for seven years. When he left, I had no job, no husband, no profession, two small children, and both my parents were dead. I had all of this on my plate at one time. I was nearly paralyzed with depression and helplessness."

As I looked at this beautiful woman, it was hard to imagine her in that position. Her brutal past was not written on her face. But Janet had answered my silent question as to why her first marriage remained such a strong presence in her life. She had been married for a major portion of her life, including entry into adulthood and motherhood. Unlike a brief first marriage, which in many cases can be sealed off if the breakup is not too shattering, an eleven-year marriage cannot be forgotten. Janet also had two children from the marriage, and they were daily reminders of her former husband and the pain of that relationship.

"How did you meet Ellis? Tell me about the beginning."

She smiled. "It was at a divorce group. I saw him there, sitting cross-legged and wearing a waistcoat made of Scottish plaid. I felt a strong initial physical attraction to him and a ray of hope."

"Were you looking for somebody?"

"Lord, no. I didn't have eyes to look. I was so miserable. This was a wonderful surprise. I noticed how good-looking he was, but I didn't dare expect it to go anywhere."

"I take it you didn't think anything would go well for you at that time."

"Absolutely. I wasn't even dating. Anyway, to get to the bottom line, we went out on a first date. It was a dazzler. It was electric." Janet laughed. "We discussed existentialism. It was an attraction of the mind, the body, and the heart. We were both bowled over. The depth of our initial emotional connection meshed with the incredible physical attraction. We came home, went to his apartment, and we went to bed on the first date. We couldn't keep our hands off each other. But in a way we were both scared of the power of our attraction, even though we were crazy for each other.

"I wasn't thinking of marrying him. We had all kinds of sexy liaisons. I'd come back to my house and be a proper mother to my children, but with the sense of a real shared treasure with him. Suddenly I had a special place, a private life that had to do with our relationship."

"That was the first time this had ever happened to you?"

"Right. I had never felt this kind of attraction. In fact, I'd had not much in the way of romance. When I married at twenty I had no experience with men."

"How hard was it to decide to take a chance the second time?"

"He wasn't yet divorced, and he was still at some level hoping to get back with his first wife. But our relationship was getting very serious. The truth is, a part of me said, 'No, no, this is too fast.' I wanted to be on my own. But another part of me said, 'Hold on, hold on.' We went on a trip together, and we stayed at a retreat where people meditate and can take long walks in the woods. It was exquisite, calm, with stone walls, a cloister, and it felt good to be there. It seemed so rich and rooted in spirituality, as if there was a spiritual aspect to our relationship. It was so different from what I'd been raised with — so calm and connected. I don't mean to be sentimental, but I felt that I had gained a part of myself I'd never had access to."

She gave her melodic laugh. "And before I knew it, he moved in. Once he got here, we bought a couch, and somehow that couch became symbolic. To get it into the house, we had to saw it in half. Once it was in place, it wasn't going anywhere. He always jokes about it and says, 'If anything happens to this relationship, I'm not leaving. I'm staying and the couch is staying.'" She laughed again and said, more seriously, "Ellis proposed and I said yes."

"Were you scared?"

"Scared doesn't capture it. All I kept thinking was why do I want to ruin this relationship by getting married? Then a friend gave me some fine advice. She said, 'You mean this guy wants you, your two kids, your two dogs, and you're worried about having his children over on the weekends? What are you waiting for?'"

I could see how much courage it had taken to come out of a dreadful marriage and take a chance on a new person, to bring to a new relationship the radiant hopes that had been ignited. Although Janet was thirty-four, it was for her a first love affair. She had zigged and zagged between hope and anxiety before marrying Ellis, but at the retreat, which she described almost lyrically, she had glimpsed the possibility of a moral, stable life with him. That began a process of recapturing her early images of idealization and requited love. Though still scared to her bones, she rejected her doubts and decided to venture into the marriage.

"You know," she said, with a new warmth and friendliness, "one reason I was so scared is that I had so few good experiences in my life, starting in childhood. I was born in Ireland, outside of Belfast, so I was surrounded by violence and hatred from the very beginning. My mother was frightened almost all the time. My father was an angry, violent man. My brothers and sisters and I spent our entire childhood in fear. He would scream. He would rage. It was terrible.

"But my mother was lovely. She was the sunshine in my early life and was a total delight. The best times were when we'd do things together, like go shopping for a pair of shoes or go to the countryside for a picnic. I thought she was perfect. I had a similar kind of relationship with my younger daughter during my first marriage. I clung to her, the way my mother held on to me."

Janet's face was terribly sad. "But then I lost both my parents in a car accident. I had just turned twelve and was completely bewildered by how fast everything changed. After the funeral, my brothers and sisters and I were shipped off to various relatives. I was sent to live with an aunt in California, in Orange County. I really didn't like her very much. She was my father's older sister and a lot like him in too many ways. I couldn't wait to get away from her, which is why I married so young.

"After my parents died, I was a loner. I had no faith I would ever become part of anything or that anyone would love me again like my mother did. That's why it was so extraordinary for me to have Ellis so in love with me. There was something curative in having him adore me. I'd never had anyone accept me that way before." She inhaled deeply and shut her eyes. "You know, now is really the sweet time of the marriage. It's good for us now. I want it to last. I worry because of our ages. We're both in our fifties. Ellis has a slight heart problem, and I worry about that. But I think this should be the home stretch. I want us to go on in the happiness we have, and I want us to keep our health."

A couple in a second marriage, as in a first, need to take time to build the marriage, to establish a loving sexual relationship, to create a safe place for conflict, to comfort and nurture each other, and much more. Eager for a fresh start, they try to learn from their mistakes and do things right. Thus second marriages begin with high hopes camouflaging the fears — and so they should. But there is important work to be done. The success of the marriage depends on redoubling the efforts that should have been made the first time. This is because every second marriage, whether it is romantic, companionate, or traditional, is also by its nature a rescue marriage. It rescues the partners not from childhood trauma but from the unhappiness of their earlier failure.

A successful remarriage begins with the promise that it will be safe for difference and conflict and, most of all, safe from the repetition of earlier suffering. During the courtship, when lovers tell each other their life stories, the ghosts from the first marriage enter the new relationship. These ghosts are especially powerful when they tap into earlier fears dating from childhood and adolescence. They remain present in the choices people make to avoid repeating their suffering.

They are implicit in the promise each person makes to the other — silently or in words — not to repeat the hurts of the past.

If the couple has chosen wisely this time, they can be explicit about their needs. Thus Ellis wanted a woman who would never reject him, whom he could absolutely trust to be there. Others have different needs: "I need a man who does not drink." "I want a husband who can hold a job." "I want a woman who is faithful." "I need a sexual, passionate man who will not bore me." "I need someone who will be married to *me,* not to her job or her mother."

It is inevitable that husband and wife will misread each other's behavior. The first night he is late for dinner, she may conclude "Here it goes again," or he may worry "Who is she out with tonight?" Fears from the earlier marriage translate easily into omens or accusations that generate counteraccusations of mistrust. Such misperceptions commonly lead to quarrels in second marriages. The task is to distinguish the ghost from the reality. Sometimes they are the same, but if not, it is critical to tell them apart; the marriage depends on it. The feeling of having fallen into the same trap a second time is intolerable.

Self-esteem is often shattered during an unhappy marriage, especially one that ends with abandonment or betrayal. Thus the nurturance task in remarriage is not only to comfort but also to reassure and restore each other's confidence. Fortunately, people who have suffered in their first marriages are often finely tuned to the need for give-and-take. Long used to giving and giving and never receiving, they know the effect of such deprivation on self-esteem, and they work to avoid this imbalance in the second marriage. Shared vulnerability and recognition of their own needs can unite husband and wife.

The external symbols of reassurance and comfort are more important in a second marriage because both people have felt humiliated and rejected. Extra praise and encouragement help heal the trauma of the failed marriage. Both Ellis and Janet needed to hear many times over that they were cherished, that their needs for nurturance would have priority. A good remarriage has the power to heal terrible wounds, break the fear of betrayal, and restore self-esteem. In building the new relationship together, two emotionally depleted people help each other, comfort each other, and soothe past traumas.

To the task of creating togetherness and autonomy in proper balance, people in second marriages bring experience and maturity. Yet because they are older and have lived independently before remarrying, they may find it difficult to yield autonomy and create the closeness that holds a marriage together. Establishing a mutual identity — the "we" in place of two "I's" — may be more difficult when separate identities are so firmly established, when each partner owns a home or has achieved economic independence. Living habits may be more rigid — many older people are less open to changing routines. Shall we go to bed in accord with your sleeping habits or mine? Shall we eat out or in? What about job requirements, careers, travel, expenses, and checking accounts? Is it old-fashioned to expect that she give up traveling with her boss? What if his closest colleague is an attractive woman whom he used to date? Where do I come in, and where does the marriage come in? How do we solve problems when interests collide, as they certainly will?

Counteracting the forces that push for autonomy is the strong and long-postponed need for togetherness, love, and friendship, for being a partner and having a life companion. It is in building togetherness that the couple relieves the painful loneliness of the years between divorce and remarriage. Remembering those lonely years, people appreciate the pleasures of sharing activities and spending evenings together, the importance of being able to reach out and know that the other is there. But because each has lived a separate, independent life, the building process takes conscious effort and planning, as Ellis and Janet intuitively realized.

An important aspect of many second marriages is the frank acknowledgment of the need for a rich sex life. Sex often begins very early in the courtship, partly because people are older and more sexually experienced — "We couldn't keep our hands off each other," said Janet. Such spontaneous combustion occurs when people have suffered sexual hunger or humiliation for many years. Although sexual love is a major task in all marriages, it has a special meaning in remarriage. Men and women are ecstatic to find that they have not forfeited their chance for sex and passion.

During the early years of the marriage people are especially concerned about whether this was a wise idea and whether it will last. Gradually, as they settle in, they feel more comfortable with each other. Both Janet and Ellis referred movingly to a moment when the second marriage felt firmly in place, when it was no longer just a temporary shelter from the storm but a safe harbor for the rest of their lives.

# 25

# Coping with Children in a Second Marriage

**H**ALFWAY THROUGH OUR INTERVIEW, I realized that Janet had been avoiding the topic of how she and Ellis had managed to raise their children in a second marriage. So when I found an opportunity, I asked her directly, "Tell me about that other chapter in your life, Janet, the one about the children."

Her answer was characteristically direct. "By now I feel I know you well enough to tell you the truth. I wanted the man, not the kids."

She looked to see if I was shocked by her confession, but my reaction was quite different. I was relieved that we had waited to talk about the children, because this was not going to be an easy topic. I was, however, taken aback by the passion of her words.

"Blending the families was the most difficult task of my life," said Janet. "We didn't have a clue how hard it was going to be. In retrospect I'm amazed at how much anxiety we were able to cope with, and I'm glad that we're here today in our marriage.

"If I'd known how difficult it would be, I might not have undertaken it. You see, the theme of this marriage has been that we are a couple. Our communication and our privacy take precedence. We come first, and the kids will do okay because we're taking good care of ourselves and providing them with an example of a loving couple. We thought it would trickle down."

"How did it work?"

She sighed. "Not so well. We realized after several years that it wasn't working. Ellis made a big compromise when we got married, at my request. To tell the truth, at my insistence. It was a very clear, on-the-table compromise. We would keep my kids, and his kids would visit. His kids were messed up royally by the time we got together, and I couldn't take it."

"What did the kids do when they visited?"

"They were hellions, full of fire, all-over physical energy, no discipline, like big dirty puppies making messes everywhere. They seemed almost deliberately to make messes and cause problems and be antagonizing."

I thought, They sound like children. To Janet they must have seemed larger than life. For her this marriage represented a last stand; she was fighting for something she had been deprived of all her life. She was fighting for an exclusive, loving, sexual relationship with Ellis. She had left her first marriage feeling helpless, like a lost child needing care. Now she also wanted to be nurtured and comforted. Instead she found herself caught up in the third act of a play starring his children and his first wife. She was expected to play the role of superparent to a pride of little lions.

"I understand now, looking back, that Ellis's kids were absolutely shattered by his divorce," said Janet. "Nobody in that family had a clue that the divorce was coming. But also, in those days, nobody knew the impact on the children. I had nowhere I could get help. This was in the seventies, when everyone said the children would be fine in a few months. So Ellis and I made this contract. It was explicit that we came first, but it was implicit that the kids came second. Of course this upset the kids even more and raised the noise level of the entire household. It's a miracle our marriage survived."

In my earlier interview with Ellis, he too had been frank about difficulties with the children. "We've had hard times dealing with the kids," he said. "This has been tough for us. All four of our kids have been deprived, in the sense that they all experienced divorce. Great as our marriage is for us, it is not the same for them. I'm sure there are many times they have felt eclipsed.

"You need to understand the situation when Janet and I decided to get married. I moved into her house, but my children stayed with their mom. Every other weekend my kids would sleep over two nights. So Janet's two children gained a full-time father, and my own kids had a part-time father."

Ellis looked pained. "Early on my kids experienced themselves as outsiders and visitors. Her kids resented them as intruders, even though each child had a private room. Nothing worked. The weekends that my children came were a living hell. Everyone was at their worst. Janet, her kids, my kids — and I'm afraid I did nothing but stand by and worry. It was at least three or more years before we were able to pull our two families together. During those first years, parenting was very taxing for both Janet and me — but especially for her."

"How so?"

"Sometimes the thing you do best can actually be your Achilles heel," said Ellis. "That's what I think happened with my wife. She's really good with children, but somehow, when it came to being a parent to her own kids or helping me think about parenting my children, she just missed the beat, and I wasn't able to call her on it. I deferred to her. I gave away more than I should have as a parent."

"Why do you think that happened?"

"My sense of myself as a parent was destroyed by my divorce, by my first wife. My sense of competence was undermined. I don't know if my kids have had gobs of problems or if they were just a little wild. After all, they'd just come through a divorce." He paused. "It's tough looking back, however. And painful. Fights over my kids went on for the first three years of the marriage. The kids tattled and fought. Everyone blamed the other. All the kids were doing poorly at school, and they got into a lot of trouble, some of it serious. Janet yelled and I despaired. But I was an optimist. I had the idea that we would just pull all the kids together, and we would end up with one big happy family. I held on to this vision, this dream, this hope. It took time for it to sink in that we were not all going to be one happy family in an instant or even in a year or maybe ever."

I was saddened by what Ellis said. Obviously his children had suffered, and he wanted to ease their grief by bringing them into a loving, stable family. That fantasy was deeply rooted in his own up-bringing as well as in guilt stemming from his first marriage. Yet the happy family did not materialize when he moved in with Janet.

More powerful than any ghosts of the first marriage are the flesh-and-blood children of that union. But why are children such an issue in second marriage, and why do they threaten to derail it?

No experience can prepare a couple for blending children into the marriage; this is new territory for adults and for children. Everyone comes to it without a dress rehearsal, and what transpires is always a surprise. Except for babies and preschoolers, who are more easily integrated into a new family, children are almost always a threat to a second marriage. To put it bluntly, children and parents in such a marriage have many colliding interests. What the couple wants and needs during their early years is not what the children want and need. Although the children, parents, and stepparents can come together, this is not always apparent to everyone when the marriage begins.

Explosions erupt over who has priority — adults or children, his children or her children. In many families this translates into the very real problems of how to allocate time and money. Do we accommodate our schedules and our lives to his former wife's wishes or to ours? Do my husband and I take a vacation this year, or do we send the money to an orthodontist for his daughter in a distant city? Do we move with the new job offer or stay here to be near her children? How do we plan for the holidays and birthdays? Should I send my son to Yale, where my father and I both went, or will a public university do just as well? And the effects of these decisions can last a long time. Lacking a King Solomon, how can we decide these divisive questions?

Such complex problems are particularly hard to address when two bruised and hurting adults are just beginning to feel their way with each other and are focusing on their own needs. One of the great advantages of the early years of marriage before children are born is that husband and wife have privacy. That time is not a luxury; it is needed to address the many tasks of marriage and lay down a strong foundation together. It is time for play and exploration of each other's bodies, hearts, and minds. But in a second marriage with children underfoot, this period of undisturbed peace doesn't exist. Many remarried couples complain that they've never had a chance to be just two, to enjoy what couples in a first marriage enjoy — being alone together.

The issues of the blended family vary with the personality, age, and sex of each child, the number of children, and the kinds of custody and visiting arrangements. How the first marriage ended — in a fury or by mutual agreement — makes a difference, as does the money available in each family. Almost every aspect of the first marriage, including the events leading up to separation and divorce and the current living arrangements of all the adults and children, has a direct bearing on the situation.

Considering the individual differences among such families, what is striking is their similarities. Most new stepparents cross the threshold with the hope that Ellis expressed so well: "I thought we'd be one happy family." The new couple wants peace and as few hassles as possible. They want desperately for the second marriage to be a success. Like Ellis, parents also want to comfort their own children and assuage any damage caused by the divorce.

The children, in their turn, wonder what the new stepparent will be like. He or she is clearly an intruder but also a potential source of interest, affection, and special treats. The children worry about losing the full attention of the newly married parent, who has come to seem like a close best friend as well as a mom or dad. Janet said that when her first marriage was in turmoil, she turned to her youngest daughter for comfort; we can assume that the little girl did not readily welcome Ellis as her replacement.

Many children hold on to the fantasy that their parents will reconcile, and they resent the stepparent for interfering with that dream. Moreover, children feel torn in their loyalties between the biological parent and the stepparent. The adults may not intentionally fuel the conflict, but many fail to help their children recognize that they can love both parent and stepparent.

The job of being a stepparent is utterly demanding and full of surprises. The stepmother faces a special dilemma with a blended family. Almost inevitably she sees the new children as intruders. She may feel that everyone's life is governed by the petulant demands of the former wife. The house must be readied periodically for the children's visits, extra food must be bought and cooked, laundry done, and plans made. The household undergoes continual upheaval to accommodate the needs of the ungrateful stepchildren. Even women who are attuned to the ways of children complain about their new family's messiness, aggression, and rudeness. In their hearts, of course, these mothers know that the children are just acting like children. As one woman said, "I'm ashamed of myself for resenting them." Another said, "I'm disappointing myself all the time. I thought I could do it."

Indeed, children who have recently experienced divorce are not on their best behavior. They are likely to be capricious, suspicious, demanding, belligerent, and very frightened. Undoubtedly they need extra care, understanding, and patience. Feelings are easily hurt. Fights erupt among siblings and stepsiblings. Tears fall quickly. Children who have come through a difficult divorce — and few divorces are easy — typically exhibit distress symptoms, including sleep problems, temper tantrums, learning difficulties, and other behaviors that keep parents awake late at night trying to decide what to do and where to turn for help.

Children often feel rejected by the newly married couple; they feel left out when their parent and stepparent have dinner à deux and shut themselves away in the bedroom for the rest of the night. Several children have confessed to me that they spent many evenings peeking through keyholes, consumed with curiosity and hurt at being shut out of a circle that they thought would include them.

Money is another area of escalating conflict. With two sets of children to support, fathers are spread too thin, and they feel guilty about both families. Should I pay for college for my children from the former marriage, or should I pay for my stepchildren — when I have no legal financial obligation to any of the children after they reach eighteen? What is enough, and what is too much? Should a stepmother's salary be used to pay for children of the first marriage? Can the new family afford a second child? How much easier it would be if the children of the previous marriage went away. In this fertile environment, the stepparent's anger at and resentment of the former spouse blossoms.

One drastic solution to these stresses is for a father to emotionally abandon his children from the first marriage — and several men in these happy second marriages had taken that road. Although they sent regular child support, they did not visit their children or have them visit the second family. These men believed they were protecting the second marriage by turning their backs on their children; they did have an easier time in some ways, but they lived with a constant veil of guilt. They had a real sense of having sinned and of having hurt their children, but they felt they had no alternative. In some cases the second wife wanted those ties cut. Some men realized they could not maintain a relationship with the children without having some contact with the first wife, and they could not stand the pain of that. In their second marriages, however, these men were devoted, loving fathers to new children of that union and to their stepchildren.

"My son was seven when I left," said one man. "He doesn't think much of me. I literally packed and left in front of him, which is very hurtful to a child. Absolute rejection, I know that, and it's something

I'm sorry about. Whatever feelings he harbors toward me to this day, I understand. Children can't hurt you. You hurt them. You see, children are innocent. They come to you totally dependent, so they can't hurt you, but you can reject them. I paid child support through my son's college, but I didn't go to his wedding. It would have been too much, too stressful on the family. I want him to be happy."

Fortunately, most divorced fathers value regular contact with their children from the earlier marriage and try to maintain it. Although joint custody has become more common, it is still customary for children to live with their mother and visit their father in his home two or more weekends a month. But as everyone soon learns, visiting a parent and having a child visit are new and strange experiences for both children and adults. To succeed, visiting must be fine-tuned to the individual child's capacities and interests. This takes time and thoughtful, sensitive planning.

Janet and Ellis faced the most challenging situation in that each brought two children into the remarriage. Although they were sophisticated and intelligent people, they mistakenly thought that blending the family would be a quick and painless process. But the fantasy of peace and harmony blew up in their faces. The household almost came apart under the onslaught, and both sets of children did poorly. The marriage that meant so much to Ellis and Janet was seriously threatened.

I asked Janet, "What did you do to maintain the marriage and the family? It must have been difficult."

"Let me tell you what we tried," she said, "because I still believe in it, although what we did at first wasn't enough. We figured out, rightly I think — and I would do this again — that the kids didn't have a chance in hell unless we were a solid couple. And we did give them an important gift, which is a couple that endures and is in good shape. But we went too far with our own needs, and the children got lost."

"How much did it have to do with your fear that you would lose out?"

"Everything," she said. "I knew it then, but I know it better now. It takes time to feel secure. We were all frightened — Ellis, the kids, and me."

"Frightened of what?"

"Each of us had a nemesis. Ellis and I were afraid of another failure.

My kids had just been abandoned by their father and were afraid of losing me to this new man. His kids, who never expected the divorce in the first place, were really scared and depressed. They were getting nothing from their mom, who was not a happy person. They were afraid of losing their father to this new woman, namely me, and to the new children, who they figured had taken their place."

"And how did that change?"

She sighed. "To put it straight, there was an internal shift in me, in my feelings, and that made a big difference."

"What do you mean, an internal shift?"

"I started to soften and began to feel very badly for the children. And I began to understand his children. I especially began to appreciate what his daughter had been through. My changing had to do with my feeling safe in the marriage. It had to do with my not feeling hungry anymore. I was content. I became a more generous, more giving person. You might say I became ready to be a stepparent."

Janet looked out the window briefly, then returned her gaze to me. "The other thing was that I realized my own children were suffering. It was a shock to realize that my two angels were not angels at all. They were behaving terribly and keeping the house in an uproar just as much as his kids were. I became alarmed over what I saw as really bad behavior in my own children. The whole scene forced me to look at myself and especially at my own children."

"So you broke the logjam?"

"Yes, we did. And everything became not easy but much easier, because the fear and competition subsided. And my anger lessened, and when that happened Ellis and I could consider each child as an individual. We also realized that one of his children needed therapy, so we dug deep down and found the money. We never became a truly blended family — whatever that is — but there is affection and caring and probably hurt that will remain. The kids now are in pretty good shape." Janet smiled. "There's no magic. I just really started to try hard."

"Where was Ellis in all this?"

"He's an optimist. He always is. What more, from the start he was a real dad to my kids. He had so much to give them. It was immense, and he was loving and caring for all of the children after I stopped blocking his relationship with his kids. We've talked about it over the years many times, and we both agree that he should have been more firm in standing up to me for his kids' sake. But he couldn't, because he needed me so much for himself."

Janet and Ellis's experiences are instructive for anyone embarking on a second marriage with children. As they so poignantly related, it is a far more complex task than building a first marriage. The early years, when every marriage is most fragile, are the hardest, because the couple and the children have problems that must be dealt with right away.

The adults are pulled powerfully in two directions at once. They need privacy and time to create physical and emotional intimacy and a sense of togetherness. But the children also need their parents' time, attention, and affection. They need to be reassured that they're not going to lose out in this family. When they feel excluded from the couple's relationship, they become frightened and are likely to become obstreperous and wild or withdrawn at home and at school. It's easy for one adult to blame the other, or for both to blame the children, or for the children to play one parent off against the other. Frustrations in the couple's relationship can ricochet into the stepparent-stepchild relationship, just as problems with the children can ricochet into the fledgling marriage. Although building the new marriage and the new family do not have to proceed perfectly in step, they do have to march along on the same front. Unless both tasks are addressed simultaneously, the marriage may go under.

But the two tasks can also strengthen and enrich each other, and that is what eventually turned a difficult situation around for Janet and Ellis. As they built their marriage into a strong and lasting union, they felt more relaxed and could then help the children. They could be generous and admit the children into their inner circle. This is what Janet meant by her "inner shift." Initially she made the mistake of trying to accomplish one task at a time. Understandably, she gave priority to her own needs and excluded the children as competitors. When she felt ready to become a stepparent, she suddenly felt softer and more open, able to perceive their needs and to respond with compassion and love.

Stepparent-child relationships are different from parent-child relationships in that both child and adult begin with separate histories. Moreover, the biological parent is still a strong presence and may direct the child's responses or try to influence the new relationship. Within this context the stepparent and the child look each other over carefully, both feeling anxious and eager as they seek common ground and try to overcome their reluctance and find pleasure in each other's company.

The relationship takes many forms. It can be central: "He is my real father." It can be peripheral: "He is my mom's husband." There are no guidelines. This makes the relationship both a challenge and a hardship. It can work if both adult and child give it time, respect each other's pace, and find or create common bonds. Many stepchildren are profoundly grateful to the stepparent — after initial hesitations and doubts — for being the benevolent figure they had never found in their biological parent.

Finally, adults and children have to recognize that the goal in remarriage is not to create one big, happy family. Many people bring to remarriage the idea that a happy family will just spring into being. Such a vision may have comforted them in unhappier times, and it dies hard. Once the new marriage begins, this hopeful vision can harm the family, because it keeps adults and children from getting down to the serious business of building on what they have.

Building the new marriage while achieving harmony in the relationship with stepchildren takes courage, patience, understanding, honesty, and sacrifice. But the potential rewards are enormous. I asked Janet and Ellis, "How close were you to calling it quits in those early years?"

Janet said, "This is the foundation of my world, to have Ellis so overwhelmingly in love with me. He gave me something I never could have anywhere else. I think that answers you."

He said, "I would lose the center of my universe if I lost her. I've always known that."

In terms of what was lacking in their first marriages, Janet and Ellis realized their fondest hopes in their remarriage. But far more than that, they fell in love and created a lasting romantic marriage. They ran into difficulties with children and finances, but these were minor compared to what they achieved. They retained luminous memories of their first meeting and their first date, and they returned to those memories often to recapture that happiness. They woke daily to the pleasure of having beaten the odds in finding each other.

Their experience is not uncommon. A happy second marriage often has an aura of magic, of a special blessing. The couple has the sense of having been given a wonderful second chance that they hardly dared hope for, intensified by the bittersweet feeling that they found each other just in time.

Two years after these interviews, I had a charming, unexpected post-script. After lecturing to a group of medical students, I was ap-proached by an attractive young woman. "Do the names Ellis and Janet Boulden mean anything to you?" she asked.

"They mean a lot to me," I replied.

"Well," she said, "I know they're part of your study on marriage. I'm their daughter."

I noted that she didn't say stepdaughter. Looking for a way to engage her, I said, "It hasn't always been easy in your family."

"That's so true," she said. "But that's history." She smiled brightly. "You were right to include them in your study. They are so happy together."

# 26 &

# Fred and Marie Fellini

*A Retirement Marriage*

L
EAVING THE WORLD OF WORK marks an end and a new beginning. It is a time when a couple once again negotiates the fundamental tasks of marriage for their final years together. What happens during the retirement chapter of the marriage depends on a mix of physical, emotional, and economic factors. Much depends on how each person computes the balance of satisfactions and disappointments of life and how they feel about spending time together. Some retired couples look forward to a rich harvest. "I think that our marriage has made aging more acceptable, and aging has made me appreciate our marriage more," said one woman. For others, retirement is a time when lifelong deprivations rise for a final curtain call, when people nurse their grievances in isolation and bitterly blame each other for their sorrow.

I decided to treat the small number of happily married retired couples as a special group because they confronted similar issues, which they resolved in similar ways. All had embarked on traditional marriages in the 1950s. After their children left home, the women had reorganized their lives around new careers. Most continued to work part-time even though their husbands had retired. All of the couples shared a sharp awareness of aging and approaching death. All were spending more time together than ever before, which meant that each individual had to change, and the marriage had to change to meet their new circumstances. Relinquishing the responsibility and status conferred by a job was for some a welcome relief and for others a wrenching loss.

As a group, these older couples were fortunate to be physically active and in reasonably good health. Although financially comfortable, they all had started in much poorer circumstances and remained keenly aware of their difficult beginnings. Much of their satisfaction stemmed from the feeling that they had done well and had done it together. A phrase I heard often was "Everything we have we created together." They were united by shared memories that included serious crises, such as the deaths of their parents, severe illnesses, and financial hardship, as well as happy times for themselves, their children, and their grandchildren. They also had a sense of having lived together through unprecedented changes in the world.

A colleague of my son's had urged me to include his parents in the study because he had always admired their marriage. His admiration was well placed. I chose Marie and Fred Fellini to represent the group of retired couples because they were articulate about the worries they had had before retiring and the rewards they were enjoying. They were able to face their fears of death and to talk about what it would mean to lose the other person.

I arrived at their large but modest home in Walnut Creek expecting to interview Marie. But when I rang the doorbell at nine in the morning, both Fred and Marie were waiting. They had apparently misunderstood the arrangement. I decided to reverse my customary procedure and see them together first; later I arranged to talk to them separately.

From the questionnaire they had filled out earlier, I knew that the Fellinis had married in 1950, when she was twenty-one and he was twenty-three. Fred had retired four years earlier from his job in the wholesale appliance business. Marie still ran a cooking school out of her large, well-equipped kitchen, which she had remodeled when her children were in high school.

From the moment I entered the bright, airy kitchen, where the interview took place, I had the sense that unlike the younger couples in the study, the Fellinis were not in a hurry. Their sense of time had changed. Marie was pleasingly plump and lively; her dark hair was streaked with white. Fred was short, sturdy, and balding. Both were willing to take the time to review the whole marriage, from their first meeting to that morning. They talked happily, occasionally interrupting each other, mostly agreeing but also recalling strong disagreements in their past.

I asked about the beginnings of the marriage.

"For over forty years he's been a good husband to me," said Marie, looking at Fred warmly. "I recall vividly our first meeting. He was gorgeous, so absolutely handsome. There was a tremendous attraction immediately. Everyone held him in such high regard. I was twenty when we met. What attracted me was that he had such a strong sense of who he was. He's sensitive, morally impeccable, and loving. We share a moral sensibility. He is very loving with his family and his friends."

She chuckled. "Thank God he's not perfect, but he has special qualities that make him special to me, to our children, and to other people. I guess I've always felt lucky to be married to him when I look around the world. Some instinct moved me toward him very quickly."

Fred's memories were darker. "We both grew up in poor immigrant homes," he said. "Her family strongly opposed the marriage because I was too short and too poor and had no prospects. My family opposed the marriage because they wanted me to get more education so I could do better and rise out of poverty. We defied them both and got married in a civil ceremony." Fred went directly to work, and Marie was soon pregnant.

"How did you meet?"

"We met at a summer camp," he recalled. "We just hit it off together in our first meeting, and that was it. You know, a summer love affair can be pretty intense, and we saw each other every day. But I was sure from the moment I heard her laugh" — he threw his arm out in a gesture of song — "from across a crowded room."

"What made you both so sure?"

Marie said thoughtfully, "I don't think we ever intellectualized our relationship the way young people do today. I think we worked from a different script, and we moved more quickly into our relationships, knowing they were going to take or not take, in terms of marriage." She smiled at Fred. "The other thing is that when I met him, he made me feel comfortable about my body and myself."

"Well," said Fred, "to tell the truth, I never felt she was so good-looking when I married her" — he paused — "as she is today." Marie pretended to throw a bread stick at him. "I think," he continued, poker-faced, "she's gotten better looking. But I was not dazzled by her beauty. It was probably her character, or that she is a character. Anyway, I liked her. I wanted to be with her. Of course, real sex was out.

But petting and necking and long canoe rides were in." Marie looked at him in mock despair.

It was a lovely interplay, and I felt privileged to be there. I was impressed not only with their flirtatious teasing but with their memories of first meeting, as if it were yesterday. I especially loved her saying, "He was gorgeous."

"Did you always get along so well?"

"Certainly not," she said tartly. "Both of us can get very angry. As a matter of fact, because we see each other all the time — much more than we used to — we bicker. Our children think we're quarreling, but that's how we talk." Fred was nodding. "We certainly haven't always agreed on a lot of things," she continued. "He thought I was too lax in raising the children and that I catered to them. Whenever he went out of town, he worried that even their homework wouldn't get done."

I turned to Fred. "I was trying to think of the worst fight we ever had," he said, "and I can't remember it. But we really did fight. I just can't remember what we fought about. One of us would flare up at the other and then get over it. None of that is important now."

"Has retirement made a difference?" I said.

They looked at each other, and by some silent signal that eluded me, she spoke first. "I used to worry about when he'd retire. What was he going to do? He had no hobbies to speak of and was so preoccupied with his job that he wasn't interested in anything. The truth is, since he retired he's a changed man. He's now a soup expert." She laughed. "Every week he makes soup. And he invites people over to eat it, too. So now I'm not the only one who wants friends around. Maybe he's forgotten, but we used to have big fights about my having a crowd over. Mostly our children and their friends. I loved having ten youngsters drop in and stay for dinner. But he complained that it was like Grand Central Station."

They exchanged amused glances. "We enjoy our lives much more, and finally we get to do many of the things we postponed, like going on trips. We spend more time together, but I don't feel any need to get away from him. If I want to spend the day doing my own things, I do it. I love the theater and he doesn't, so I go with a friend. Sometimes I'll go see a movie by myself or with a friend."

"So retirement's been pretty good for you?"

"I don't mind him being retired," said Marie. "My younger women friends ask me point-blank how I can stand having him home. They always ask, 'Who makes lunch?' I say, 'Whoever gets hungry makes lunch. Whoever has time goes to the store to buy groceries.'" She shrugged. "We don't get in each other's hair. It's been a pleasure. He does what he does. I do what I do. We don't keep busy, we *are* busy. My friends say their husbands hang around the house all day — I don't know what they mean. I would like it to go on this way forever."

I turned to Fred. "She's right. We're much freer now. My days are very full. It hasn't been any problem at all. We don't get in each other's way, and she and I have a lot of things we do without each other. I like to play golf. She's very athletic, but she's always resisted it. I don't push her. I like to go with her to art shows, but I certainly can't spend my whole day that way. I like to read. She doesn't. The kind of thing I love doing with her is going out to dinner, to the movies, going on trips."

Marie reached across the table and put a hand on Fred's forearm. "I have one friend," she said, "who complains all the time that whenever she leaves the house, her husband asks her where she's going. She doesn't mind telling him, but she doesn't want to be asked this question every time she goes out. That's not our relationship at all."

The central psychological task in retirement is the need, once again, to define issues of togetherness versus autonomy. How close and how separate shall we be? How dependent and how independent? Who nurtures whom? When is closeness a burden and when is it a pleasure? And although the questions sound familiar, their meanings are not the same as earlier, and the answers have different consequences.

Togetherness is not a conscious choice in retirement; it's a given, unless the couple's plans lead in separate directions. Autonomy, too, has a different meaning when it is no longer tied to the demands of work or community. It becomes a voluntary movement into separate pursuits. There are new questions. Will all this togetherness open a Pandora's box of conflicting wishes and frustrations? Will too much autonomy lead us far apart just when we need each other's support? Will being alone in the house when the other is out raise fears of loneliness and abandonment? Will being together result in a childlike dependency? Thus the familiar task of balancing togetherness and autonomy is now negotiated under the onus of aging. The options are fewer, and the shadows are deeper.

The task of nurturance is also redefined in retirement. As people age, they need more loving care and encouragement, and when they are less vigorous physically and mentally, they need more help. They may become more dependent. Sometimes they regress — "I'm getting old, take care of me!" is a familiar theme. Childhood memories may become stronger, along with recurring dreams of loss and death. Whereas earlier in the marriage the needs for nurturance and encouragement were sporadic, in the retirement marriage they are ongoing.

Women especially worry about what they see as the increasing emotional neediness of their retired husbands, afraid that they will become more demanding and childlike. The wives don't want to move into the "mommy" role. The ubiquitous question, "Who will make lunch?" reflects their fear that they will have a new child at home to care for. But both men and women fear that their established routines and friendships will be disrupted by the other's dependency.

This is no idle fear. In many divorces at this life stage, the wife's chief complaint is of being sucked dry as caregiver and mother to an aging husband. The main complaint of many an aging man, on the other hand, is that he receives little acknowledgment, praise, and loving care from his wife. Each blames the other for providing little and demanding all. The wish for greater closeness and the fear of too much closeness mark the retirement marriage.

Another major concern is loss of privacy. A woman in the study said, "My husband retired three years ago. At first I experienced his being around all the time as an intrusion. He was quiet, but I felt he was somehow interrupting me. So two things happened. He became more sensitive about not talking when I was using my computer. And gradually I became more dependent on his company. What used to feel intrusive began to feel important and necessary." Her anxiety about his presence was initially so high that she felt even his silences as an interruption. But gradually she not only included him in her personal space but grew to depend on his close presence.

Marie and Fred addressed these complex questions head-on. First they acknowledged their initial concerns to each other. What will Fred do all day? Will we get in each other's hair? Will I lose my freedom? They resolved them by establishing a loose togetherness along with busy individual routines. They encouraged each other to pursue the activities that interested them. There was no false autonomy and no fake unity; they shared activities that truly engaged them both. As a result, there was a new balance in the marriage, making it less traditional and more companionate. Both participated in doing household chores, cooking, and shopping. They were aware of their achievement as they contrasted their situation with that of friends who found the partner's presence irksome. Indeed, many couples spend their retirement years in nonstop bickering because these issues remain unresolved.

As Marie got up to make tea for the three of us, I asked Fred if he missed his work. His mood turned more serious. "The biggest disappointment in my life was my work," he said sadly. "It was difficult and unsatisfying to me. The truth is, when I was working, I felt trapped, and I didn't know how to get out of it. I used to envy people who loved their work. I never cared how much I sold or how much people bought. But it made a good living. No diamonds, no Cadillacs, but no real money problems either. The real meaning of my job was to take care of my family. Looking back on my life, I got more satisfaction from Marie and the kids. So now I stay home and enjoy what I have."

The loss of the demands and rewards of work can have far-reaching effects on the individual and on the marriage. For many, retirement signifies being cut off from the world of peers, from a sense of identity, and, of course, from an income. Men, especially in traditional families, often fear that their wives will no longer love and respect them now that they are not carrying the responsibility for maintaining the family. And all working people depend on the job to structure their day; they tend to feel at a loss with so much time on their hands.

But for Fred, as is true for many others, retirement was welcome. He felt liberated from a burden he had carried for many years. Because retirement was a gift and not a banishment, he was spared the psychological crisis so many men and women face when they end their careers. That was one reason why he found it relatively easy to change and grow by taking on new activities.

Marie changed too to some extent. Because Fred helped around the house, she could continue her part-time work more easily, and this, too, created a new balance in the marriage. They joined together in grandparenting and in taking trips to Europe, which they couldn't do when he was working full-time.

One of the serendipitous results of the way they used their new freedom was that they were able to avoid boredom and isolation — the great hazards of the retirement years. When connections to the workplace end, couples need to work harder to keep up their other interests and remain connected to the community. Ties to groups, friends (including younger people), family, and grandchildren are more critical. Strong connectedness to the outside world is necessary to protect the inner world of the marriage.

I asked the Fellinis about their children and grandchildren.

Marie said, "The high points in my marriage were the births of my children and the births of our grandchildren. The grandchildren have brought enormous pleasure to both of us. In fact, two of our grandchildren are coming for dinner tonight and are sleeping over. It's wonderful that they live close by and we can be a part of their lives."

Fred said, "The children strengthen our marriage. We spend a lot of time with them. Parenting was wonderful and difficult. We were never professional parents like some of our friends, who spent hours analyzing every little act of each child. We took care of them and had fun with them. Now we spend weekends with our kids and grandkids, and I guess our kids are among our best friends."

Marie chimed in. "I loved being a mother and taking care of my home."

Fred nodded. "I genuinely loved being a father, and I love being a grandfather even more. I spend as much time with my grandkids as I can. It's fun for me, and I love baby-sitting them. I do a day each week now in my grandson's preschool. I change diapers." He chuckled. "I do everything."

"You say you love being a grandfather even more than being a father. What's the difference?"

"I don't have any responsibilities," he said, grinning. "I'm like a visiting uncle. I don't even have to pay for their school or make sure their homework is done. It's just a lot easier. The commitment is not as great. I do the fun things with them. I don't take them to the doctor. I take them to the ball game."

At retirement the task of parenting expands for those who are grandparents. Once again Fred and Marie were united in a parenting role, one that was both familiar and new. Although typically there are differences of opinion between the generations about how to raise the grandchildren, when the younger couple become parents they develop a new appreciation for their parents. The inner conflicts of adolescence and young adulthood fade. Both generations can create new ties and share common concerns, becoming, as Fred said, "best friends."

Fred and Marie loved playing with their grandchildren and taking care of them. Watching them grow brought back happy memories of the time when their own children were little, but without the tension and fatigue. Unlike parents, grandparents are able to set limits on their time and their availability. Grandparenting is the least ambivalent of all family relationships. The grandparent-grandchild relationship is filled with pleasure and provides the aging couple with a symbolic link to the future.

For Marie, being an active grandmother in a growing family was a continuation of her central role as mother in a traditional family. For Fred, and many other active grandfathers, this new relationship represented a major change. Many men shine in this role, ministering to the younger generation with devotion, expressing a soft and loving maternal side that was not always evident when their own children were young. The satisfaction of being in charge of little children is now fully acceptable and rewarded with genuine appreciation and praise. The great reward for these grandfathers is access to the emotional world of children, from which they were earlier excluded by work, time pressures, their own reluctance, and the traditional idea that the world of young children is the woman's domain.

When I asked about their sex life, Fred responded frankly. "We have sex less frequently now, but it's satisfying to me. Now that we are both home, we could spend all our time in bed. But it's still more amorous when we go away. When we travel, it's like a honeymoon."

"Are there sexual problems?" I asked.

"Not really," said Marie. "Sex has been important in our marriage, but not the most important. The most important thing has been our personal relationship, our fondness, respect, and friendship."

Sex was a source of continuing pleasure and comfort in these retirement marriages, although it no longer had the imperious drive of earlier years. Most couples said that they had sex about once a week. Some men suffered from transient or extended bouts of impotence, and women reported that they were slower in reaching orgasm. But temporary inhibitions did not reduce the deep comfort provided by their continuing sex life.

I turned to Fred and Marie and asked, "What about the future?"

After a pause Marie said slowly, "I think about this often. I think about it all the time. I have a dear friend whose husband just died of cancer. They are younger than us." She sighed. "I think I would go on living and be fine. I try a fantasy of what it would be like without Fred because these are realities coming down. Either I'll go first or he'll go first. I think I'll be able to live without him because I've already lived without him in certain kinds of ways when he was on the road. And also I have so many support systems with my family and friends. I would be able to make a life with my cooking school. I don't feel alone. I've never been bored with my life. I'm a very social person. But I would be devastated."

Although I hadn't mentioned death, Marie took my question about the future in those terms. After a hushed silence, she continued, "I think there would be an enormous loss of the person who has been central to my life for forty years, who's really precious and dear and more. My lover and my husband, and we really are friends. We always enjoy being together."

She looked at Fred, and we waited for him to reply. "I don't know what I would do," he said after an awkward silence. "I've thought about it. I have a feeling I would not remarry."

Marie said she thought about death all the time. Fred was more reserved, but he too admitted, "I've thought about it." His first remark was about whether he would remarry. Although that sounded unfeeling, I realized he could not deal with the question directly, as Marie had, and was blocking the powerful emotions brought up by thinking about the loss of his wife. Yet both Fred and Marie, despite their courageous plans, were talking about the impossibility of filling a great void in their lives.

"I don't know what I'd do," Fred said. "I guess I'd continue doing what I'm doing now. The children would be there, and so would friends." He gave a nervous laugh. "Whenever Marie and I talk about death, she says I'd be married in one year. But I don't think I would be. I've never met another woman whom I think I'd want to marry. I like women, but I can't believe I'd ever have another relationship like this. It wouldn't be the same. It couldn't be the same."

At retirement a couple's relationship is more and more influenced by thoughts of their own death and the death of their partner. Marie and Fred and the other retired couples in this study were able to keep these thoughts from overshadowing their lives, but they remained as a hovering presence. The preoccupation may be conscious or more subliminal.

One woman said, "What I see myself doing if I lost him is becoming a recluse. I would much prefer that we died together." People note how friends have coped or failed to cope with the death of a spouse. Some read obituary columns regularly, looking for the names of people they know. One retired couple took turns driving so that each would be prepared to take full responsibility for driving when that became necessary. Women are more likely to plan how they will conduct their lives as widows; they tally up their resources and realize how much they will rely on other women.

Men are less likely to make plans. Like Fred, they think about whether or not they will remarry, which may represent an erotic daydream to some extent. It is taken for granted that remarriage is not the same option for widows. But neither men nor women are truly able to contemplate their grief or to push it completely away. It is too overwhelming. They are prepared for death in their heads but not in their hearts — and it may well be that this is all that human beings can do. But the task of separation looms dramatically at this time. Both partners are preparing but are unprepared for the final separation from the central relationship of their lives.

As the interview drew to a close, I asked Marie and Fred if they had advice for young people thinking about marriage.

Delighted by the question, Marie spoke about how to choose a partner. "You think you're going to change someone. But really, you have to feel very solid and good about what that person is about. If they fill most of your requirements, you can feel pretty safe. But if there are pieces missing — things you think you're going to change — forget it. Look for a generous person, look for a loving person, look for a person who can handle stress. If you see a person who is too fragile under conditions you observe them in, stay away. I tell my kids, 'If you're not whole when you marry, it's no good. You can't expect another person to make you whole.'"

Fred said, "You really have to like the person, that's the most important thing, even more than loving them. I love Marie, but what's held us together even more is that I really *like* her. We like to be together. I like to see her. You also have to be able to compromise, be able to give in once in a while and expect the other person to do the same. After a time you get an instinctive sense of what's important to each of you. The amazing thing is that all the things you fight about

— they don't amount to anything. When you look back on it, it's insignificant." Fred put down his teacup with a clatter. "The other thing young people have to realize is that you have to stay tuned to each other, and if you don't you're going to have problems."

Fred smiled. "I think our relationship now is as good as or better than it ever was."

# 27

# The Ninth Task

*Preserving a Double Vision*

M ARIE FELLINI WAS TELLING ME about their courtship. "My children and I never tire of hearing Fred tell how he decided to marry me." She flushed with pleasure at the memory. "We were both working at a summer camp. He walked into a room where I was talking to friends and heard me laugh. He says he decided at that moment that I was the woman he wanted to marry." She laughed. "Of course, he was only twenty-two years old, but he says he knew that I was the woman he wanted, and he followed his instincts from that moment on."

Marie described more early memories; in one, she and Fred strolled at midnight along Riverside Drive in New York, carrying a steel box with one hundred dollars inside. "Fred was the treasurer of some organization," she said with a laugh, "but all we could think about was how lucky we were to have found each other, about how much in love we felt. There we were, easy targets for muggers, and we were deliriously happy." She paused, savoring the memory. "That image captures so much of our marriage. I have thought of it often through the years, and it's very much a part of our love today." She chuckled. "Even though we sure as hell don't look the same!"

Marie's story beautifully illustrates the ninth task of marriage, which is to carry in one's head a simultaneous vision of past images and present realities. It involves holding on to the early idealizations of being in love while realizing that one is growing older and grayer and cannot turn back the clock.

Many couples in the study told me about their first impressions of each other, using images that expressed the passionate fantasies of their courtship, their dreams of love and sexual pleasure, and their hopes of being comforted and treasured. Some memories were of an entire scene; others fastened on fleeting impressions that had become enshrined as symbols of what came later.

Thus Sara remembered Matt's Santa Claus laugh and the way he smelled when she first met him. Thirty years later Matt remembered Sara's white bikini and a day and night of sexual passion in their hotel room. Janet remembered seeing Ellis in a plaid vest, sitting cross-legged on the floor at a meeting for divorced parents. "I can't explain it," she said, "but I suddenly felt hope and joy." Keith recalled meeting Helen: "When I first saw her, she looked so lovely. And I said to myself, 'That's the kind of woman who would never be mine. What could she possibly see in me?'" Beth talked about "Kit's kind eyes," and Nicholas described Maureen's "soothing hands."

One man, who had been married for twenty-eight years, said, "I remember when I first saw her. Her legs were propped up on a chair, and she had those high cheekbones I have loved all my life. She looked so pert and vibrant, and I said to myself, 'This is the one.'" A woman recalled how, decades before, she and her fiancé had come together after a lover's quarrel. "It was raining hard when I got off at the station, and he didn't care because he was so happy to see me. He didn't notice that the rain was streaming down his face or that his shirt was soaking wet, because he was wild with joy." Another woman said of her husband of sixteen years, "When I first saw him I was terrified because the attraction was so strong. I could feel my heart beating. I never had that feeling before, but in one crazy moment I knew that he was the man I would want to have a child with. Thank God I didn't run away."

Happily married couples treasure these images and episodes. The story of how they met and courted is given special status and dignity, set apart from everyone's else's history. Told again and again, the story reaffirms the couple's early pleasure and their present togetherness. This is what toasts and flowers and anniversaries are for — to celebrate us, our history, and, by logical extension, our future. Retelling the stories brings a rush of feelings and provides a vital link between the wishes of the past and the needs of the present.

The final task of marriage is to hold on to those idealized images of courtship and early history along with a realistic view of the present, including the changes wrought by time. A couple creates this double vision by weaving the early idealizations into the fabric of daily life, giving the relationship a meaning that lifts it above the mundane. When Sara said that Matt was magic for her, she meant that daily life with him was suffused with a magical glow. She was describing her own perception of the transformative power of love and fantasy that defined their relationship. Matt and Sara and other couples continued to have the same subliminal perceptions of each other that they had when they first were lovers. Each person felt proud of possessing the prized partner. Each man and woman felt blessed to have gotten their choice and doubly blessed to have been chosen.

When these feelings become a part of daily life, they help to mute the inevitable disappointments that occur in every relationship. The powerful memories provide a reservoir of past indulgences on which people can draw when things look dark. Beloved recollections of a better past soften the blows of the present. When a couple who have never idealized each other encounter disappointment, they have a bitter sense of déjà vu. They have a hard time forgiving each other for failing, because they have no reason to hope; they conclude bitterly that this is all there was and all there can be in the relationship.

Of course a marriage cannot live on memories of courtship and fantasies alone. But if their life together has some genuine gratifications along with the idealizations of the past, a couple is better able to accept deprivations in the present. They are able to forgive a partner for not delivering on all that was promised by keeping in mind what they have received and by hoping for future fulfillment.

Sensual memories particularly can remain alive over a lifetime and soften the impact of midlife and aging. A man in his seventies said of his wife, "I remember how her whole body vibrated like a sweet harp when we made love." Such early images were especially vivid in romantic marriages, but they also occurred in the cooler companionate marriages. "She is exactly the woman I fantasized about all through my adolescence," said Kit, drawing happily on his memories.

The men and women in these happy marriages idealized different characteristics. Men spoke of their wives' expressiveness, beauty, honesty, nurturant qualities, sexual passion, intuition, and compassion. One man said, "She has the softness of a woman and the strength of a man." Women spoke of their husbands' honesty, tenderness, compassion, good looks, parenting skills, passion as a lover, and absolute trustworthiness. Often a man's first take on his future wife was of her liveliness and her smile, whereas the women responded to a man's sexual attractiveness or kindness. More often than not, spouses valued the same virtues in each other.

The common view that idealization blocks realistic thinking and good judgment was not true among these couples; rather, idealization enhanced reality and did not interfere with accurate assessments of the here and now. They realized that no one can fully live up to early promises or remain young and beautiful forever. But each partner's store of intensely private, loving images from the past allowed them to have a double vision of their partner.

While all of the couples in the study retained images and memories of courtship, in my experience the same is not true of unhappy couples who divorce. Such images are extinguished by anger or are transformed into bitterness by humiliation and loss. People who discover that reality is completely at variance with their earlier idealizations feel betrayed — both by their own perceptions and by the other person's treachery.

One major hazard of infidelity is that its discovery can shatter idealization. Even if the infidelity is forgiven, the couple may be unable to restore the ideal image that once enriched the marriage. If that image was entirely at odds with the discovered reality, the relationship may be broken beyond repair. "Not only is he not honest," said one divorced woman, "he is corrupt." The ex-husband replied, "She's a liar. I left town for a business trip, and she neglected the children."

Every relationship holds the possibility that the dreamed-of loving rescue will turn into its opposite. The angel becomes a demon, treacherous and rejecting; the once idealized partner is perceived as destructive, dangerous, evil. This demonization of the ideal lies at the core of the severe disorganization that often accompanies divorce. In many divorces the projection of all that is good and admired onto the beloved turns into the projection of all that is most feared and hated. The anguish of experiencing one's own worst nightmare replaces the euphoria of the beginning love affair. Disappointment and rage may break the marriage or may keep the two people bound to each other for many years or for life.

The other side of retaining the early idealization is maintaining a reasonably accurate perception of the partner and oneself. Without a healthy sense of reality, a marriage based on idealization can become a hothouse in which the partners glorify each other, with sentimentality taking the place of genuine respect. In decades gone by, women were expected to look up to men uncritically, and this is still the fashion in public posturing, as when the adoring and attentive wife of the political candidate stands slightly behind her husband on the podium and gazes at him worshipfully. (I have not seen the same pose by the husband of a woman candidate; I presume it might detract from her public persona.)

The great strength of a marriage that is sensitive to changes in each partner's needs and circumstances is that it enables the man and woman to help each other at crisis points and at life's major milestones. If this flexibility is inhibited, their capacity to be responsive to each other and to recognize change in themselves is crippled. The marriage is a hollow shell in which the partners continue their stale routines without a sense of connectedness. Such marriages are most likely to fail at midlife, when the mutual venture of child rearing no longer unites the couple. And that is precisely the time when the individuals need to draw on the deep wells of imagination and feeling that drew them together originally, to reach back to the images of the way they were so that they can move forward together on a new basis.

Both parts of the vision — the symbolic and the real — are powerful weapons for combating impoverishment in the marriage and for buffering the inevitable disappointments in oneself and in the other that are inherent in all long-lasting close relationships.

Thus the last task of marriage is to celebrate a shared history, to refurbish the light-filled early memories that drew the two people together in the first place while recognizing that each is a human being with both virtues and flaws. This is the double image that sustains a happy marriage. Without fantasy, the relationship is mundane. Without a healthy dose of present reality, it is sentimental and hardly worth fighting for.

# Conclusion

*Marriage as a Transformative Experience*

AS I COME TO THE END of writing this book, I think about my own marriage, as I have so often in the course of the study. I am aware of the physical changes of aging in my body: my right knee is getting stiff with arthritis, and I walk more slowly than before. When my husband and I walk together, as we do daily, I notice that he has slowed his pace because of my infirmity. Of course he is aware that he is getting less exercise, but that thought is not at the center of his consciousness, and he does not expect me to express my gratitude. It goes without saying that he will accommodate to my need and we will both walk more slowly.

When we return home, he usually has some tasks he urgently wants to attend to, and that is fine with me; I know that if he doesn't do them he will be unhappy. I am also aware that he, too, is less flexible than he used to be. So I postpone conversation until he has finished his work. I expect no appreciative comment from him. This is the give-and-take of life, and this is what marriage is about: keeping up, not getting too far ahead and not falling behind.

Marriage is made up of little things, and it is the little things that count, both the good and the bad. The little changes, too, add to the important rhythms of life. The changing interactions between my husband and me are part of this major chapter in our married life. We are building a marriage now just as surely as when we were younger, as surely as when we returned from our honeymoon and started out on our life together. The thousand and one changes in our relationship, in observing each other and adjusting to each other, are no different today. Except that we are better at it — we have had a lot of practice. Strangely enough, it is these little things, the ebb and flow of the relationship, that so many couples cannot manage.

I bring this book to a close with mixed feelings of exhilaration and sadness. From my encounters with the couples in the study I have learned a great deal about building a happy marriage, even beyond my own high expectations. I have also learned about the rigors of maintaining one's adulthood and of being a parent amid the pressures of contemporary society. It has been a wonderful experience to spend time with couples who are thriving, who have held on to friendship and love for each other and for their children in a society in which divorce has become commonplace.

The people in these good marriages did not all start off with advantages. They came from a wide range of backgrounds: a few rich, most modest, some dirt-poor. A lucky few had parents who loved each other, but more came from marriages they perceived as unhappy. Most were eager to create a marriage that would be different from and happier than the one in which they were raised. In this they succeeded. Each couple created an emotionally rich, enduring relationship that was designed to their liking. They were frank with me about the pleasures of the marriage and also about the areas in which they felt pinched or disappointed. Their generosity has led me to new knowledge that can be put to immediate use by other married couples. I take leave of them with affection and deep gratitude.

I will miss having almost everyone I meet at social gatherings ask me anxiously, "What have you found out?" — and then wait for a one-line answer. It is truly distressing to hear over and over again how worried most of us are and how eager we all are for a message that will give us some control over the most intimate aspects of our lives.

I shall also miss the wonderfully condensed responses I received when I turned the question back to the asker. My all-time favorite: "Do I know what makes a happy marriage?" said a woman, laughing. "A bad memory." She had a point. Surely, being able to forget the day-to-day disappointments and keep one's eyes on the big issues is what is needed to make a marriage go. And in fact separating the trivial from the important is one of the great gifts of a sense of humor. No one would gainsay the usefulness of humor in sweetening the stresses of marriage and raising children. But in truth there are no one-line answers to the question of what makes a marriage happy.

What then are the secrets? How do a man and a woman who meet as strangers create a relationship that will satisfy them both throughout their lives?

First, the answer to the question I started with — what do people define as happy in their marriage? — turned out to be straightforward. For everyone, happiness in marriage meant feeling respected and cherished. Without exception, these couples mentioned the importance of liking and respecting each other and the pleasure and comfort they took in each other's company. Some spoke of the passionate love that began their relationship, but for a surprising number love grew in the rich soil of the marriage, nourished by emotional and physical intimacy, appreciation, and fond memories. Some spoke of feeling well cared for, others of feeling safe, and still others of friendship and trust. Many talked about the family they had created together. But all felt that they were central to their partner's world and believed that creating the marriage and the family was the major commitment of their adult life. For most, marriage and children were the achievements in which they took the greatest pride.

For these couples, respect was based on integrity; a partner was admired and loved for his or her honesty, compassion, generosity of spirit, decency, loyalty to the family, and fairness. An important aspect of respect was admiration of the partner as a sensitive, conscientious parent. The value these couples placed on the partner's moral qualities was an unexpected finding. It helps explain why many divorcing people speak so vehemently of losing respect for their former partner. The love that people feel in a good marriage goes with the conviction that the person is worthy of being loved.

These people were realists. No one denied that there were serious differences — conflict, anger, even some infidelity — along the way. No one envisioned marriage as a rose garden, but all viewed its satisfactions as far outweighing the frustrations over the long haul. Most regarded frustrations, big and small, as an inevitable aspect of life that would follow them no matter whom they married. Everyone had occasional fantasies about the roads not taken, but their commitment to the marriage withstood the impulse to break out.

Above all, they shared the view that their partner was special in some important regard and that the marriage enhanced each of them as individuals. They felt that the fit between their own needs and their partner's responses was unique and probably irreplaceable. In this they considered themselves very lucky, not entitled.

Their marriages had benefited from the new emphasis in our society on equality in relationships between men and women. However they divided up the chores of the household and of raising the children, the couples agreed that men and women had equal rights and responsibilities within the family. Women have taken many casualties in the long fight to achieve equality, and many good men have felt beleaguered, confused, and angry about this contest. But important goals have been achieved: marriages today allow for greater flexibility and greater choice. Relationships are more mature on both sides and more mutually respectful. A couple's sex life can be freer and more pleasurable. Today's men and women meet on a playing field that is more level than ever before.

Unlike many unhappy families, these couples provided no evidence for the popular notion that there is a "his" marriage and a "her" marriage. On the contrary, the men and women were very much in accord. I did not see significant differences between husbands and wives in their goals for the marriage, in their capacity for love and friendship, in their interest in sex, in their desire to have children, or in their love and commitment to the children. They fully shared the credit for the success of the marriage and the family. Both men and women said, "Everything we have we did together."

Although some men were inhibited in their expression of feelings at the beginning of the marriage, as compared with their wives, I did not find much difference between the sexes in their ability to express emotions over the course of their relationship. Both spoke easily of their love for their partner. In response to my questioning, both men and women cried when they contemplated losing the other.

The children were central, both as individuals and as symbols of a shared vision, giving pleasure and sometimes unexpected meaning to the parents' lives and to the marriage. As the couples reported to me in detail, the children reflected their love and pride. And this powerful bond did not diminish when the children left home.

As I compared the happily married couples with the thousands of divorcing couples I have seen in the past twenty-five years, it was clear that these men and women had early on created a firm basis for their relationship and had continued to build it together. Many of the couples that divorced failed to lay such a foundation and did not understand the need to reinforce it over the years. Many marriages broke because the structure was too weak to hold in the face of life's vicissitudes. The happy couples regarded their marriage as a work in progress that needed continued attention lest it fall into disrepair. Even in retirement they did not take each other for granted. Far too many divorcing couples fail to understand that a marriage does not just spring into being after the ceremony. Neither the legal nor the religious ceremony makes the marriage. *People* do, throughout their lives.

What is the work that builds a happy marriage? What should people know about and what should they do? On the basis of the study I proposed nine psychological tasks that challenge men and women throughout their life together. These tasks, the building blocks of the marriage, are not imposed on the couple from the outside; they are inherent in a relationship in today's world. If the issues represented by each psychological task are not addressed, the marriage is likely to fail, whether the couple divorces or remains legally married. The tasks begin at the start of the marital journey and are continually renegoti- ated. A good marriage is always being reshaped so that the couple can stay in step with each other and satisfy their changing needs and wishes.

The first task is to detach emotionally from the families of child- hood, commit to the relationship, and build new connections with the extended families. Husband and wife help each other complete the transition into adulthood or, in a second marriage, detach from a prior relationship and commit emotionally to the new partner.

The second task is to build togetherness through intimacy and to expand the sense of self to include the other, while each individual carves out an area of autonomy. The overarching identification with the other provides the basis for bonding. As one man put it succinctly, "In a good marriage, it can't be Me-Me-Me, it's gotta be Us-Us-Us." Exactly! But within the new unity, there must be room for autonomy; otherwise there is no true equality. These two early tasks launch the marriage.

The third task is to expand the circle to include children, taking on the daunting roles of parenthood from infancy to the time when the child leaves home, while maintaining the emotional richness of the marriage. The challenge of this task is to maintain a balance between raising the children and nurturing the couple's relationship.

The fourth task is to confront the inevitable developmental challenges and the unpredictable adversities of life, including illness, death, and natural disasters, in ways that enhance the relationship despite suffering. Every crisis carries within it the seeds of destruction as well as the possibility of renewed strength. Managing stress is the key to having a marriage that can reinvent itself at each turning rather than one that becomes a shadow of its former self.

The fifth task is to make the relationship safe for expressing difference, anger, and conflict, which are inevitable in any marriage. All close relationships involve love and anger, connectedness and disruption. The task is to find ways to resolve the differences without exploiting each other, being violent, or giving away one's heart's desire. Conflict ran high among several couples in this group, but I saw no evidence that conflict by itself wrecks a marriage.

The sixth task is to establish an imaginative and pleasurable sex life. Creating a sexual relationship that meets the needs and fantasies of both people requires time and love and sensitivity. Because a couple's sex life is vulnerable to interference by the stresses of work and by family life, and because sexual desire changes, often unpredictably, over the life course, this aspect of the marriage requires special protection in order to flourish.

The seventh task is to share laughter and humor and to keep interest alive in the relationship. A good marriage is alternately playful and serious, sometimes flirtatious, sometimes difficult and cranky, but always full of life.

The eighth task is to provide the emotional nurturance and encouragement that all adults need throughout their lives, especially in today's isolating urban communities and high-pressure workplaces.

Finally, the ninth task is the one that sustains the innermost core of the relationship by drawing sustenance and renewal from the images and fantasies of courtship and early marriage and maintaining that joyful glow over a lifetime. But these images, nourished by the partners' imaginations, must be combined with a realistic view of the changes wrought by time. It is this double image that keeps love alive in the real world.

I have learned from these happily married couples that marriages come in different shapes and sizes. Under today's looser rules a marriage can be custom-made by the couple to an extent their grandparents never dreamed possible. I have therefore suggested a typology of marriage to capture what I have observed in this study. This typology includes romantic, rescue, companionate, and traditional marriages. Second marriages can belong to any of these groups. I suspect that more types will emerge in the future as marriage continues to reflect people's changing emotional needs and values.

No marriage provides for all the wishes and needs that people bring to it. Although every good marriage provides many satisfactions, each type maximizes different rewards and exacts a different price. In each type the psychological tasks are resolved differently. The kind and degree of togetherness and autonomy vary, as does the importance of children, work, and sexual passion. The values on which the marriage is built differ among the types, although they overlap. Children growing up in each kind of marriage have quite different experiences.

Moreover, the various types of marriages require different kinds of support from society. For traditional marriages to succeed, society must offer jobs that pay enough money for one parent to support the family while the other raises the children. Society also must provide economic and educational opportunities for the child-rearing parent when the children have grown up. Similarly, for companionate marriages to flourish, society must ensure that workplace demands are not allowed to overwhelm the marriage and the family. Companionate couples also need good-quality child care and enlightened personnel policies so that they do not have to make anguished choices between the demands of work and of family, especially at times of crisis.

I have tried to show the importance of the fit between the couple and the kind of marriage they create. The idea that different people seek different kinds of marriages has important practical implications. If couples understand in advance that each kind of marriage poses different hazards and requires different tending, they can anticipate where problems are likely to develop and take steps to resolve them. The deepest satisfaction of the romantic marriage is that it gratifies the desire for passionate love, which in some cases is reinforced by the powerful wish to restore a beloved figure lost in childhood. By their nature, romantic marriages absorb most of a couple's emotional investment, and one hazard is that the children may feel peripheral to the couple's relationship.

The rescue marriage is often less emotionally intense than the romantic marriage; its great contribution is in allowing people to revise their sorrowful expectations of life. People who have suffered severe traumas are freed to pursue their lives, because the marriage gives them strength. But there is danger that the old problems will reemerge, either in the couple's relationship or between parent and child. Romantic and rescue marriages are not subject to voluntary choice, but in each type the tasks can be resolved and the marriage shaped to avoid the most likely hazards.

Companionate marriage does represent a choice, based on the couple's commitment to two careers or economic necessity or both. At its best, companionate marriage provides the gratifications of family life and the rewards of a successful career for both partners. But each individual's separate path may supersede the togetherness that happy marriage requires, leading to the loss of intimacy and emotional connectedness. Or child care may be delegated to others to the point that neither parent is primary in the child's upbringing.

Traditional marriage can meet people's needs for a home and a stable family life and provide comfort and nurturance for both adults and children. But the danger in a traditional marriage is that the partners' lives may become increasingly separate. And at midlife, when the all-absorbing tasks of child rearing are over and the tasks of the marriage need to be negotiated anew, the partners may feel estranged from each other.

A good marriage, I have come to understand, is transformative. The prevailing psychological view has been that the central dimensions of personality are fully established in childhood. But from my observations, men and women come to adulthood unfinished, and over the course of a marriage they change each other profoundly. The very act of living closely together for a long time brings about inner change, not just conscious accommodation. The physical closeness of sex and marriage has its counterpart in psychological closeness and mutual identification.

As the men and women in good marriages respond to their partner's emotional and sexual needs and wishes, they grow and influence each other. The needs of one's partner and children become as important as one's own needs. Ways of thinking, self-image, self-esteem, and values all have the potential for change. The second marriages show clearly that the capacity of men and women to love each other passionately revives in their relationship despite early disappointments. The power of marriage to bring about change is especially evident in rescue marriages. As I have described, people who have been severely traumatized during childhood are able, with the help of a loving relationship, to restore their self-esteem.

A willingness to reshape the marriage in response to new circumstances and a partner's changing needs and desires is an important key to success. All of the couples in the study understood that unless they renegotiated the tasks of the relationship at key points, one or both partners would be unhappy. There are shaky times in every marriage. Many life-course changes, such as the birth of a baby or a child's adolescence, can be anticipated, but others, such as major illness or job loss, cannot. At all of these times, emotional changes in the individual coincide with external changes. If the couple does not take steps to protect it, the marriage may be in peril. These couples succeeded in reshaping their relationship at each major crossroads so that it continued to fit their needs. All mentioned that they had experienced many different marriages within their one enduring relationship.

I have learned a great deal about the intimate connectedness of a good marriage. It became clear to me early on that popular notions about marital communication failed to capture the subtlety of the daily interactions between these men and women. They had learned that a little tact goes a long way, that sometimes silence is golden, and that timing is everything. They listened carefully to each other and tried to speak both honestly and tactfully. But they recognized intuitively that true communication in marriage extends far beyond words. It involves paying attention to changing moods, facial expressions, body language, and the many other cues that reveal inner states of mind. It means knowing each other's history and catching the echoes and behaviors that reverberate from the past. It includes knowing enough about the other so that at critical times one can take an imaginative leap inside the other's skin. That is what empathy in a marriage is about.

These were not talents that came naturally to all of these people, nor were these individuals necessarily empathic in other domains of their lives. They learned to listen and to be sensitive to their partner's cues because they wanted the marriage to work; they had learned that by anticipating a partner's distress, they could protect themselves and the marriage.

These couples also understood that symbolically a marriage is always much greater than the sum of its parts. It is enriched by the continued presence of fantasy. When the marriage is successful, it represents a dream come true, the achievement of full adulthood. Tragically, when it fails, the symbolic loss may cause enormous suffering. The home these couples created gave them both real and symbolic pleasure because they felt strongly that it was their own creation. Their pleasure in each other, especially during times of leisure and reflection, represented more than current satisfaction; it represented the fulfillment of wishes extending way back to the dreams of early childhood.

Finally, I learned again, as I have learned many times over from the divorced couples I have worked with, the extraordinary threats that contemporary society poses to marriage. The stresses of the workplace and its fierce impact on the couple are writ large in the lives of these families, no matter what their economic level. Their stories told and retold how few supports newly married couples have to keep them together and how many powerful forces pull them apart. As the younger couples made clear, the whole world seems to invade the couple's private time together.

Americans today work long hours, yet during the early years of marriage, money is often hard to come by, even in professional occupations. Working for a big firm can be exciting for someone ascending the ladder of success, but it does not provide the latitude for creativity that many crave or the individuality that everyone needs. And because the corporate world is so impersonal, the emotional bonds of the couple and family are even more important, but the time and energy to enjoy them are substantially and cruelly curtailed.

Marriage is hard work partly because raising children is hard work; there is insufficient time before bedtime each day and not enough hands for the tasks that were supposed to have been cut by laborsaving devices but somehow weren't. Marriage is also hard because so many people come from unhappy families, whether the family split up or remained together; those who grew up in such families often carry deep hungers from childhood. Marriage is a high-risk venture because the threat of divorce is everywhere, as these couples all knew.

Because of societal pressures and the essential loneliness of modern life, marriage serves many purposes in today's world. It is our only refuge. The couples in the study were realistically aware that they had to fulfill many needs for each other; there are not many opportunities at work or elsewhere in society for gratifying our desires for friendship, comfort, love, reassurance, and self-expression. These couples wanted a marriage that could respond to all these complex needs without breaking. They discovered anew each day the many ways in which they helped each other and how pleased and proud they were of the marriage they had created.

A good marriage is more than the happy possession of an individual couple and their children. It is this unit, which represents us at our civilized best, that shapes adults and children. More than any other human institution, marriage is the vehicle for transmitting our values to future generations. Ultimately it is our loving connections that give life meaning. Through intimate relationships we enlarge our vision of life and diminish our preoccupation with self. We are at our most considerate, our most loving, our most selfless within the orbit of a good family. Only within a satisfying marriage can a man and woman create the emotional intimacy and moral vision that they alone can bequeath to their children.

These findings on marriage are hopeful and reassuring. The guidelines I have developed to help couples as they start out and at later points along the way are realistic. But given the pressures of contemporary American society, it is clear that marriage is a serious game for adult players, whether they begin as adults or become adults in the play.

As I write these final paragraphs, my thoughts turn to my grandmother and to Nikki, my youngest grandchild. My grandmother, who brought her three young children to the new land in the hold of a ship and raised them by herself, knew exactly what she wanted for me. When I was growing up, she used to sing Yiddish folk songs about love and marriage, about mysterious suitors from distant lands. Whom will you marry? the songs asked. Her hopes for me were built on her own tears. My future happy marriage and my unborn healthy children made her sacrifice worthwhile.

Nikki has just turned four. She has recently demoted her twenty or so stuffed bears, puppies, kittens, even her beloved tiger, to the foot of her bed. They who were her special joy hardly have her attention now. She has entered a new phase. I am to address her as "Princess" when I call. (The great advantage of grandmothers, I have discovered, is that they follow instructions, whereas mothers issue instructions.) She is

Princess Jasmine, and she awaits Aladdin. She is practicing at being a grown-up young lady, preparing for the future with all the energy and devotion that she brought to caring for her animals. No one works harder or with greater purpose than a child at play.

What do I want for Nikki? The roads that were so clear to my grandmother have become harder to follow. They fork often and sometimes lead to a dead end. Some directions, however, are still visible. I, too, want my granddaughter to be strong and brave and virtuous. I want her to love and be loved passionately and gently and proudly by a man worth loving. I want her to experience the joys and terrors of raising children. But far beyond what my grandmother envisioned for me, I want Nikki to have the choices in life that I and many others had to fight for, real choices that the community will respect and support. And I want her to know how to choose wisely and understand how to make it all work. I hope that Nikki finds the Aladdin that she has started to look for. If he comes flying into her life on a magic carpet, so much the better. This book contains her legacy, a set of annotated maps for their journey.

APPENDICES

NOTES

ACKNOWLEDGMENTS

# The Study Population

The study sample consisted of fifty married couples who volunteered to be interviewed about their marriages. The criteria for selection were as follows:

1. the legal marriage was of at least nine years' duration
2. the couple had one or more children
3. both husband and wife regarded the marriage as happy
4. both were willing to be interviewed individually as well as together*

The concept of *happy marriage* was subjectively defined. Couples accepted into the study were not required to agree on a definition; rather, each partner needed only to regard the marriage as a happy one.

The participants, drawn from the San Francisco Bay Area, were Caucasian, except for one Asian. At the beginning of the study they ranged in age from thirty-two to seventy-four, with a mean age of forty-eight. The men and women were urban, well educated, middle class or upper middle class; they were in fair to excellent health. The couples had an average of 2.2 children, ranging in age from newborn to forty.

At the time of the initial interviews, the couples had been married an average of twenty-one years, within a range of nine to forty years. The mean age at marriage was 25.5 years for women and 28.5 years for men. Twenty percent of the couples had married in the 1950s, 30 percent in the 1960s, 30 percent in the 1970s, and the remaining 20 percent in the 1980s. Twenty-one of the fifty couples had lived together for one or more years prior to the marriage. Among the couples who married in the 1970s and

---

*Four couples were eliminated at the initial interview when it became clear that only one partner in each couple felt the marriage was happy.

1980s, the cohabitation period had lasted from several months to nine years. In thirty-two cases the marriage was the first for both husband and wife. In seven cases both husband and wife had previously been married. In the remaining eleven, one spouse had had a previous marriage.

Twenty percent of the couples were single-income families with the husbands employed and the wives working as homemakers. In two families the wife was employed full-time and the husband was the homemaker. Annual family incomes ranged from $18,000 to over $100,000, with an average of $82,000. Women reported personal annual incomes ranging from zero to over $100,000, with a median category between $25,000 and $50,000. Men reported incomes ranging from $5,000 to over $100,000, with a median category between $75,000 and $100,000. Sixty percent of the women and 75 percent of the men held professional degrees. Ninety percent of all participants were college graduates.

The economic backgrounds of the participants covered a wide range. Less than 20 percent had been raised in upper-middle-class circumstances. Forty-four percent of the men and 46 percent of the women had been raised in poor or modest circumstances.

The largest religious group was Protestant (46 percent), then Jewish (40 percent), and Catholic (12 percent). One person was Buddhist. In 38 percent of the marriages the partners came from different religious traditions; 14 percent of the couples were Protestant-Catholic, 18 percent were Protestant-Jewish, and 4 percent were Catholic-Jewish. For 20 percent of the adults the religion of the family of origin was of major importance in their lives; a greater number had joined religious institutions to give their children a religious education.

*Procedure.* The couples were interviewed between May 1990 and April 1991 by one of five experienced clinicians, including myself. The clinicians scheduled and conducted at least one interview with each spouse and then one interview with both spouses together. Each participant was assured full confidentiality from the other spouse as well as from the community at large with respect to the material elicited in the individual interviews. Each interview lasted several hours; many went on for three to four hours.

All of the initial interviews took place in the participants' home or workplace, in order to observe the individual and the couple in their own milieu. Prior to being interviewed, individuals filled out a four-page questionnaire that covered personal and family background.

The clinicians took notes and, in most cases, made audiotape recordings of the interviews. The comprehensive record of each interview included these verbatim materials combined with detailed clinical observations of body language and emotional expression, the individual's interaction with the interviewer, the clinician's impression of the person's motivation, and impressions about information that might have been withheld.

The individual interviews were based on a semistructured format in that the clinicians covered a general outline of key areas. However, the interviews were conducted as oral histories, and participants were encouraged to tell their stories in the way that was most meaningful to them. All of the interviews opened with the question "What is happy for you in this marriage?" This was followed by the question "What is disappointing to you about the marriage?" The following general areas were then addressed:

1. childhood experiences in the family of origin, including earliest memories
2. characterization of the interviewee's parents' marriage, including parent-child and sibling relationships
3. romantic relationships in adolescence and young adulthood, including previous marriages and cohabitations
4. attraction to and courtship of the current spouse
5. factors in the decision to marry
6. expectations, fears, and doubts about the marriage
7. reactions to the marriage by the family of origin
8. history of the marriage, including salient events such as moves, work history, and the birth of children
9. assessment of major satisfactions, dissatisfactions, compromises, successes, and distresses across the major domains of marriage, including love, sex, parenting, conflict, money, health crises, in-laws, and infidelity
10. understanding of or personal theory about what makes the marriage a good, happy, or satisfying one
11. characteristics of the children, the parents' relationship with each child over the years, and the nature of the parenting arrangements

Interviewing individuals in their own home or workplace enhanced the degree of intimacy and offered access to the complexity of the participants' personal lives. In many cases the interviewers had opportunities to meet the children, observe family interactions, and take the pulse of the household. Contrasts between the individuals as they presented themselves in familiar surroundings were noted, as were contrasts between spouses when seen separately and when interacting during the joint interview.

The joint interview was conducted after the two individual interviews were completed. A number of projective tests and drawings were used at this interview, and participants were encouraged to discuss all aspects of their marriage, including differences and consistencies in their individual perspectives. The follow-up interviews were conducted by the same clinician two years later. All of the couples participated in the follow-up; some of these interviews were conducted by telephone.

# The Children

In deciding to concentrate on the adults and the marriage, I have had to forgo descriptions of the children. The knowledge I have about the children of these couples I will note here briefly.

I talked at some length with each parent separately about each child, and I had direct interviews or play sessions with several of the children. There were ninety-six offspring altogether, ranging from one child who was born a week after we interviewed her mother to one man who was forty years old. Many of those couples who married in the 1950s had three or more children. Those who married in the 1960s and 1970s had an average of two children. In the marriages that began in the eighties, most couples had one child, but one family had three children with another on the way, and two families had two children. Two women in this last group became pregnant in the interval between the initial interview and the follow-up. These newer families may well become larger, although the parents said that this was not their current plan.

There had been some tragedies before the study. One child had died in infancy of sudden infant death syndrome. Two children had been diagnosed with cancer and had undergone extensive treatment for several years. Two had been born with severe birth defects and had required multiple surgeries and devoted care throughout childhood.

Most of the children in first marriages were on target developmentally and doing well in school and with their friends. Several were advanced beyond their years in academic achievement. A few showed special talent in theater, music, math, or sports. Those children with special artistic or academic abilities usually received special coaching either at school or in extracurricular activities arranged by the parents.

Nevertheless, several children in first marriages showed psychological problems of sufficient severity and duration to require treatment. One child, after being trapped in a fire, developed obsessive-compulsive symptoms that lasted for many years. Another had severe posttraumatic symptoms following an earthquake. Two children had learning difficulties that required special educational programs at school.

The parents in first marriages were generally very satisfied with their offspring. Parent-child relationships were affectionate and mutually respectful. There were no reports of child abuse, neglect, or sexual molestation by parents or others. Disciplinary methods were restrained, even by those parents who had themselves been severely disciplined or abused, abandoned, or molested as children. None repeated these painful experiences with their own children.

Adolescence was marked by the usual conflicts and rebellions, none of which appeared excessive. The acting out took the form of a few episodes of marijuana smoking, including one arrest for possession of marijuana, and some moderate drinking. There were no teenage pregnancies and no eating disorders.

In overall psychological adjustment the children in second marriages who had experienced their parents' divorce differed from the children of first marriages. Although 34 percent of the marriages were second marriages for one or both adults, only 24 percent of the entire group had children from the prior marriage. Of the children who had experienced divorce, half showed moderate to severe psychological difficulties. The children born within the remarriage did not exhibit similar problems. The problems experienced by many children and adolescents in divorced and remarried homes have been described in my previous work and that of several other researchers. These young people were no exception, despite the very good relationships of the couples in remarriages. Stepparents expressed concern about their difficulties with stepchildren, both those who lived with them and those who visited.

Because I did not personally interview all of the children in this study, I cannot comment on the advantages or limitations of the children's experience according to the marriage type of the couple. The children's experiences surely differed among the marriage types as well as within each separate family. But it is important to bear in mind that any child's experience depends upon a wide range of personal and family factors and upon the sum total of their relationships with those who are significant in their lives.

Public policy questions about whether children benefit significantly by growing up in one type of marriage rather than another could be resolved only by a careful study of children grouped by age, gender, and many other relevant categories. In any case the answers would have to be interpreted by each couple for each individual child.

# Notes

### 1. Happy Marriages

page

5  Studies in which Americans are asked what they value most: Angus Campbell and Philip E. Converse, *The Sense of Well-Being in America: Recent Patterns and Trends* (New York: McGraw-Hill, 1980); Angus Campbell, Philip E. Converse, and Willard L. Rodgers, *The Quality of American Life: Perceptions, Evaluations and Satisfactions* (New York: Russell Sage Foundation, 1976).

6  The longest study done on divorce: Judith S. Wallerstein and Sandra Blakeslee, *Second Chances: Men, Women, and Children a Decade after Divorce* (New York: Ticknor and Fields, 1989).

7  Demographic information about the incidence of divorce: Patricia H. Shiono and Linda Sandham Quinn, "Epidemiology of Divorce," in *Children and Divorce*, vol. 4, *The Future of Children* (Los Altos, Calif.: David and Lucille Packard Foundation, 1994), pp. 15–28; Frank F. Furstenberg, Jr., "Divorce and the American Family," *Annual Review of Sociology* 16 (1990): 379–403.

10  Number of divorces peaks in the early years of marriage: Shiono and Quinn, "Epidemiology of Divorce."

14  Jung told us that marriage . . . : Carl Jung, "Marriage as a Psychological Relationship," in *Collected Works*, vol. 17, *The Development of the Personality* (London: Routledge and Kegan Paul, 1925).

16  Glenn . . . concluded that we need more qualitative research: Norval D. Glenn, "Quantitative Research on Marital Quality in the 1980s: A Critical Review," *Journal of Marriage and the Family* 52 (1990): 818–31.

17  In predicting divorce a husband's body language: John M. Gottman, *Why Marriages Succeed or Fail* (New York: Simon and Schuster, 1994).

*page*
17  Interesting recent studies: John M. Gottman, "Predicting the Longitu-
    dinal Course of Marriages," *Journal of Marital and Family Therapy* 17,
    no. 1 (1991): 3–7; John M. Gottman and Lowell J. Krokoff, "Marital
    Interaction and Satisfaction: A Longitudinal View," *Journal of Consult-
    ing and Clinical Psychology* 57, no. 1 (1989): 47–52; Arlene Skolnick,
    "Married Life: Longitudinal Perspectives on Marriage," in *Present and
    Past in Middle Life,* ed. D. H. Eichorn, J. Clausen, N. Haan, M. Honzik,
    and P. Mussen (New York: Academic Press, 1981); Robert H. Lauer and
    Jeanette C. Lauer, "Factors in Long-Term Marriages," *Journal of Family
    Issues* 7 (1986): 383–90; Florence W. Kaslow and Helga Hammerschmidt,
    "Long-Term 'Good' Marriages: The Seemingly Essential Ingredients,"
    *Journal of Couples Therapy* 3 (1992): 15–38; Jerry M. Lewis, W. Robert
    Beavers, John T. Gossett, and Virginia A. Phillips, *No Single Thread: Psy-
    chological Health in Family Systems* (New York: Brunner-Mazel, 1976).
18  Culture of divorce: Karla B. Hackstaff, "Divorce Culture: A Breach in
    Gender Relations" (dissertation, University of California at Berkeley,
    1994).

## 2. Patterns in Marriage

26  Erikson's blueprint of the life cycle: Erik H. Erikson, *Identity and the
    Life Cycle,* monograph vol. 1, no. 1 (New York: International Universi-
    ties Press, 1959).

## 3. Matt and Sara Turner

41  What psychologists call transferences: The psychoanalytic concept of
    transference was first developed by Sigmund Freud in a classic 1912
    paper, "The Dynamics of the Transference," in *The Collected Works of
    Sigmund Freud,* Standard Edition, vol. 12 (1957), pp. 97–108.

## 8. Helen Buckley

92  Each person influences the other: Joseph Sandler, "Countertransfer-
    ence and Role-Responsiveness," *International Review of Psycho-Analy-
    sis* 3 (1976): 43–47.
98  For a person whose childhood was traumatic . . . : Leonard Shengold,
    *Soul Murder: The Effects of Childhood Abuse and Deprivation* (New
    Haven: Yale University Press, 1989).
99  Complementarity: This concept was first used in the psychotherapy
    of unhappy marriage by Henry V. Dicks, Marital Tensions (London:

*page*

Routledge and Kegan Paul, 1967) and more recently elaborated by
Christopher Clulow and Janet Mattinson, *Marriage Inside Out: Understanding Problems of Intimacy* (Harmondsworth, U.K.: Penguin, 1989).

## 9. Keith Buckley

112  The anniversary effect: Josephine R. Hilgard, "Anniversary Reaction in
Parent Precipitated by Children," *Psychiatry* 16 (1953): 73–80.
113  Differences in children's resiliency: Norman Garmezy and Michael
Rutter, eds., *Stress, Coping and Development in Children* (New York:
McGraw-Hill, 1983).

## 14. Beth McNeil

174  Divorce rate among couples who live together before marriage: Wil-
liam G. Axinn and Arland Thornton, "The Relationship Between Cohabitation and Divorce: Selectivity or Causal Influence?" *Demography*
29, no. 3 (1992): 357–74.

## 16. The Unforgiving Workplace

194  Work intrudes on family life: Juliet B. Schor, *The Overworked American: The Unexpected Decline of Leisure* (New York: Basic Books,
1993).

## 20. The Eighth Task

241  Continuing dependency needs: Takeo Doi, *The Anatomy of Dependence: The Key Analysis of Japanese Behavior* (Tokyo: Kodansha International, 1971); Frank A. Johnson, *Dependency and Japanese Socializa-
tion: Psychoanalytic and Anthropological Investigation into Amae* (New
York: New York University Press, 1993).
247  Remark about ensemble work: Jim Downey, San Francisco Bay Area
actor.

## 22. Infidelity in Fantasy and Reality

262  Most recent study of infidelity in America: John H. Gagnon, Edward
O. Lauman, Robert T. Michael, and Stuart Michael, *The Social Organization of Sexuality* (Chicago: University of Chicago Press, 1994). For a
much higher estimate of infidelity, see Janet Reibstein and Martin

*page*

Richards, *Sexual Arrangements: Marriage and the Temptation of Infidelity* (New York: Scribner's, 1993).


### 23. Confronting Change

271   Psychological and social changes . . . during midlife: Calvin A. Colarusso and Robert A. Nemeroff, *Adult Development: A New Dimension in Psychodynamic Theory and Practice* (New York: Plenum Press, 1981); Daniel J. Levenson, C. M. Darrow, and E. B. Klein, *The Seasons of a Man's Life* (New York: Alfred A. Knopf, 1978).


### 25. Coping with Children in a Second Marriage

301   Children an issue in second marriages: Shiono and Quinn, "Epidemiology of Divorce."

# Acknowledgments

My greatest debt is to the fifty couples who participated in this study. They were cooperative subjects as well as valued allies in the effort to generate a body of knowledge about happy marriage that would be helpful to others. Although they lead very busy lives, they were generous with their time and admirably forthcoming and candid in their comments. I want to thank them for their generosity and willingness to share their experiences and wisdom. I hope they will be pleased with my formulations and will consider their efforts worthwhile.

In the interests of protecting the privacy of the participants, I have disguised each one carefully. The heavy disguise enabled me to quote their comments directly, along with their expressions and gestures. I have presented each marriage exactly as it was perceived by both partners, as observed on several occasions in different settings. To further conceal the identities of the participants, I have used composite portraits in certain situations.

I am equally indebted to my colleagues on the research team for their rich intellectual and clinical contributions to the study. For purposes of coherence and structure, I have presented each interview as if I personally had conducted it. This, of course, was not possible. The interviewing was shared by a small group of senior clinicians, including myself. I would like to express my profound appreciation and gratitude to Karen Fagerstrom, Ph.D.; Karla B. Hackstaff, Ph.D.; Alice S. Steinman, M.A.; and Susan S. Zegans, M.A., M.S.W., who brought sensitivity, compassion, and high clinical skills to the work.

I want to acknowledge the contribution of Karen Fagerstrom, who was responsible for the statistical analysis of the data and shared in the literature review. She and I spent many hours poring over the findings to discern patterns and to discuss hypotheses.

I would also like to thank the Rockefeller Study Center at Bellagio on Lake Como, Italy, where as a Fellow in the spring of 1992 I formulated the concept of the tasks of marriage and developed the central ideas for this book. I also want to express my appreciation to the *American Journal of Orthopsychiatry* for permission to use material from my article "Early Psychological Tasks of Marriage, Part 1," published in November 1994.

I want to thank Benjamin Tucker Friedman, my seven-year-old grandson, who served as my consultant on the toys that children enjoy.

Sandra and I are very grateful to Katrina Kenison for her careful reading of the manuscript, the perfect pitch she brought to this task, and her enthusiastic support of our renewed efforts. We also want to thank Peg Anderson, our manuscript editor, for her sensitive and respectful editing and Barbara Lehman, editorial assistant, for her competent help. I want to express my appreciation to Houghton Mifflin's director of publicity, Irene Williams, for her sensitivity and wisdom. Sandra and I wish to thank our respective agents, Ginger Barber and Carol Mann, for their thoughtful advice and unflagging support. We are especially grateful to John Sterling, our editor, for his remarkable calm, unfailing good humor, sensitivity to our purpose, and excellent editorial guidance.

Finally, my husband, Robert, was the mainstay of this work. His love, encouragement, and confidence in me have infused every part of my life throughout our forty-eight years together.

*Judith Wallerstein*
*November 21, 1994*